THE HOLOCAUST YEARS:
The Nazi Destruction of European Jewry, 1933–1945

By
Nora Levin
Associate Professor of History
and
Director, Holocaust Archives,
Gratz College,
Philadelphia, Pennsylvania

AN ANVIL ORIGINAL

under the general editorship of
LOUIS L. SNYDER

ROBERT E. KRIEGER PUBLISHING COMPANY
MALABAR, FLORIDA

1990

Original Edition 1990

Printed and Published by

ROBERT E. KRIEGER PUBLISHING COMPANY, INC.
KRIEGER DRIVE
MALABAR, FLORIDA 32950

Library of Congress Cataloging-in-Publication Data

Levin, Nora
    The Holocaust years: the Nazi destruction of European Jewry,
    1933–1945/ by Nora Levin.
        p.   cm.
    ISBN 0-89464-223-5
    1. Holocaust, Jewish   (1939–1945)   2. Jews—Germany—
History,—1933–1945.   3. Germany—Ethnic relations.
    4. Holocaust, Jewish (1939–1945)—Sources.   5. Jews—
Germany—History—1933–1945—Sources.   6. Germany—
Ethnic relations—Sources.   7. World War, 1939–1945—
Underground movements, Jewish—Sources.   I. Title.
    D804.3.L49   1990
    940.53'15'03924—dc 19   89-2315
                                                                                    CIP

10   9   8   7   6   5   4   3   2

For
Kimberly, Brett, Stacy, Melissa, and Scott
And Their Generation
of
Children Born After 1945

CONTENTS

INTRODUCTION

The twentieth century has witnessed astonishing achievements in science, technology and information science, but, paradoxically, it has also produced and witnessed the most destructive genocides in human history, including the Turkish slaughter of Armenians during World War I, the Nazi destruction of European Jews during World War II, and the Cambodian genocide of the 1970s. The Holocaust has stimulated a quantitatively greater literature than the other genocides, and possibly more controversy as well. The issues debated range from the definition of the word, to the documentation, the relationship of the Nazi years (1933–1945) to earlier and later German history, Hitler's precise role in the implementation of the annihilation process, the nature of the Nazi dictatorship, and the economic and social classes that supported Hitler.

These, among other questions, have stirred an immense volume of scholarly research as well as popular treatments, fictionalized accounts, film and TV versions, and collections of survivor testimony, diaries, and memoirs. New materials are continuously being uncovered and translated into English, and many Holocaust centers and archives have been established throughout the United States, Europe, and Israel. Questions regarding the place of Holocaust study in university and high school curricula have also been discussed. Each year sees an increasing number of teachers and students undertaking an admittedly difficult subject, revealing imaginative, surprising approaches in fields such as literature, religion, psychology, political science, art, and philosophy, as well as history.

What can such studies mean to a new generation, a half-century away from the events described, events which some would like to consign to ''the dustbin of history''? We leave this new generation to ponder the issues in individual and collective introspection and exchanges, and to add to the ''commentary'' suggested by the British historian Sir Herbert Butterfield:

. . . when the human race has gone through one of its colossal chapters of experience, men in the after-period have been so appalled by the catastrophe, so obsessed by the memory of it, that they have gone back to the story again and again, finding new angles of research, new aspects of the matter to reflect upon, as one generation succeeds another—a process of thinking and rethinking which in special cases is capable of continuing for a thousand years or more. As a result of this, there piles up (with the passage of the generations) a tremendous accumulation of commentary on any single great historical theme.

I believe that the Holocaust is such a chapter. Furthermore, I believe that it belongs most profoundly and appropriately within the discipline of history. I have attempted to describe the experiences of Jews in Nazi-occupied Europe during the years 1933–45, using official documents and readings to further elaborate the brief text. I am dubious that past history provides us with so-called lessons that can be applied to the present. However, an examination of the Holocaust years forces each of us to peer hard at the debasement of traditional Western values at the hands of a highly developed society, a society which made mass murder a civic virtue. In our struggle to understand such an inversion of values and behavior, we should also exert every effort to strengthen and sustain democratic and humanitarian values, indeed to reclaim them from the past, which still casts its dark shadows over many lives.

I should like to express my thanks and appreciation to Dr. Louis L. Snyder, general editor of the Anvil series, for his expert advice in preparing this manuscript. Thanks, too, should go to Elaine S. Rudd, editor at Krieger Publishing Company, for her assistance. For the maps I am indebted to the careful work of Judith Stehle who reworked my rough drawings. I am also grateful to Howard Fertig, Inc., for permission to use selections from George L. Mosse, *Toward the Final Solution: A History of European Racism,* c 1978.

Nora Levin
Philadelphia, Pa.

PART 1

A BRIEF HISTORY OF THE HOLOCAUST

CHAPTER ONE

THE COLLAPSE OF THE WEIMAR REPUBLIC

The collapse of the Weimar Republic in 1933 gave Hitler the opportunity to take, sustain, and enlarge his power until the state was poured into Nazi hands, agencies, and an ideology that made anti-Semitism its centerpiece. His ascent to power and subsequent political and military aggressions also gave Hitler full scope to put into practice his fanatical anti-Jewish obsession, ultimately materializing in the death camps and gas chambers.

It is generally agreed that anti-Semitism in early twentieth century Germany was indeed palpable, conspicuous, and, at times, alarming, but that it was not as pervasive as in Russia, Poland, or Romania, or, in fact, as widespread as in France. German Jews, it has often been said, had had an unrequited love affair with Germany, but, if they were never fully accepted, they had achieved a high degree of acculturation and had made distinctive contributions to German cultural, intellectual, and economic life. Their most important victory in the struggle for full civil and political rights, they believed, had been won in 1871 with German unification. At times of alarm, they could appeal to the principle of the *Recht-staat,* a state based on guaranteed rights. What they could not have envisioned was the sweeping elimination of all of their rights in the early years of the Hitler regime, and much worse later.

The Weimar Republic, born in humiliating military defeat in 1918, laid bare raging forces of vindictiveness, scapegoating, and embitterment and revealed a society unhinged from its most valued traditions and unable to master the burdens and responsibilities of democracy in a period of severe economic and political crisis.

On September 29, 1918, the German Army High Command advised Kaiser Wilhelm II that Germany must sue for peace, marking a traumatic reversal of General Ludendorff's confidence in a German victory the previous spring. The Kaiser had to abdicate in the last days of the war and discipline in the armed forces broke down, beginning with a mutiny among naval units in Kiel—the first of numerous revolts that spread throughout Germany. Workers' and soldiers' councils emerged. Socialist parties, agitating for an end to the war and political and social reforms, pressed their aims in the disintegrating monarchy.

The smaller, more radical party, the Independent Social Democrats (USPD) joined the larger party, the German Social Democratic Party (SPD), in a new government under the SPD leader Friedrich Ebert, but wartime differences and disagreements over economic and social policies made the coalition fragile. A republican form of government was announced, but Ebert, who was called Reich Chancellor, and most of the other social democrats, although they were good labor movement leaders, lacked political experience. Almost at once they were taxed with maintaining order and discipline in a dissolving army and creating a force that would be loyal to the Republic. This involved Ebert in a fateful deal with General Wilhelm Groener, of the old Imperial High Command. Groener offered to place the army at Ebert's disposal if the government agreed to put down any revolutionary outbreaks. This pact immediately radicalized the left wing of the USPD (Spartacists), who formed a separate German Communist Party and caused the USPD as a whole to resign from the government.

Groener may have wanted to honor his pledge, but other officers did not. The army did not serve the government loyally. Instead, the officers betrayed it to Hitler, when they realized that he could restore Germany to military greatness. The army was also allowed to raise a corps of volunteers, the *Freikorps*, under the new Defense Minister, Gustav Noske, to put down any revolts. These units were led by the old Army Command and paid by the Prussian War Ministry. They attracted rootless, frustrated men who later formed the nucleus of Hitler's Storm Troops. Their first action was to crush the Spartacist rising in Berlin; later they began to support plots for the overthrow of the Republic. In 1920, one of their brigades—Brigade Ehrhardt—occupied Berlin, flaunting swastikas and singing an anti-Semitic marching song:

> *Wir sind keine Judenknechte,*
> *In Deutschland soll immer nur ganz allein*
> *Ein Deutscher unser Führer sein.*
>
> *(We are no slaves of the Jews,*
> *Forever and ever in Germany*
> *Shall only a German our leader be.)*

It was this brigade that assassinated the man who signed the armistice—Matthew Erzberger. Their 1920 plot failed, but the treatment of the traitors is significant. Over 700 were charged with high treason, but only one received a sentence—five years of honorary confinement—and continuation of his pension.

The Army High Command, through General Ludendorff, also recommended that responsibility for peace negotiations be placed on civilian politicians. Blaming the home front for the military collapse, he said, "They must now eat the dish which they have prepared for us." The defeat of Germany was referred to as "the stab in the back," and was identified as the work of criminal conspirators—Jews and socialists. Hitler was later to call them the "November criminals."

Weaknesses of the Weimar Republic. In 1923, when Hitler made his first bid for power, he failed miserably, was mocked, and imprisoned for attempting to overthrow the republic. But by 1933, he was hailed as Germany's savior. In those ten years, the Weimar government was so weakened and battered that it could not cope with the serious economic, social, and political crises of the early thirties. The question of causation is a question still debated by historians: How was it possible for the Nazis to come to power in a society of advanced intellectual and scientific culture? Some find "wrong turns" or unfortunate characteristics in earlier German history: the authoritarian tradition from Martin Luther on; belated unification; accelerated industrialization in a largely feudal society; philosophical contempt and popular distaste for democracy; excessively high values placed on the military virtues. Many Germans scorned values associated with individualism, dissent, and pacifism, which were considered cowardly and weak. The German hunger for a deep, ultimate reality, embodied in the state, was contrasted with a simple Western optimism and belief in political action. However, these older elements, however they may have contributed to Germany's acceptance of Hitler and Nazism, were hardly responsible by themselves. As most historians have interpreted the coming of Nazism, it was certain historic roots *in combination with* the crises of the early thirties, or the crises themselves that must be examined in trying to answer the question: why Germany?

Among the elements of the immediate pre-Nazi period were the unstable coalition governments; the ruinous depression; the acute, general fear of Communism; the cunning exploitation by Hitler of grievances and ambitions of the Junkers, industrialists, peasants and workers; the vehement struggle between German Communists and Socialists; the pent-up frustrations over the Versailles Treaty; the lax treatment of opponents of the Republic; the widespread hankering for the old order—Reich and Kaiser—or something like it. Despite the turbulence of the Weimar period and the fundamental changes promised by the radical parties, much remained the same: the nobles kept their large estates, the old civil servants kept their jobs, the judges their posts, and the industrialists their factories. The generals also remained. Weimar produced no new heroes and the republican government failed to arouse strong national devotion. No new authority inspired popular respect or obedience.

The Weimar period was also marked by a climate of lawlessness. Political groups attacked each other on the streets with their own military units, including the Nazi Storm Troops. Assassinations became common. Among the victims were Matthias Erzberger, a leader of the Catholic Centrist Party, who had led the German delegation that signed the peace treaty; and Foreign Minister Walter Rathenau, a Jew, who had successfully organized the supply of scarce raw materials during the war. At his trial, one of the assassins said that Rathenau was a "creeping Bolshevik," and "one of the 300 wise men of Zion," who wanted to apply the theories of the "Jew Lenin" to Germany.

Growing Anti-Semitism in the 1920s. The reference to the "wise men of Zion" is significant. It refers to a notorious forgery known as the Protocols of the Elders of Zion, describing an alleged scheme for a Jewish worldwide conspiracy. (*See Reading No. 1.*) In spite of conclusive proof that the Protocols—like the ritual murder charges against Jews—had been fabricated, they had sensational popularity and large sales in the 1920s and 1930s. They were translated into many different languages and sold widely in Arab lands, England, and the United States. But after World War I they had their greatest success in Germany where they were used to explain all the disasters that had occurred: the defeat in the war, hunger, the destructive inflation. In 1920, a Jewish reporter described several meetings which he attended, completely devoted to the Protocols: "The speaker," he wrote, "was usually a professor, a teacher, an editor, a lawyer, or someone on that level. The audience consisted of members of the educated class, civil servants, tradesmen, former officers, ladies, above all students—students of all faculties and years of seniority . . . Passions were whipped up to the boiling point." This forgery was later to become the very center of Hitler's message and was used as a manual in his war to annihilate Jews.

The identification of the Jew as utterly alien, outside the pale of normal citizenship or membership in the German *Volk* was a central point in the platform of the German Workers' Party, whose name was changed to that of National Socialist Workers' Party—the Nazis—in 1920. Point Four reads: "None but members of the nation may be citizens of the state. None but those of German blood, whatever their creed, may be members of the nation. No Jew, therefore, may be a member of the nation." Point 24 adds that the party "combats the Jewish-materialist spirit within us and around us." In Articles 5, 7, 8, and 23, which mention "non-citizens" or "non-Germans," Jews are meant.

The conservative, nationalist German National People's Party took a stand in the same year "against the predominance of Jewry in government and public life." During the next ten years, dozens of anti-Semitic associations and societies were formed and over 400 anti-Semitic periodicals were issued. Anti-Jewish bills were regularly introduced into state and national legislatures. The German youths in the universities, the declassed low middle-class, and the uprooted and dislocated throughout German society were becoming increasingly susceptible to anti-Semitic appeals and arguments. Earlier layers of Christian anti-Semitism had created the image of the Jew as Christ-killer, Satan, part of a rejected pariah people doomed to wander, despised money-lender, incapable of salvation. Over these layers were added images of the Jew as the symbol of everything frightening to many Germans in the shifting, uncertain world of the 1920s: the loss of national honor and power, the loss of imperial order, the threat of revolution, loss of one's place in the social order, the dangers of a permissive, unrestrained urban culture, the breakdown of familiar traditions.

The Aryan Myth. Hitler used all of these imagined threats with intuitive cunning and political shrewdness. He also exploited the cult of race and the myth of Aryan supremacy, which had been preached by the German oriental scholar Paul de Lagarde; Houston Stewart Chamberlain, (*See Reading No. 2*) author of *Foundations of the Nineteenth Century;* the social Darwinist philosopher Eugen Dühring; and racist journalist Wilhelm Marr, among others. Appeal of this myth lay in its power to recall the world of Teutonic glory, with its pagan gods and heroes. Race is now all-important. Good and evil are in one's blood; they are implanted biologically and cannot be changed. (*See*

Reading No. 3.) Supporting the racial myth was also the *Volkisch* strain that is so strong in German history—the mysterious essence and soulfulness of Germanness which no outsider can share but which gives supreme meaning to national life. One of the main elements of the *Volkisch* force was the glorification of the supposedly pure, simple, honorable life style of the Middle Ages, when people worked and loved the land and lived in peaceful harmony. By contrast, the Jews were seen as rootless phantoms who had no contact with the land, and who were spoiling the dream of communal peace by their restlessness.

Under Bismarck, Germany had become an aggressive, expanding, intensely nationalistic power. The idea of a ''master race'' gripped many Germans. Darwinian biology gave it a pseudo-scientific basis. By contrast, Jews were considered a negative race, inferior and undesirable. Aryan supremacists said that Jews polluted and defiled the pure German stock and must be eliminated. Hitler, who had an obsessive hatred of Jews, took up these ideas literally and translated them into genocidal destruction—the Holocaust. However one interprets the frustrations or ''wrong turns'' in Germany history, or the severe crises of the early 1930s, it is impossible to overestimate the factor of Hitler in the decision to physically annihilate European Jewry. He was the architect, the driving force, and single-minded center of the war against Jewry. What others had merely dared to suggest—the elimination of Jews from Germany, then, the world—Hitler dared to implement. The essential emptiness of Nazi ''ideology,'' as well as the inconsistencies and fuzziness of the party program, were revealed soon after Hitler consolidated his power and made war. Hermann Rauschning, a Nazi leader in Danzig who soon left the party, spoke of Nazism as a ''revolution of nihilism.'' Naked power and exploitation of conquered peoples and the German people as well came to be the stark features of the regime. Europe was not re-made; it was destroyed. Early doctrines and pledges were abandoned or reversed. But anti-Semitism remained an unchanging core-hatred. The Jew objectified and embodied all of the specific problems and evils targeted by the Nazis; hatred of the Jew was Hitler's consuming obsession.

Hitler's Obsessive Anti-Semitism. In the autobiographical sections of *Mein Kampf,* Hitler locates the origins of his violent anti-Semitism—his experiences in Vienna from 1909 to 1913, (*See Reading No. 4*) where he lived a hand-to-mouth existence, hoping to be admitted to the city's Academy of Fine Arts. The city's political life was dominated by a rabble-rousing anti-Semitic mayor, Karl Lueger, whom Hitler came to admire. Later he was to use with uncanny skill the tricks of manipulating masses of people which Lueger had perfected on a small scale. In Vienna, Hitler also began to read the large quantities of anti-Semitic propaganda which abounded. For a time he was fascinated by a deranged racial mythologist named Lanz von Liebenfels, who had visions of creating a blond master race. In his writings, Liebenfels depicted the struggle between blond Aryan heroes and the ape people representing lower races. Between these two groups there raged continual warfare. Thus, the biological necessity of destroying all inferior people. Liebenfels deplored the racial shame of blond women living with lesser humans and urged marriage helpers for breeding colonies of racially pure children. The destruction of the inferior races was to be achieved through X-rays, sterilization, starvation and death—all of which the Nazis later practiced. In Vienna, Georg von Schönerer had also left a legacy of anti-Semitism within the Pan-German movement, which wanted union between Austria and Germany and German supremacy over the many nationalities in the Austro-Hungarian empire. These ideas also influenced Hitler, especially the anti-Semitism of the movement, which, he said, ''was based on a correct understanding of the importance of the racial problem, and not on religious ideas.''

In Vienna, Hitler also encountered east European Jews for the first time. They repelled him by their black caftans and sidelocks. They were unclean and lived wretchedly. Hitler blamed them for prostitution and the white slave traffic. He could not bear the thought that such Jews could be Germans, that they might have sexual relations with German women. In Vienna, he also became disgusted by the cosmopolitan features of the city, by the mixing of so many different ethnic groups. He also noticed that many Jews were active in the city's cultural and artistic life, in the liberal press, and in the social democratic movement, and these associations further sharpened his revulsion. His family background may also have contributed to his obsession with racial purity and with Jews as defilers of German blood.

Some psychoanalysts have suggested that Hitler's vehement hatred of Jews may have been a projection of his own self-hatred and guilt-provoking fantasies. Considerable uncertainty surrounds his own origins. His father Alois was illegitimate, and the identity of his father remains in doubt to this day. Hitler's father and mother (Alois' third wife) were blood relatives; his mother was a second cousin or niece.

The boy Adolf knew something about this blood relationship (the marriage needed special church sanction), creating doubts about his own identity and feelings of fear and guilt. In a massive projection, he may have thrown these unconscious feelings onto the Jew as defiler and blood-poisoning criminal. It would then be an easy step to imagine a plan of world Jewry to undermine the racial vigor and purity of the German people.

Hitler left Vienna in 1913, went to Munich, fought in World War I, and afterward worked as an education officer in the Political Department of the Army Command in Munich. His job was to help indoctrinate army recruits against the dangers of Bolshevism. In 1919, he was assigned to make a report on the newly-formed German Workers' Party. The next year he himself joined the party and was mainly responsible for drawing up its platform. By this time, Hitler had added Germany's defeat in the war to the list of things the Jews were responsible for, and within the next few years he met a number of like-minded Germans. He was also introduced to Alfred Rosenberg, a Russian emigré from the Bolshevik Revolution who returned to Germany with a copy of the notorious forgery, *The Protocols of the Elders of Zion.* Rosenberg became Hitler's intellectual guide on anti-Semitic and anti-Bolshevik thought and the concept of living space—*Lebensraum*—as a factor of power. His ideas about Jews began to crystallize and he began making public speeches urging the removal of Jews from the nation. Germany's defeat, the evils of bolshevism, war, depressions, financial crisis—everything was blamed on the Jews. Of the 25 points in the Nazi Party platform—a hodge-podge of vague appeals to workers, peasants, and the middle class—six dealt directly or indirectly with Jews.

Build-up of the Nazi Party. Hitler was imprisoned after the unsuccessful Munich *Putsch* in 1923, but used the subsequent trial to attack Weimar democracy. He was sentenced to five years in prison, but was released by Christmas 1924. Admiring women brought flowers and special foods to him during his brief imprisonment and he spent much of the time dictating *Mein Kampf* to Rudolf Hess and other idolizing secretaries. After Hitler's growing popularity in 1930, the book became a best-seller. However, the years from 1925 to 1929 were lean ones for Hitler and the Nazis. Germany enjoyed relative political stability and economic recovery and there were ideological and personality conflicts within the Nazi movement. Hitler began to work furiously to put his stamp on the party and build support. By 1926 he had won over Josef Goebbels and made him *Gauleiter* of Berlin. In time Goebbels created a new type of political journalism—the printed word as pure agitation. He caused an uproar in ''Red Berlin,'' disrupting meetings, denouncing the so-called ''Jew Press,'' printing outrageous cartoons and placards, manipulating facts and symbols to spread the myth of the Jew as arch-enemy. Early in 1930 he became head of Nazi propaganda and in 1933, Minister of Propaganda, the Nazi evil genius who saturated Germany with anti-Semitic newspapers, films, radio programs and posters. The notorious anti-Semite, Julius Streicher, was building support for Hitler in Bavaria. In 1927, Hermann Göring returned to Germany and introduced Hitler to some upper-class social and industrial contacts. In 1928, both Goebbels and Göring were among the twelve Nazis elected to the *Reichstag*. Membership in the party grew slowly to 178,000 in 1929, and in that year Hitler had his first important political opportunity.

Assuming continued economic growth, the so-called Young Plan projected payment of German reparations until 1988, but by the summer of 1929, unemployment was ominously high and investment was falling. The vociferous leader of the anti-Young Plan forces was Alfred Hugenberg, head of the German National Party and owner of a newspaper empire who was determined to bring down the Republic. He formed a right-wing front with Hitler and other anti-republican elements and the Nazis, as a consequence, gained funds, respectability, publicity, and new members. The economic and political crises that followed the American stock market crash of October 1929 made the Nazi party a major political factor in Germany.

From March 1930 on, it was no longer possible to create a coalition with a majority in the *Reichstag,* and after July 1930, under Article 48 óf the Weimar Constitution, the Chancellor, in effect, ruled by decree. Hitler stepped up his attacks on the Republic, corrupt politicians, Reds, and above all, Jews, and increased his appeal to farmers, small shopkeepers, and workers no longer loyal to Marxist ideas. In the September 1930 elections, the Nazis won an astonishing 107 seats in the *Reichstag*—over 6 million votes, now the second party in the country.

An important element in the drift to Nazism was the hope of some army officers that Hitler could help restore Germany's military might and erase the humiliations of the Versailles Treaty. However, they also feared that his army of Storm Troops (SA) might eventually displace the *Reichswehr*. Hitler understood this ambivalence and skillfully bid for army support at a trial in Leipzig a few days after the 1930 election. Three young men in an artillery regiment were accused of distributing political leaflets among soldiers, contrary to the law that the armed forces were to avoid party politics. Three young officers, however, admitted that they would not fire on Nazis in case of a Nazi uprising and they were charged with treason. Hitler appeared as a witness for the defense and used this opportunity to announce his political intentions. He said the idea of an armed revolt was madness, and that the Nazis would come to power only by legal means. He also predicted that out of the small *Reichswehr,* a great army of the German people would arise. He stirred the court and army officers with his prediction of the coming German National Revolution and the rescue of the enslaved nation. Many generals now began to feel more sympathetic toward a movement they had formerly regarded with suspicion or contempt. They began to wonder if National Socialism might not be just what was needed to unite the people, to make the army great once more and restore the old German Reich. All three officers were given light sentences and the Nazis increased their infiltration of the *Reichswehr.*

The End of the Republic. Meanwhile, politics and violent military action took to the streets of Germany in the form of noisy demonstrations, disorderly parades, brawls among rival paramilitary organizations, and assassinations. Unemployment passed the 5 million mark by the end of 1931, while Nazi membership rose to over 800,000. Moreover, Hitler captured over 13 million votes in the 1932 presidential election. The chancellor, Heinrich Brüning, was contemptuous of Hitler, but an influential general, Kurt von Schleicher, advised the aging and declining President Hindenburg to open discussions with him and work out some accommodation. Brüning had been fully aware of the danger of admitting Nazis into the government and "framing them in," but neither Schleicher nor Brüning's successor Franz von Papen was. Shrewd and manipulative, von Schleicher believed that a von Papen government, which was his idea, could be used by him, but Chancellor von Papen went his own way, destroying the last bulwark of German democracy—the Prussian government. (*See Reading No. 5.*) In the process he became Reich Commissioner for Prussia and took over the resources of the largest federal state and a police force of 90,000.

In new elections in July 1932, the Nazis increased their number of seats to 230, but lost 34 in the November elections. (*See Reading No.*

6.) In the meantime, reparations payments had been cancelled and many Germans were revolted by brutal street fighting by the SA. Radical Nazis wanted to seize power, but Hitler held fast. He insisted that he would come to power legally and would accept nothing less than the chancellorship, but a chancellorship unshackled by a coalition.

The internal political situation was ominous. The Communists had increased their vote in the November elections and were joined by the Nazis in a Berlin transit strike, threatening civil war. Schleicher, upholding his steady concern for the army, declared that it no longer had any confidence in von Papen, and he became chancellor himself on December 2, 1932. But von Papen played the last card. On January 4, 1933, he and Hitler met in the home of the Cologne banker, Kurt von Schröder. Von Papen intrigued with Hitler to replace von Schleicher; von Schröder pledged funds; and a group of industrialists and bankers urged Hindenburg to let Hitler form a presidential cabinet. Von Schleicher meanwhile had failed to form a government and had to resign. After hard bargaining, Hitler and von Papen came to an understanding, strengthened by their common desire to defeat von Schleicher. By January 30, von Papen had reassured the reluctant Hindenburg that he could restrain Hitler in a coalition if Hitler were made chancellor and he, von Papen, vice-chancellor, who would always accompany Hitler in his talks with Hindenburg. Moreover, there would be only two other Nazis in the cabinet: Wilhelm Frick, Minister of the Interior, and Göring, Minister without Portfolio. The Conservatives were complaisant; the army was in place with Field-Marshal Werner von Blomberg as Defense Minister; the Communists did not call for mass strikes and were swiftly repressed when they tried to demonstrate; the SPD trade unions and *Reichsbanner* forces remained inert. The explosive potential danger of Hitler's legal ascent to power was unperceived—in Germany and internationally. Shoddy wheeling and dealing had brought him to this power which he would now use to destroy the Republic, unleash violence and terror of unimaginable dimensions, and begin the process of physically destroying the Jews of Europe.

CHAPTER TWO

PERSECUTION OF GERMAN JEWS, 1933–1938

Parliamentary Democracy Destroyed. Hitler quickly revealed the political cunning and autocratic will behind the early facade of compromise. He convinced Hindenburg to dissolve the Reichstag and hold new elections in March in the hope that the Nazis could win a clear majority. In February he lectured the generals on the identity of interests between them and an authoritarian government, and in the same month, Göring, acting arbitrarily, purged the Prussian police and added SA auxiliaries who terrorized citizens in the streets and political meetings. Hitler also persuaded Hindenburg to sign a decree prohibiting any public meetings, publications, or statements that allegedly endangered the vital interests of the state. This decree was used immediately against Communists, Socialists and other anti-Nazi groups and individuals. On February 27, the *Reichstag* building went up in flames. Although the cause is still somewhat disputed, the fire was very likely instigated by the Nazis and blamed on Marinus van der Lubbe, a half-witted Dutch Communist who had committed arson. There was no sign whatsoever of a revolution, but van der Lubbe gave the Nazis the dupe they needed and the pretext for new emergency measures. Hitler induced a confused and frightened Hindenburg to sign a decree euphemistically called ''For the Protection of the People and State,'' suspending all of the basic rights of citizens, and imposing the death sentence for arson, sabotage, resistance to the decree; and disturbances to public order. Arrests could be made on suspicion and imprisonment without trial or the right of counsel. The suspension was never lifted throughout the entire course of Nazi rule and the decree of February 28 destroyed fundamental guarantees under Weimar democracy.

During the next few days, up to elections on March 5, the Nazi Brown Terror broke loose. By making the trumped-up Communist threat ''official,'' Hitler threw millions of Germans into panic. Arbitrary arrests multiplied while truckloads of Storm Troops rampaged through the streets, broke into homes, rounded up victims, including many Jews, and took them to SA barracks where they were beaten and tortured. Freely using the resources of the national and Prussian governments, and the wealth contributed by business and industry, the

Nazis carried on an election campaign unprecedented in Germany. But despite the frenzy of terror and propaganda, the Nazis received only 44 percent of the vote. Hitler then decided on a scheme to pass a law enabling him to govern without any check by the *Reichstag*, but first, on March 21, in a dramatic gesture, he opened the new *Reichstag* in the Garrisonkirche in Potsdam, where Frederick the Great was buried. The church was a hallowed shrine, to which many Germans had made pilgrimages. In formal dress and top hat, Hitler paid homage to the aged President and the old Reich, reassuring the barons and generals and loyalists of the imperial regime that he would not break with the traditions. The chair reserved for the Kaiser was left empty. The SS and SA forces stood in disciplined ranks on one side with the honor guard of the Army on the other. Just the day before, Heinrich Himmler, then provisional police president of Munich, completed arrangements for setting up the first concentration camp at Dachau, near Munich. (*See Reading No. 7.*)

It was at Dachau, beginning in May 1941, that medical experiments on prisoners were begun, including high altitude tests with oxygen and freezing experiments to see how much a human being could endure before dying. Later, in many camps experimentation included sterilization and various lethal injections.

On March 23, the first and last *Reichstag* of the Third Reich met in the Kroll Opera House. Outside were massed black-shirted SS men; inside the corridors were lined with the brown shirts. A huge swastika banner draped one wall. Most of the Communists and a number of Socialist deputies had already been arrested. The votes of the Center Party were crucial for Hitler in getting enough—a two-thirds majority—to pass an Enabling Act and this they supplied, thus giving him the arbitrary power he craved. He could now use this power without the *Reichstag,* and ignore the constitution and the president. He could also enact laws, unchecked by any other authority.

Now, one by one, Germany's institutions began to surrender and crumble. All political parties were destroyed or dissolved themselves. The federal structure of the *Länder* was torn down and Reich, i.e., Nazi commissioners were put in charge of the states. Trade unions were dissolved. Opposition clergy were arrested. The Nazi Party had, in Hitler's words, become the state. Only one sphere remained: the command of the armed forces, which pledged allegiance to the President. But in August 1934, Hindenburg died and Hitler became Chief Commander as well as President and Führer of the German Reich to

whom every officer and individual in the armed forces pledged unconditional obedience and willingness to lay down his life.

The Anti-Jewish Boycott. After the Enabling Act was passed,
Hitler turned his attention to Jews and instructed Goebbels to organize
a large-scale boycott of Jewish shops and business, in retaliation
against a boycott of German goods that had been organized abroad, for
which German Jews were held responsible. Julius Streicher, editor of
the viciously anti-Semitic newspaper *Der Stürmer,* was told to form a
boycott committee and lists of specific businesses and individuals to
be boycotted were published. (*See Reading No. 8.*) On April 1, Nazi
pickets were posted in front of stores and factories belonging to Jews
and in front of Jewish professional offices to prevent anyone from entering. Göring, meanwhile, had ordered German Jewish leaders to
deny reports of Nazi atrocities committed against Jews. Germans who
tried to buy from Jews were shamed and exposed publicly.

The boycott lasted only one day but it had important implications
and consequences. Moreover, it revealed the completeness and efficiency of Nazi information on Jewish economic life. It also strengthened the idea that it was permissible to damage and even destroy that
life with impunity. Later measures were based on this assumption.
Yet, throughout March, so many Jews had been dismissed from positions in civil service and professions that Hindenburg himself wrote
to Hitler, complaining about the cases of Jews in public service who
had been wounded in World War I being dismissed. Hitler replied by
promising that the solution to this problem would be ''carried out legally and not by capricious acts,'' but this was a hypocritical gesture.

The First Anti-Jewish Laws. On April 7, 1933, two days after
Hitler's reply, the first anti-Jewish law was passed, removing all
Jews—referred to as non-Aryans—and political opponents of the regime from civil service. To meet Hindenburg's objections, Jews employed before 1914 and World War I veterans were exempted for the
moment.

Eventually, 400 anti-Jewish laws and decrees were passed. To sim-
plify matters, the definition of ''non-Aryan'' established guidelines,
April 11, 1933. A person of non-Aryan descent was defined as someone who had one Jewish parent or grandparent. This formed the basis
of the Aryan paragraph which was soon applied by many private individuals and organizations as well as government agencies and re-

moved many Jews from educational, cultural, and social institutions. It became a point of honor with many Germans to put Aryan clauses into effect and bar Jews from work or membership. On April 21, a law banned *shechita*, the Jewish ritual slaughtering of animals, and in July, laws canceling naturalization of "undesirables," specifying east European Jews in Germany, were passed.

The Nazi Apparatus of Terror.

In 1933, ten concentration camps were set up in Germany, the functions of which were carefully concealed from the world, and the Nazi terror apparatus began to expand and take on a menacing face. Terror, of course, is not new in history, but under the Nazis, terror was revolutionized. Hitler used it not only against opponents, and not merely as a deterrent, but as a permanent weapon aimed at the German people as a whole. Opponents of the regime had enormous difficulties resisting. (*See Reading No. 9.*)

The concentration camps were intended not only to break the prisoners as individuals and to spread terror among the rest of the population, but also to provide the *Gestapo* with a training ground, a way of conditioning them so that they would lose all familiar human emotions and attitudes. In talks with a Nazi leader even before he became chancellor, Hitler had said: "We must be ruthless. . . . Only thus shall we purge our people of their softness . . . of their Gemütlichkeit . . . and their degenerate delight in beer-swilling. . . . I don't want the concentration camps transformed into penitentiaries. Terror is the most effective political instrument . . . It is my duty to make use of every means of training the German people to cruelty, and to prepare them for war. . . . There must be no weakness or tenderness."[1]

There were a number of systems of terror in Nazi Germany, some overlapping, often feuding with each other in ruthless conflict over power, influence and the spoils of victory. The first system was the *Gestapo,* organized by Göring, who, as Minister of the Interior of Prussia, administered two-thirds of Germany and controlled the Prussian police. After purging the regular police and replacing them with Nazis, he added a small unit of his own called the *Geheime Staatspolizei,* the Secret State Police, or *Gestapo.* The *Gestapo* was first used against Göring's political opponents, but was then aimed at any so-called enemies of the regime and could seize and arrest anyone at will without

[1] Hermann Rauschning, *The Voice of Destruction.* New York, G. P. Putnam's Sons, 1940, pp. 16, 83.

regard for court or law. Under Heinrich Himmler, it quickly expanded as an arm of the dread SS, the Black Shirts.

Himmler had been a chicken farmer and fertilizer salesman before the war. In 1923 he joined the march during the attempted *Putsch* of 1923 and for a time worked in the party office in Landshut under Gregor Strasser, a leading Nazi ideologue who broke with Hitler in 1932 and was later murdered. In this job Himmler began to collect confidential reports on party members made by his spies, thus building up secret files later used by Reinhard Heydrich in the Security Service (SD). The SS (*Schutzstaffel*) was originally set up under Himmler in 1929 as a protective guard for Hitler and other leading Nazis, but Himmler ultimately developed it into a vast empire of terror. He had helped to secure Bavaria for the Nazis and fell under the spell of blood and soil cranks who wanted to breed a future race of blond Nordic leaders as world overlords. For a few years, the SS was subordinate to the SA, but Himmler steadily built up his force into a combination private army and police force, enlisting only the most loyal followers of Hitler and racial fanatics like himself. The open membership reached 52,000 by 1933, but, in addition, Himmler recruited a shadow corps of SS officers who kept their affiliation secret until Hitler fully controlled the state as well as the party, but who then filled huge parts of the government machinery.

Purge of the Storm Troops, June 30, 1934. Himmler's ascendancy came after the purge of the SA under Ernst Roehm. In 1933, Roehm's troops number over four million men, arousing fears among army leaders that they might replace the army. Roehm indeed had proposed that his forces be made the basis of a new people's army—an intolerable idea for the old officers' corps. Roehm also wanted radical social and economic changes—a Second Revolution after the Nazis came to power. But such changes would be intolerable to industrialists and other conservative elements whose support Hitler needed. A power struggle brought Himmler and Göring together against Roehm. They told Hitler that he was plotting against him and urged drastic action. It came on June 30, 1934, the "Night of the Long Knives," when Roehm and several hundred men in the SA and a number of marked men, branded as traitors, were murdered. Hitler made much of the depraved morals of the men who were killed and the danger they posed to the state. The cabinet legalized the slaughter as a necessary measure for the defense of the state, and Hitler and Göring were thanked by Hindenburg. The army, of course, was pleased with the elimination of the SA as its rival, but showed itself unwilling or incapable of challenging the gangster-like powers under Hitler's control. Moreover, it deluded itself into thinking that it could hold on to its traditional perogatives. However, in place of the SA came the SS.

Himmler's Rise to Power. As a reward for carrying out the executions on June 30, Himmler advanced in rank and prestige. Göring named him chief deputy of the Prussian *Gestapo* and he immediately began to build a police empire of his own—the terrible machine of terror that was to become the scourge of the continent and the annihilator of Jews. After the Roehm purge, the concentration camps were turned over to SS control. Guard duty was given to the SS Death Head units, whose members were recruited from the toughest, most sadistic Nazi elements. By 1936, the *Gestapo* was absorbed into the SS and in the same year Himmler gained control of the entire police force in Germany, which he pushed into the framework of the Nazi Party. Later, Himmler created an SS Supreme Command, consisting of twelve departments which duplicated many of the departments of government, including a huge army and a department that organized huge population upheavals after the war started.

A third system of terror during the Third Reich was the SD (*Sicherheitsdienst*) or Security Service. This substructure was also within the SS, and did not number more than 3,000, but its intelligence and counterintelligence systems pried into the lives of all Germans through the use of thousands of part-time informers. Under Reinhard Heydrich, the head of the SD, security and terror were brought to murderous effectiveness. After the June purge of the SA, Heydrich began to penetrate the political police with personnel and build up dossiers on great and small Nazis, including Hitler himself, for blackmail purposes. Many of his recruits were bright, university trained men who were unable to find jobs, but their civilized backgrounds were no barrier to later assignments carrying out orders in the murderous *Einsatzgruppen,* or mobile killing squads that accompanied the German army into Russia, or enforcing the sinister Night and Fog decrees whose victims vanished without a trace. Toward the end of 1934, a so-called expert on Zionism, named Adolf Eichmann was hired by the SD to work in its department for Jewish affairs. This department gathered information about prominent Jews in Germany and abroad and monitored the Jewish press. It also made studies of Jewish organizations and books about Judaism. Jewish organizations in Germany, their meetings and members came under close SD surveillance, and agreements were worked out between the SD and the *Gestapo*. By 1936, Himmler turned over the administration of the *Gestapo* to Heydrich and the line between the *Gestapo* and SD became extremely blurred after that time. The distinctive functions which these agencies once had all but disappeared, and *Gestapo* and SD came to be used interchangeably. By 1939, Eichmann became head of Department IV B 4 in Heydrich's huge police and terror organization (RSHA), and organized transports of Jews to concentration and death camps. (*See Reading (Chart) No. 10.*)

Intense Patriotism of German Jews. The agencies that destroyed the Jews of Europe evolved out of these agencies of terror, but the process developed slowly, with great cunning and stealth. Harsh measures were concealed by euphemisms and legalistic camouflage. Lulls followed brutal repressions, creating illusions that one could survive within prescribed limits. Moreover, between 1933 and 1938, the Nazis disagreed about what to do with and against Jews; they improvised, experimented, and were often inconsistent in their efforts to solve the "Jewish Question." Not until 1938, by which time Hitler had fully consolidated his dictatorship, did they adopt a clear policy. During those five years, German Jewry fluctuated from moods of bewilderment, shock, momentary relief, then disbelief, to a grasp of the coming or actual reality, only to be tossed again by waves of hope.

In looking back to the reactions of German Jews to the coming crisis, we must be careful not to judge from the perspective of history which has already unrolled. "In hindsight, it is easy to appear wise," as we have been reminded. Virtually all Jews at first believed—as did most observers in the West—that National Socialism was a transitory affair, something that would pass, but must not be aggravated by anti-Nazi actions. Passionately attached and long rooted to the German Fatherland, (*See Reading No. 11*) most German Jews believed they could hold on and hold out, that they could count on long-time friends and allies to help them in their negotiations and bargaining with the regime. Culturally and economically assimilated to a high degree, German Jews had faced anti-Semitism during their long history in Germany and had prevailed. They, at first, felt they could do the same in the face of Nazi anti-Semitism. Their chief organizational defense was the Central Association of German Citizens of Jewish Faith, which had battled anti-Semitism in the usual ways and even made po-litical alliances and engaged in political activity to fight anti-Semitism. The fact that they were confronting a wholly new kind of anti-Semi-tism dawned slowly. At first, the general feeling was to wait out the storm, to make a resolute defense of constitutional rights, to adjust to new situations and endure as long as there were laws.

The April 1 boycott drew the following response—quite a typical one—from the Berlin *Gemeinde*: ''The charges which have harmed our people touch most deeply our honor. For the sake of both our honor and truth, we solemnly raise our guard against the attack. We trust that the Reichspresident and the Reich government will not allow our legal rights and livelihood to be seized in the German fatherland. We stress in this hour our relationship to the German people, our obligations and most passionate wish is working for its renewal and strengthening.''

In the early and middle 1930s, most Jews stayed in the country they loved because they believed they could survive and because there were few emigration possibilities. Yet, before the end of 1933, 37,000 Jews had left Germany—the largest number to leave in any single year thereafter. Many of these were part of the exodus of the large German liberal intelligentsia and radical groups. Jewish war veterans consid-ered those who left as deserters, ''shooting arrows from secure hiding places.'' Even the Zionists, as late as June 1933, appealed to the Nazis not to snap the long historical relationship between the two peoples. ''The Jews are not enemies of the state,'' they said. ''German Jews wish for the rise of Germany, for which they have given the best of their resources.'' Late in 1933, the distinguished Jewish philosopher Mar-tin Buber told his fellow Jews: ''Today we need not dissociate from German-ness, with which we have an inner relationship which nothing that Germans do can change.'' In a short time, of course, he changed his mind and emigrated in 1938. Even so, the separation was painful for, as he later wrote, ''the symbiosis of German and Jewish existence, as I experienced it in the four decades that I spent in Germany'' was ''most extraordinary and meaningful.''

What to do with German Jews? Nazi Uncertainties (1933–1935). The Nazis themselves, at first, were at odds as to what to do about Jews. Jewish cultural as well as physical survival seemed possible and was encouraged in some quarters. For example, the *Jü-dische Kulturbund* was organized in 1933 and provided purposeful work for professional Jewish musicians, actors, and artists who had been expelled from German cultural fields. As was true of the Jewish schools, which were established after Jewish children and teachers were forced to leave regular schools, so the programs of the *Kulturbund* tried to balance Jewish themes with those from general European culture. At its peak, the organization enrolled over 50,000 members, but its early autonomy was destroyed and Party censorship banned Schiller and the German romantics, all revolutionary references, Beethoven and Mozart (after the absorption of Austria in 1938), and severely cut the plays of Moliere and Shakespeare.

However, between 1933 and 1935, there was a lull in anti-Jewish persecution and a false optimism was induced by the purge of June 30, 1934. Some German Jews actually returned to Germany after the purge. Moreover, in some official agencies that still contained holdover civil servants from the republic, Jews were still treated with great courtesy and respect, especially in the Reich Office of Migration. (*See Reading No. 12.*) After the panic emigration of 1933, these officials worked cooperatively with Jewish relief agencies until 1938, and helped emigrants prepare for new homes with proper vocational retraining, language skills, and orientation. Matters affecting Jews that were handled by the Ministry of Economy, which was still staffed with old-line officials, were also handled in a civilized manner. Some Jewish textile and clothing firms, for example, were able for a time to obtain government contacts to produce goods for the armed services. Jews also hoped for support and protection from the non-Nazi parties in the cabinet, and von Papen tried to encourage such hopes, but this illusion fell away quickly. Von Papen's office was wrecked during the June purge and he was kept under house arrest for four days; two of his advisers were shot as were a number of Catholic leaders. It is true that many individual Germans were ashamed of the anti-Jewish measures and helped their Jewish neighbors in many ways, but German institutions did not respond. After the boycott, the universities were silent and submissive, as were the courts and the churches.

The Leadership of Rabbi Leo Baeck. To Rabbi Leo Baeck, who was to lead German Jewry through its greatest trial, boycott day was the ''day of the greatest cowardice. Without the cowardice, all that followed would not have happened.'' What Rabbi Baeck meant was that Hitler's order for a boycott of Jewish business was a tentative step, almost as if he were feeling his way. How far would the German people allow him to go? Would the religious, social, and business institutions protest this officially inspired anti-Semitism?

Rabbi Baeck, the acknowledged intellectual and spiritual leader of German Jewry, was one of the few German Jews who were fundamentally pessimistic about the coming trial. Soon after Hitler came to power, while addressing a meeting of Jewish communal organizations, Rabbi Baeck said, "The thousand-year history of German Jewry has come to an end." But he did not remain passive. Quite the reverse. He assumed many roles in the sudden crisis. As rabbi, he urged Jews to maintain faith in the ultimate triumph of justice, to remember that the "essence of justice is that is exists, that it is not woven into the wheel of happenings, that is stands firm and independent from whatever happens and from whatever pulls it in the other direction." He tried to create a sense of inner freedom among Jews that could sustain them through the mounting persecution. On a more practical level, he agreed to serve as the spokesman for all German Jews, as head of the *Reichsvertretung der deutschen Juden*—the Representative Council of German Jews—in September 1933. Up to this time, German Jews lacked a central body; there were serious regional and organizational differences and hundreds of *gemeinden*, or officially recognized religious communities. (*See Reading No. 13.*) Baeck was able to command the respect of all factions. He asked Jews of Germany to forget all differences among themselves and unite with passion for Judaism. Included in the Council were Zionist groups, moderately liberal Jews, Orthodox Jews, welfare agencies, veterans and youth groups—a broad representation of agencies that carried out specific functions of welfare, emigration, education and fund-raising. The Council tried to be the political voice for all German Jewry in relation to the government. In the early months of its existence, it made contacts with government offices, documented abuses and restrictions, and appealed for redress on the basis of law.

Removal of Jewish Children from Schools. The Council also negotiated with Jews abroad for political support that would not expose them to retaliation, and for funds. One of its most important tasks was the bolstering of spirit through education and religious experience and preparation for emigration. After the Law Against Overcrowding German Schools was passed on April 25, 1933, quotas were set up and Jewish children were removed from public schools. (*See Reading No. 14.*) Soon thereafter, Jewish schools had to be provided for them. The

Council allocated one-fifth of its budget to education and set up a network of Jewish schools which became a fortress and refuge for Jewish children, shocked and bewildered by the turmoil invading their lives and the rejection they experienced from teachers and classmates.

Children who had grown up in a land they loved now had to learn to bear rejection and hatred in their regular schools and neighborhoods. City after city raced to set up Jews' benches in their schools to meet quota limits. "Racial science" became compulsory; every subject made ugly connections with the so-called dangers of Jewish influence and the entire Nazified course of study created unbearable emotional tensions for Jewish children. (*See Reading No. 15.*) Once enrolled in new Jewish schools, great adjustments had to be made by both students and teachers. The new world of the Jewish school had to compensate for the loss of the old familiar school and the depressing atmosphere at home.

A broad educational system for Jewish adults was also developed, to help them find new sources of strength within Judaism: the Bible, Jewish history and literature and Hebrew, as well as European humanistic subjects. But there was very little time in which to fortify either child or adult in Nazi Germany.

The Nuremberg Laws, September 15, 1935. On September 15, 1935, came the first frontal attack on every individual Jew in Germany—the "Law for the Protection of German Blood and German Honor," and the "Reich Citizenship Law," the so-called Nuremberg Laws to mark the ceremonial closing of the party congress in Nuremberg. (*See Reading No. 16.*)

These laws defined Jews negatively as persons ineligible to citizenship because they were not of "German blood," and effectively isolated them psychologically and socially from other Germans. Jews were not permitted to marry or have sexual relations with Germans, or display a German flag. Citizenship thus became a matter, not of individual rights, but a right derived from membership in the *Volk*. (Thirteen supplementary laws followed to July 1943 and further elaborated Hitler's anti-Jewish war.) Jews were further defined as persons having three Jewish grandparents, or two, if they belonged to the Jewish religious community (*Kultusgemeinde*) before September 15, 1935, or if they were married to Jews as of that date.

No Jew could possibly envision the sinister implications of these laws, for no Jew was physically harmed by them. But we now know that they had a much greater built-in danger than the earlier acts of Nazi violence, or even the rioting of *Kristallnacht* in November 1938. For the Nazis now had a definition that was the first of a chain of measures, one leading to another, escalating in severity and leading ultimately to the physical destruction of European Jewry. For, once Jews could be defined and identified, they could be and were segregated socially, politically, and economically from other Germans. Their property could be and was confiscated. They had become pariahs, outside the protection of the state. They were, in fact, to become the state enemy by state decree. "Race defilement is worse than murder," became the new commandment for many Germans. Much of this poisonous propaganda was carried by the leading Jew-baiter of Nazi Germany, Julius Streicher, ex-school teacher, *Gauleiter* of Franconia, organizer of the April 1933 boycott, and publisher of *Der Stürmer*.

Der Stürmer was first issued in 1923, with a small circulation, but it had an enormous growth after 1933—thousands heard Streicher at party rallies—and by the end of 1935, it had 500,000 subscribers. However, the readership was much larger, for each copy was read by several others and copies were read in public display cases, at bus stops and factory canteens. Special editions were devoted to racial defilement by Jews and ritual murders. Typical headlines read, "He Who Buys From a Jew Is a Traitor to the Nation," and "German Women and Girls: The Jews are Your Destruction." Streicher kept personal files and letters from correspondents. In a special "Pillory" column, he listed the names and addresses of Germans called "Stürmer Guards" who patronized Jewish shops, doctors, lawyers, and dentists, and mobilized Germans who acted as informers, obtained subscriptions, and filled the display cases. It is known that special editions for children had a noxious influence on German children, and that articles from *Der Stürmer* were used in school textbooks. Millions of minds were now suffused with horror and fear of Jews, giving rise to easy blackmail schemes. A casual encounter between a Jew and "Aryan" could lead to arrest of the Jew and confiscation of his shop; many Jews—without any hard evidence—were accused of having sexual relations with non-Jews and were arrested or subject to blackmail.

The devastating effects of the Nuremberg Laws soon swept over German Jewry. There were large-scale dismissals in business and factories. Jews still employed in civil service were fired. Jews and Jewish organizations were no longer "German" but "Jews (or Jewish) in Germany." German "Aryans" began to take over Jewish shops and business under voluntary "aryanization" measures. Long-term contracts with Jews were cancelled; some were denied food and drugs in certain stores. Most Jews now had to face the daily ordeal of being shunned, ostracized, and insulted, as well as hear and read the ugly propaganda. How was one to cope?

Some Jews, younger ones particularly, began to seriously prepare for vocational changes, hoping they would be able to emigrate and build new lives. Some found intellectual and spiritual comfort in the sense of being part of a community of faith and fate. Rabbis tried to counsel against despair and instill hope and strength. After the passage of the Nuremberg Laws, Rabbi Baeck composed a special prayer for the somber Yom Kippur service in 1935: "We stand before our God. With the same courage with which we confess our sins, individual and collective, we shall declare with deep aversion that the lies against us, and the defamation of our religion and its teachings, are beneath our dignity. We stand by our faith and our fate . . . We stand before our God . . . Before Him we bow, but we stand upright before men . . . "

Dr. Otto Hirsch, director of the *Reichsvertretung,* distributed copies of the prayer to all synagogues in Germany to be read, with the result that both he and Baeck were arrested and the prayer, described as "revolutionary," was forbidden to be read.

In the summer of 1936, there was another temporary lull in persecution while the Olympic games in Germany masked reality and deluded foreign visitors into believing that Hitler and the Nazis were solving German party factionalism, unemployment, and social embitterment. The games also obscured the significance of the German occupation of the Rhineland in March. Everything was available to visitors except military installations, concentration camps, and *Gestapo* cellars. And all anti-Jewish signs and propaganda were momentarily withdrawn, to be swiftly restored after the games were over. By the end of 1936, 25,000 Jews emigrated, and by the end of 1937, 129,000 Jews had left—a little over one-fourth of all German Jewry. In the following year 1938, conditions worsened and the urgency to leave Germany became sharper. But the opportunities diminished.

CHAPTER THREE

1938: THE CRUCIAL YEAR

The events of 1938, which mark the great divide between emigration and annihilation of European Jewry, must be understood against the background of Hitler's consolidation of power in that year and his foreign policy objectives. At a meeting of military and political leaders in November 1937, Hitler announced that he intended to go to war to acquire Austria and Czechoslovakia and eliminated the generals who opposed this policy. He no longer had to cultivate the allegiance of the army. After the war began, more and more Jews were to become victims, diminishing the possibilities of escape or resistance.

The year 1938 left the Jews of Germany increasingly vulnerable. A storm of decrees fell upon them. (*See Reading No. 17.*) They had to add the names Sara and Israel to their own names, and register their property, foreign as well as domestic, including the property of non-Jewish spouses. For these purposes, various lists of Jews were drawn up by tax offices and local police stations. The official recognition of all Jewish religious communities and their central organizations was abolished, thus losing their tax-exempt status and the power to tax members. By October 1938, 25 percent of all such bodies had to dissolve. On June 9, the great synagogue of Munich was destroyed on the personal order of Hitler, followed by the destruction of synagogues in Nuremberg (*See Reading No. 18*) and Dortmund. In mid-June there began the compulsory ''aryanization'' of Jewish businesses.

Failure of the Evian Conference. The German absorption of Austria in March 1938 led to mass arrests of Jews there, confiscation of their property, rampant Nazi terror and forced expulsion under the direction of Adolf Eichmann. Before the end of 1938, some 45,000 Jews fled from or were expelled from Austria. The failure of the Evian Conference in July 1938, originally called by President Roosevelt to spur international efforts to provide new homes for refugees, further strengthened Hitler's hand. (*See Reading No. 19.*) The Jews of Germany and Austria, many already stripped of their resources and desperate to find refuge, hoped for relief and rescue. However, the invitation to the 33 governments specified that no country would be expected to receive a greater number of emigrants than was permitted by existing legislation. Moreover, Roosevelt made it clear that it would be up to private groups to finance emigration projects. What was not known at the time was an inside State Department effort to control the outcome. An inner departmental memorandum said that it was preferable for the department ''to get out in front and attempt to guide the pressure, primarily with a view toward forestalling attempts to have the immigration laws liberalized.''

The contrast between the setting of the conference at Evian-les-Bains, France, a luxurious resort on the shore of Lake Geneva, and the plight of those trying to leave, was stark. The challenge of Evian was eloquently put by Anne O'Mare McCormick, columnist of *The New York Times:* ''It is heartbreaking to think of the queues of desperate human beings around our consulates in Vienna and other cities waiting in suspense for what happens at Evian. But the question they underline is not simply humanitarian. It is not a question of how many unemployed this country can safely add to its own unemployed millions. It is a test of civilization. Can America live with itself if it lets Germany get away with this policy of extermination, allows the fanaticism of one man to triumph over reason, refuses to take up this gage of battle against barbarism.''? Unknown to Miss McCormick and other reporters covering the conference, the Americans had been pressured by Britain into refusing to allow Chaim Weizmann, head of the Jewish Agency, to present the case for immigration to Palestine (*See Reading No. 20*), which was the one seemingly available place for Jews. Of all the nations, only the Dominican Republic offered any encouragement by offering unspecified areas for agricultural colonization. (Later, an area called Sousa, financed largely by Joint Distribution Committee funds, provided a haven for about 500 refugees, but by 1940, wartime transportation problems restricted arrivals.) No other country offered any increased acceptance of refugees. The United States agreed only to accept its combined German-Austrian quota of 27,370 immigrants under the existing law.

Within a week, the conference was over, with nothing accomplished except the creation of an Intergovernmental Committee on Refugees, which was to deal directly with the German government.

One particularly ominous chord was struck at Evian by the Swiss representative, Dr. Heinrich Rothmund, the former chief of the Swiss Federal Police. Rothmund spoke about the threatening refugee ''inundation'' of Switzerland following the German occupation of Austria. Three or four thousand refugees had crossed the border into Switzerland—some were interned, others were returned to Germany. The Swiss increased their police guards and patrols at the frontiers and mountain passes and set a new machinery in motion. They insisted on visa controls or special passports for Jews. The Germans carried this suggestion to the limit by marking the passports of all Jews with a large red "J," regardless of their destination. Jews living outside of Germany were not immune and were trapped by their passports when Hitler occupied countries to which they had fled.

Expulsions to Poland. Meanwhile, Hitler had acquired the Sudetanland in Czechoslovakia as a result of the Munich Pact in September 1938. The German people were elated and relieved that the danger of war had passed. But Hitler needed to whip them to a war-like state. "With such a people," he had said, "one cannot go to war." A pretext for violent rioting came late in October, when suddenly, thousands of Polish Jews who had been living in Germany were expelled. They were seized on the streets and in their homes and crowded into trucks and trains which took them to the Polish border at Zbaszyn, near Posen. Money, jewelry and luggage were taken and Polish officials then took them to a military camp where they were put into stables. In this mass of human misery was the Grynszpan family who had had a small grocery store in Hanover. They wrote to their 17-year old son Herschel who was in Paris, and the youth, overwrought by his family's suffering decided to shoot the German ambassador and thus shock the world into some action to save Jews. He went to the embassy, but instead of the ambassador, he was seen by a minor official named Ernst vom Rath. Grynzspan fired at him and two days later on November 9, vom Rath died.

The Pogroms of November 9–10, 1938. There followed the pogroms of *Kristallnacht,* the night of broken glass, an orgy of arson, plunder and murder of Jews. (*See Reading No. 21.*) One hundred ninety five synagogues were burned, more than 800 shops were destroyed and over 7000 looted. Twenty thousand Jews were taken off in the dead of night to concentration camps; many of them died under torture. *The New York Times* called the wave of destruction "unparalleled in Germany since the 30 Years' War." The Austrian Nazis, not to be outdone, joined the carnage and burned all of Vienna's synagogues and sent many Jewish men to concentration camps. American and

British consuls reported the horror of midnight arrests, the cold indifference of German police, and the beatings of Jews waiting in lines for the opening of consulates the following morning.

The Western press expressed outrage at these events and many civic and religious groups demanded action and rescue, but the governments did not respond. Propaganda Minister Goebbels challenged the democracies: ''If there is any country that believes it has not enough Jews, I shall gladly turn over to it all our Jews.'' But the doors were fast closing. President Roosevelt summoned Ambassador Hugh Wilson home for consultation but did not break off diplomatic relations with Germany. Although there was a very effective unofficial boycott of German goods, official trade relations continued. However, pressure for more decisive action came from many quarters. For example, 36 of the most prominent writers in the country sent a collective telegram to Roosevelt, saying: ''We feel we no longer have any right to remain silent. Thirty five years ago, a horrified America rose to its feet to protest against the Kishinev pogroms in tsarist Russia. God help us if we have grown so indifferent to human suffering that we cannot rise now in protest against pogroms in Germany.'' The President extended visitors' visas to about 12,000 German Jews whose visas had expired, so that, as he said, they would not have to return to Germany and concentration camps. Beyond that, he said, he looked to the Intergovernmental Committee on Refugees for new approaches and solutions. He also believed in the possibility of resettlement of Jews in sparsely settled lands. Many plans were explored but none materialized.

The Nazis, of course, gloated over Western failure to act—a reaction predicted by the American Ambassador to Poland, Anthony Drexel Biddle. Right after *Kristallnacht,* Biddle said that according to reliable sources in Germany, ''Nazi officials consider world opinion bankrupt. They believed people abroad would undoubtedly throw up their hands in horror, but they would do nothing about it.''

Biddle was right. The timing of the pogroms is significant. Hitler had shrewdly gambled on Western passivity, without opposition. His triumphs were already considerable. In 1936 he had occupied the demilitarized Rhineland and flexed German military muscle in the Spanish Civil War. In 1937, the Rome-Berlin axis was forged, and German and Italian military power swelled. In 1938, Hitler absorbed Austria without hindrance and bullied the Western powers into sacrificing Czechoslovakia at Munich. The Evian Conference in July had failed dismally to provide refuge. Nazi policy could now become radical, completely oblivious to Western moral outrage. Germany could now dare take extreme measures against Jews under its control. First came further economic punishment: a collective fine of one billion Reichsmarks (*See Reading No. 22*), a so-called indemnity for the death of vom Rath, as well as 250 million Reichsmarks to cover insurance benefits for their destroyed property. (These monies were immediately fed into the German rearmament program.) Then followed further deprivations: all telephones and radios owned by Jews were seized. In Munich, Leipzig, and Nuremberg, Jews could no longer buy food.

Future ominous actions were outlined at a meeting of the Council of Ministers, called by Göring on November 12. Göring's opening words indicated the nature of the meeting. "Today's meeting," he said, "is of decisive importance. I have received a letter which Bormann sent me by order of the Führer, asking that the Jewish question be now, once and for all, treated in its entirety and settled in some way. Yesterday the Führer telephoned me to point out again that decisive measures must be undertaken in a coordinated manner." Jews were to be completely eliminated from the economy, but there would be no more wasteful riots which destroyed goods badly needed by the German economy. The meeting was stunned to hear that millions of dollars of plate glass had been destroyed, belonging not to Jews, but to their non-Jewish landlords. Jewish insurance claims were paid by the insurance companies, but the money was then confiscated by the government, and Jewish property owners were ordered to make repairs themselves.

Reinhard Heydrich was also present at the meeting, but economic matters were not his concern. The main problem, he said, was to force Jews out of Germany. He boasted that Eichmann's Center for Emigration in Vienna had already eliminated 50,000 Jews from Austria and he wanted a similar machinery in Germany. Heydrich also wanted the remaining Jews isolated and he mentioned ghettos and movement controls. When Göring interrupted to say that Jews should not be allowed to starve, Heyrich said, "We'll have to decide whether we want that or not." Göring ended the four-hour meeting on a threatening note: "If in the near future the German Reich should come into conflict with foreign powers, it goes without saying that we in Germany should first come to a showdown with the Jews." He also added, "The Führer wants to say to other countries, 'Why are you always talking about the Jews? Take them.' "

German newspapers then picked up these themes. One proclaimed in its leading editorial that the German people had embarked on "the final and unalterably uncompromising solution of the Jewish problem." *Das Schwarze Korps,* the organ of the SS, was more explicit: In a lurid first-page article, the paper argued that "the Jewish problem should have been solved completely and with the most brutal methods in 1933 . . . but we lacked the military power we have today. . . . Because it is necessary, because we no longer hear the world's screeching and because, after all, no power on earth can hinder us, we will now bring the Jewish question to its totalitarian solution." It went on to detail Heydrich's plans and predicted the end of German Jewry.

Ironically, *Kristallnacht* was the last occasion of physical violence directed against Jews in Germany. There were serious repercussions abroad. The foreign press had reacted strongly and the boycott against German goods was spreading. Besides, the economic losses were too great. In the future, Nazi actions were to be taken systematically. They would allow for proper and thorough planning, through memoranda, correspondence and conferences.

This decision marks a revolutionary change in the history of anti-Semitism. Bureaucrats, with the air of confident specialists would now deplore "crude" anti-Semitism and excesses and put into action muderous action camouflaged by coded language. Mass murder was to become an administrative process. Professionals like Eichmann frequently condemned crude and vulgar anti-Semitism as they perfected assembly line techniques of mass murder. To the end, Eichmann denied that he was anti-Semitic.

Excesses in Austria. Meanwhile, Austrian Jews experienced shocking excesses as the Germans invaded Austria. (*See Reading No. 23.*) An American newspaper correspondent, G. E. R. Gedye, who witnessed the days following the Anschluss in March 1938, wrote: "For the first few weeks, the behavior of the Vienna Nazis was worse than anything I had seen in Germany. There was an orgy of sadism. Day after day, large numbers of Jewish men and women could be seen scrubbing . . . signs off the sidewalk and cleaning the gutters. While they worked on their hands and knees, with jeering storm troopers standing over them, crowds gathered to taunt them. Hundreds of Jews . . . were picked off the streets and put to work cleaning public latrines and toilets of SA and SS barracks. Tens of thousands more were jailed." Overnight, from playing a large role in the cultural and economic life of the city, Viennese Jews lost their property, their means of livelihood, and in many cases, their sanity. In many homes suicide was discussed as the only way out of the horror. In Austria, on November 10, 680 Jews committed suicide: About 15,000 Jews were taken to concentration camps. Eichmann meanwhile was perfecting the efficiency of his so-called Jewish Emigration Center in Vienna.

Instead of requiring a dozen or more different documents from separate offices—as was the process for German Jews—Eichmann, head of the Jewish Section of the Security Service, pushed Austrian Jews into a conveyor belt system to speed up their expulsion. The model was copied in Prague and Berlin and after the war started, these "emigration centers" became centers of deportation to the death camps. Eichmann, too, made the leap from "crude" anti-Semitism to an "objective" solution to the Jewish problem. He told a Dutch journalist: "I saw the Jewish problem as a question to be solved politically. It was not a matter of emotion. My SS comrades and I rejected the crude devices of burning temples, robbing Jewish stores and maltreating Jews on the streets. We wanted no violence."

The Struggle to Emigrate. In their effort to emigrate to the United States, (*See Reading No. 24*) Jews faced openly expressed anti-Semitic hostility, unemployment, congressional opposition, a weak and vulnerable American Jewry, and obstructionist American consuls. Technically, there were 25,000 emigration permits per year available to German Jews, yet only a fraction of this number was allowed to enter: fewer than 2,500 in 1933; slightly over 4,000 in 1934; and fewer than 5,000 in 1935. In the period from 1933 through 1938, only 26,000 German Jews were admitted. This number was lower than the number of Germans in the United States who emigrated to Germany in the same period—37,000!

The American consuls demanded affidavits from police officers (i.e., *Gestapo*) who may have arrested them and who had to attest to their good character. Applicants also had to prove that they would not become public charges—understandable enough in light of the depression—but consuls chose to ignore guarantees of work or support on the part of American relatives. One particularly perverse interpretation involved the cases of Jews who were assured of jobs, but who were then accused of violating an old Contract Labor Law, which was originally passed in order to protect immigrant workers from becoming indentured servants to unscrupulous employers. Many refugees turned down by the United States fled to England, France, the Low

Countries, and Italy, but substantial numbers of these were later caught in the Nazi net. Adding immeasureably to the desperation of German Jews was a regulation passed in October 1934, drastically reducing the amount of money they could take out to ten Reichsmarks—about $4.00. After the pogroms of November 9–10, 1938, at the Stuttgart consulate alone, there were 110,000 applications from German Jews trying to leave.

The unwillingness of the nations to challenge Hitler at the time of the Anschluss and the Munich Conference in 1938, and their unwillingness at Evian to ameliorate the refugee situation not only strengthened Hitler's hand in foreign policy, but gave the most rabid anti-Semitic Nazis a free hand in determining the fate of Europe's Jews. The last voice of relative moderation in emigration policy was that of Dr. Hjalmar Schacht, Minister of Economic Affairs, who had objected to the drastic anti-Jewish measures because of foreign repercussions and subsequent harm to the German economy. He wanted to squeeze the most he could out of Jewish assets, ease the drain of foreign exchange, and exploit Jewish emigration for the purpose of increasing Jewish German exports. He was in constant conflict with Göring and Heydrich, and finally resigned as Minister of Economic Affairs. However, he remained head of the Reichsbank and developed a plan to freeze the remaining assets of German Jews and use them as security for a long-term loan to Germany, to be raised abroad by Jews or by an international committee. (*See Reading No. 25.*) He believed that a billion and a half marks could be raised, enough to finance an orderly emigration of Jews within three to five years, while the interest could be used to buy German goods.

However, Heydrich would have none of this. In January 1939, Schacht and Hitler had a violent quarrel. Schacht's proposals would have had considerable economic benefits for Germany, which was in a serious economic crisis that was effectively concealed from the world, and would have saved many Jews. But they would have slowed down Hitler's war timetable.

The Gestapo Controls "Emigration." Schacht was dismissed on January 20, 1939, and four days later, Heydrich became head of a *Reichszentrale für die jüdische Auswanderung* (Reich Central Office for Jewish Emigration), to "solve the Jewish Question by emigration and evacuation in the way that is most favorable under the conditions prevailing at present."

Thus, Heydrich and his destructive intentions had won. The *Gestapo* now had complete control over all Jews in Germany and in German-controlled lands and would have no inhibitions in their treatment of Jews. Orderly emigration would no longer be an option.

Hitler's Views on Palestine. Meanwhile, unaware of the ominous implications of radical Nazification of the "Jewish Question," German Jews had been forming long lines in front of the Palestine Office of the Jewish Agency and foreign consulates each day. About 135,000 Jews, including 23,000 German Jews, had been allowed to go to Palestine in 1933–35, but beginning in 1936, Britain, which held a mandate over Palestine, reacted to Arab opposition, and itself opposed Jewish immigration. However, immigration was increased by a special agreement called *Ha'avara,* or the transfer agreement, signed in 1933 between the Nazi Ministry of Economic Affairs and the Jewish Agency. Under this agreement, which lasted until 1938, Jews who had sufficient assets, could deposit them in a special blocked account in Germany. Once in Palestine they would be paid half the amount in Palestine pounds. The other half would be credited toward the purchase of German goods by the Jewish Agency. It is estimated that approximately 50,000 German Jews were saved by this arrangement, although it was severely criticized by some Jews because it gave help to the German economy and diminished the efforts to boycott German goods—one of the many issues that caught well-intentioned people in inescapable conflicts and arguments rooted in different perspectives on a tormenting dilemma.

However, Hitler's view of Palestine, which crystallized just before the *Anschluss*, opposed the migration of Jews to Palestine, while Britain's White Paper of May 1939 sharply curtailed Jewish immigration to 75,000 for the next five years, thus making the transfer agreement academic. Desperate efforts at *Aliyah Bet*—so-called illegal immigration—then became the route some young German (later Austrian, Czech, French and eastern European) Jews tried. This involved negotiating for ships—many of them unseaworthy cattleboats—and the struggle to outmaneuver the pursuit of the British navy as well as the greed of unscrupulous agents who sold worthless documents at exorbitant prices.

From 1933 to January 1936, a rare humanitarian, James McDonald, served as League of Nations High Commissioner. During this time he carried on a tireless search for havens and support for rescue schemes, warning that considerations of diplomatic correctness must yield to common humanity, but finally resigned in great frustration. Throughout 1939–40, President Roosevelt sponsored or encouraged many resettlement investigations, including possible projects in Alaska, the Belgian Congo, Cyprus, Equador, British Columbia, Lower California, Mexico, Haiti, Brazil, British Columbia, Angola, the Philippine Islands, among others. All of them collapsed due to technical problems, poor climate, poor soil, anti-Jewish attitudes, (*See Reading No. 26*) poor return on investments, and/or insufficient will to succeed.

Refugees Blocked at Sea. An important agency for the rescue of Jews was organized by Palestinian Jews in 1937, called *Mossad le Aliyah Bet*—the Committee for Illegal Immigration. The *Mossad* sent emissaries to Europe to organize convoys of Jews bound for Palestine. But by 1936, Britain signalled its intention to cut off this escape route. Strict immigration restrictions caused a drastic decline in the number of Jews admitted to Palestine from 61,000 in 1935 to fewer than 30,000 in 1936, and to under 11,000 in 1937. The young emissaries—Moshe Auerbach, Pino Ginsberg, and Ehud Avriel—began to make deals with the *Gestapo* and shipping agents, paying huge sums for any ships they could buy or lease. Their work was often wrecked by freak accidents, missed contacts, or British seizure. But a number of convoys got through the ports of the Black Sea, Yugoslavia, and Greece. After the British White Paper of May 1939, the struggle against the British took a heavy toll. The borders of Palestine were now closely guarded and new police stations were established. British agents were sent to search out the ports from which the boats sailed. In two months' time, over 3,000 refugees were captured. In the same period, Britain's Colonial Secretary refused Weizmann's petition for the safekeeping of 20,000 children from Poland, while admitting the "tragic consequences" of his refusal.

In May 1939, there occurred the tragic voyage of the German liner *St. Louis,* which had left Hamburg, crossed the Atlantic with 937 Jewish passengers aboard, all with American quota permits. Unable to remain temporarily in Cuba, it drifted uncertainly for 35 days and ultimately returned to Europe—only one of the numerous accounts of refugee ships in search of a port, but pressing against closed doors. Except for the refuge in Shanghai under Japanese occupation, escape from Europe became virtually impossible after the German invasion of Poland, September 1, 1939. Twenty thousand Jews found safety there in 1938–39.

CHAPTER FOUR

FORCED GHETTOIZATION—PRELUDE TO ANNIHILATION

On March 15, 1939, Hitler seized all of Czechoslovakia and stationed troops on Poland's southern border. He then had to prevent the Soviet Union from challenging his plans to attack Poland. Soviet exclusion from the Munich Conference and her failure to secure a collective agreement with the West disposed her to a separate deal with Germany. It has also been argued that Stalin needed time to prepare for a possible attack from Germany sometime in the future. George Kennan has also produced evidence indicating the possibility that both dictators planned to divide their subsequent conquests between them. Whatever the mixture of motives, the Nazi-Soviet Non-Aggression Pact, which stunned the world, was signed on August 23, 1939. It neutralized the Soviet Union, gave her eastern Poland (and over a million Jews there), and enabled Hitler to invade and conquer western Poland without any military threat from the east.

Invasion of Poland. From the first hour of the invasion on September 1, 1939, the German armies and SS forces committed a succession of atrocities on Poles and Jews. "The aim in Poland," Hitler had said, "was the elimination of living forces . . . The destruction of Poland shall be the primary objective." The fate of Polish Jews had already been foreshadowed in Hitler's address to the Reichstag on January 30, 1939: "Today I will be a prophet again: If international finance Jewry within Europe and abroad should succeed once more in plunging the peoples into a world war, then the consequence will be not the Bolshevization of the world and therewith a victory of Jewry, but, on the contrary, the destruction of the Jewish race in Europe."

In a welter of barbarity accompanying the swift conquest, Jews were easy prey. Indiscriminate torture and shooting, especially of religiously observant Jews, became a popular pastime. By the end of December 1939, a quarter of a million Jews in Poland died from shooting, forced labor, torture, starvation, or disease. For Himmler, the outbreak of war was the dawn of a new era, for he had marked out Poland as an area perfectly suited for the practical application of racial experiments. The SS and Security Police came into positions of control

THE PARTITION OF POLAND
September, 1939
SOVIET ANNEXATIONS, 1939-40

almost immediately and gave orders for movement control of Jews, round-ups for forced labor, and concentration camps.

Heydrich's Order of September 21, 1939. The blueprint was sketched in Heydrich's order of September 21, dealing with the Jewish problem, three days after Poland surrendered. (*See Reading No. 27.*) The full implications of the order would take several years to be realized, but they were ominous. Heydrich distinguished between short-term measures leading to the ultimate goal, and the ultimate goal, which must be kept secret. The first condition for achieving the final goal was the concentration of Jews in cities with railroad connections, or cities along railroad lines. In each Jewish community, a Jewish Council of 12 or 24 was to be set up, depending upon the size of the city or town. Each council was to be fully responsible for the execution of Nazi orders.

Two million Jews now under Nazi control were to be ghettoized (*See Reading No. 28*) and given a deceptive pseudo-autonomy through the Jewish councils. They were forced to leave their homes and were shoved into an area in south central Poland called the Government-General. Western Poland was to be cleansed of Jews to make room for racially pure Germans. The evacuations were sudden and chaotic, without warning or preparation. Jews were allowed to carry with them only small supplies of food and a few personal belongings. Many thousands took temporary shelter in communities that were not yet expelled and lived from hand to mouth in barracks, schools and synagogues. Uprooted from little towns and villages, hundreds of thousands more were sent to large cities such as Warsaw, Crakow, and Lublin.

Forced Labor. The potential labor productivity of Polish Jews was very great—many were skilled artisans—but the Germans made no effort to utilize their labor rationally. During the early weeks of the German occupation, Jews were seized to clear rubble, fill anti-tank ditches and shovel snow. A little later they were forced into labor columns (*See Reading No. 29*) which developed into labor camps, one of which was near Crakow, called Auschwitz. At first, Jews were used only for outdoor projects, but industrial operations were soon added and labor camps sprang up using slave labor. The survival of the hardiest gave the Germans the basis on which sick and weak Jews could be classified as ''unproductive'' and thus expendable. Progressive physical and psychological decline began at once in the labor camps and many died of exposure, hunger, and disease. On some projects the army paid two zlotys per man per day—about 40 cents. Other agencies paid nothing and workers had to rely on Jewish councils for food or wages. Many army officials, needing Jewish labor, protested the waste and destruction of Jewish workers, but they did not prevail. (*See Reading No. 30.*) Heydrich's police were in full control. Himmler, himself, admitted that he never recognized "the argument of war production." There was, moreover, rampant profiteering by Nazi looters among the police.

The Lublin "Reservation." One of the most sinister of the SS Police in Poland was Odilio Globocnik, who had helped to organize the terror in Austria, and was in charge of all population transfers in a large area of the Government-General in Poland called the Lublin Reservation. (*See Reading No. 31.*) This was one the numerous resettlement myths the Nazis promoted, but the SS had no intention of solving the problem territorially or by emigration. Their talk about resettlement and colonization was simply a device to delude the victims and keep them calm during the transfer process. Jews from Austria, Czechoslovakia, and Germany as well as Poland were deported to Lublin, where Globocnik's labor camps were to become half-way houses to death centers. In 1941, Globocnik became head of all the death camps in the Government-General: Auschwitz, Treblinka, Belzec, Maidanek, and Sobibor where preparations for the huge industry of death were made soon after the invasion of Poland.

Poland—Center of Nazi Annihilation Plans. Poland was to be the Nazi laboratory for annihilation. This was the very heartland of Jewry. Here were concentrated the great masses of Jews and the intellectual and spiritual roots of much of Jewish life. It was in Poland that Jews developed the most populous, most cohesive, and homogeneous Jewish communities in Europe. Here also existed a pervasive and widespread anti-Semitism which the Nazis could count on in helping to implement their plans. Here in Poland began the experiments in ghettoization and primitive gassings in huts where Jews in labor units were confined. Jewish property, jewelry, and other assets were seized soon after the conquest of Poland. Hostages were taken to enforce the extortion of money and goods. Synagogues were set on fire. The Nazi press reported that fire brigades would burn synagogues and books. During the first three months of occupation, massacres occurred in

GERMAN   OCCUPATION   OF   U.S.S.R.,   JUNE 22, 1941-42

———×———   Extent of German Advance
— — —   Western Boundary, U.S.S.R.,
Prior to June 22, 1941

Chmelnik, Konskie, Kutno, Lowicz, Lukow, Zdunska-Wola, and Przemsyl. In Ostrow, all male Jews were shot after being forced to dig their own graves. Pogroms erupted in many towns.

The Nazi Ghetto. On November 23, 1939, all Jews over ten were ordered to wear the Star of David, and several days later Jewish councils were created—often at gun point—and ordered to transmit Nazi orders on pain of death. The first ghetto that was sealed off was Lodz with its 160,000 Jews, in May 1940. In Warsaw, the ghetto walls were constructed during the summer of 1940 and by November, nearly half a million Jews were locked in behind the walls. (*See Reading No. 32.*) All the ghettos were eventually closed off from outside contact. Invariably they were located in the most squalid parts of the cities. Tosha Bialer, who had managed to escape from Warsaw, has described the scene before the ghetto was sealed: ''Try to picture one-third of a large city's population in an endless stream, pushing, wheeling, dragging all their belongings from every part of the city to one small section, crowding one another more and more. No cars, no horses, no help of any sort was available to us by order of the occupying authorities. Pushcarts were all we had and these were piled high with household goods. There was appalling chaos. Thousands of people were rushing around at the last minute trying to find a place to stay. The narrow crooked streets of the most dilapadated section of Warsaw were crowded with pushcarts, with their owners going from house to house, asking the inevitable question: Have you room? The sidewalks were covered with their belongings. Children wandered, lost and crying, parents ran after them, their cries drowned in the hubbub of half a million uprooted people.''[1]

After November 15, 1940, the 22 entrances to the Warsaw ghetto were closed, and no Jews were permitted to leave except those in closely guarded labor columns. Eventually, all the ghettos were closed off and the death penalty threatened any Jew leaving the ''Jewish residential districts'' illegally. The struggle for survival now raged—the struggle against hunger, merciless persecution, and despair.

The Jewish Councils. It will be recalled that Heydrich referred to short-term measures in Poland leading to the fulfillment of the ultimate goal, which was to remain secret. The ghettos were the short-

[1] Tosha Bialer, ''Behind the Wall,'' *Collier's*, February 20, 1943, p. 17.

term measures, which later became way stations to the gas chambers. The Jewish Councils were presumably to administer the ghettos, but were forced to become instruments of Nazi control. (*See Reading No. 33.*) At first, like the traditional *kehillas,* or autonomous communal bodies, they administered religious, educational, and welfare services within the ghettos, and tried to buffer the drastic Nazi orders. The Nazis cleverly created the illusion that the Councils would indeed be able to serve the community. Jews among themselves debated the wisdom of having such Councils; a few saw into ultimate Nazi intentions to exploit the Councils for their own purposes. Most, however, believed the Councils were essential to prevent utter chaos and would be able to blunt Nazi measures. The latter perceptions were true, but the results were only momentary. At the first stage, most of the Council members were traditional, prewar community leaders who were able to reassure the ghettos. Moreover, those who refused to serve were often killed. However, as Nazi demands became more and more brutal and destructive, the dilemmas became literally unbearable. Many members committed suicide.

Some Council members worked secretly with the Jewish undergrounds, after at least some Jews understood that "resettlement to the east" meant deportation to the death camps—a concept that most Jews found unthinkable. Other members debated traditional rabbinic discussions and found a wrenching rationale for surrendering some Jews in order to enable a remnant to survive. The road the Council took was tortuous and nearly always led to the abyss. Every member had to ask himself: "Shall I forsake the community and surrender the dread responsibility to someone else? Is not flight from responsibility a betrayal? If I accept the burden where must I draw the line that will release me from unbearable responsibilities?"

The Councils tried to alleviate hunger and disease, to provide shelter and work, and to organize a chaotic society. They worked under impossible odds. All of the programs undertaken in good faith were perverted by the Nazis into mechanisms of gross suffering and eventual destruction. We can see this perversion in the effort of the Jewish Council in Warsaw to regulate Jewish manpower and stop the random seizure of Jews for labor by press gangs. The Council offered to provide labor batallions at specified times and in specified numbers. The Germans agreed, but soon the burden of paying the workers fell on the Council itself. A rotation system was then set up which enabled Jews who still had money to buy their way out. Some of this money was then used to pay workers and their families. Soon dreadful conditions in the labor camps were reported to the ghetto. Bodies of beaten men and corpses were brought back and labor quotas could not be met. The Nazis then suspended the already miserable food supply for the ghetto. Penal camps were threatened, and families of workers were held as hostages. Again the Council tried to meet the new crisis. Jewish "supervisors," group leaders and police were recruited. The situation temporarily improved. Production increased momentarily and so did rations. A new cycle of more drastic demands then started and new dilemmas were created. Germans, meanwhile, were spared the police manpower that would normally have to be diverted. The Council entanglement was progressively twisted into a harmful process. In its economic and administrative collaboration, which was the ghetto's main chance for survival, lay the seeds of its ultimate destruction. Yet, no Jew in or out of the Councils in 1939, 1940, 1941, and even in the first half of 1942, before the massive deportations started, could have known that ghettoization was the beginning of their annihilation, that Nazi cunning and camouflage language deceived Jews about the intended end, that Jewish submission and compromise—approaches that had worked in earlier struggles for survival—were doomed under the Nazis. Because of their economic and geographic isolation in the ghettos, Councils had to provide functions normally handled by municipal governments: water, police, and fire protection, fuel, public health and sanitation, economic production and employment, food supplies and distribution—immense and impossible tasks under untenable conditions. The Councils had to tax the ghettos in order to provide basic services such as community kitchens, hospitals, orphanages, public baths, and disinfection centers. The Councils also needed funds to purchase drugs, to pay fines, to ransom prisoners, to bribe officials to open or re-open schools and synagogues for the time they were permitted. All manner of things were taxed by the Councils: wages of those who worked, ration cards, and rooms. But the ghettos could not survive.

Physical Attrition. Hunger, starvation, and disease soon took their toll. (*See Reading No. 34.*) Food became a continuous obsession. Beggars and children lined the streets pleading for food. Some ignored the curfew and went out at night crying for bread. Food packages were permitted until the attack on Pearl Harbor, and then were stopped, as were all mail and telephone contacts. Official food rations were set at

800 calories a day—half those given to the Poles—and meant little more than moldy bread, potatoes, which were often rotten, and fat. Smuggling became an absolute necessity and smugglers of all ages and sizes, including very small children, crawled through sewers or dug holes near the walls, in the struggle to make contact with Poles and barter for food. If not for smuggling, the ghetto residents would have quickly starved to death.

Hunger also wrought a severe psychological and emotional toll, making the victims depressed, inert, mentally confused, enraged, demoralized. Under famine conditions, some would live, and some would die. Even the sternly moral historian, Emanuel Ringelblum, who frequently criticized the Warsaw Jewish Council, was forced to admit that there was simply not enough food to go round. The people being fed at the public kitchens were dying out. "What are we to do?" he asked. "Dole out spoonfuls to everyone, the result being that no one will survive? Or are we to give full measure to a few, with only a handful having enough to survive." The dilemma had no answer.

Doomed Strategies. In some ghettos such as Lodz and Bialystok, the Councils tried to use Jewish productivity to ensure survival. Chaim Rumkowski, head of the Council in Lodz, offered to produce finished goods for the Germans if they would provide raw materials. He believed that his plan would provide work and income for the ghetto and make Jewish workers so valuable to the Germans that they could not afford to lose them. At the peak of production, Lodz had 117 factories, workshops, and warehouses which brought in over 16 million reichsmarks. Rumkowski became obsessed with his work program, and was hated and feared by the ghetto. He had an insatiable need to control everything—smuggling, culture, schools. In trying to make Lodz a model ghetto of efficiency, he became an obedient instrument of the Nazis—tragically so in January 1942, when they ordered him to select Jews for "resettlement elsewhere." The Germans said that the deportations were necessary in order to eliminate the unemployables, and Rumkowski found the reason plausible. Neither he nor anyone else in the ghetto knew at the time that transports were going to the death camp at Chelmno. At the end of 1943, 80,000 Jews were still alive in the Lodz Ghetto, and they were still alive in 1944—the only ghetto in Poland that had survived to that date. All of the others had been liquidated. But in August, Lodz, too, met the same end. Rumkowski joined the others in the transports to Auschwitz. Yet, at this very time, the

Russian army was rolling westward through Poland, but stopped 75 miles from Lodz. Ironically if it had continued its momentum, many Jews in Lodz would have been saved, and Rumkowski would perhaps have become a kind of hero, and his policy justified.

Each of the hundreds of ghettos in Poland and elsewhere underwent its own particular ordeals and must be studied as a special case, (*See Reading No. 35.*) with its own history, sociology, leadership, political composition, and relations with non-Jews. In each case, there were always diminishing possibilities for human existence, and the inability of Jews to grasp the reality that they were doomed to die. However, each ghetto struggled in its own way to fathom the meaning of Nazi decisions, the sudden reversals and inconsistencies, deliberately circulated rumors, population changes, the quixotic concessions followed by brutal persecution. No rationality could be discerned and the baffling irrationality kept the victims in a continuous state of fear, anxiety, and disequilibrium. Yet, each ghetto strove to maintain the rudiments of a human community as long as that was possible. Cultural and religious life at times was astonishingly vigorous, especially in Vilna, Warsaw, and Theresienstadt in Czechoslovakia. There were theater presentations, concerts, literary evenings, and lectures. There were classes for children—clandestine when the Nazis forbade them—religious services, and Jewish holiday celebrations. Children wrote poems and made drawings. Teachers were determined to pretend that there would be a future for them. The underground press also helped to sustain morale. (*See Reading No. 37.*)

The Need to Document the Unthinkable. There was also a passion to record the disintegrating life of the ghettos, to document the terrible present in smuggled notes, diaries, and sketches. The famous Jewish historian Simon Dubnow, as he was dying after being shot in the Riga Ghetto, appealed to the living: ''*Schreibt un farschreibt!*'' (write and record).

There are many diaries and notes that have been translated and published, giving the appearance of a quite ordinary book. Each effort required snatched moments, hiding places, access to paper, and great risk-taking. One of the most important testimonies of this kind was undertaken by the Polish Jewish historian Ringelblum in his *Notes from the Warsaw Ghetto,* and collection of materials for an archive. His *Notes,* which he started in November 1939, are literally notes toward a history of the coming catastrophe, not a personal diary. At the outset, the author does not know the end of the story, but perceives the fatal design only gropingly, and intermittently, as he moves from day to day, week to week. The scope of the entries is very broad, encompassing every facet of life in the ghetto and much of what was happening in the rest of Poland. Ringelblum's aim was to record the whole truth, however bitter, with as much objectivity as possible, and he steeled himself, as he enjoined his volunteers who helped amass the archive, to avoid preconceptions, even about the abominable enemy. The archive was gathered by a large group, called *Oneg Shabbat* (pleasure of the Sabbath), who produced diaries, reports, chronicles, and monographs on the life and history of Polish Jewry. (*See Reading No. 38.*) Their work was secret, of course, and continued until the massive deportations in the summer of 1942 when the materials were buried in crates and discovered in the rubble after the war. Ringelblum escaped to the ''Aryan'' side of Warsaw, but was caught by the Germans and shot together with his wife and 12-year old son. Chaim Kaplan, another diarist in the Warsaw Ghetto, perished in the deportations, while Adam Czerniakow, chairman of the Jewish Council there and author of one of the most remarkable of the journals, committed suicide July 23, 1942, after failing to save children from the deportations.

In Warsaw, Lodz, (*See Reading No. 39*) Vilna, Bialystok, and numerous other ghettos, writers and community leaders gathered and prepared materials documenting the life and death of Polish Jewry. Elsewhere in Europe, with the German conquest and occupation, individuals scribbled their impressions, partly to escape from dread experiences, partly to document them for oneself and then, for the sake of history. At first, notes were written in an atmosphere of hope and expectation of deliverance by the Allies. Later, as it became clear that no help was coming, the record-keeping became a kind of resistance against engulfing death, a gesture against oblivion.

While the Jews in western Poland were undergoing ghettoization and intensified persecution from September 1939 to June 1941, when the Germans invaded the Soviet Union, Jews in eastern Poland, under Soviet control, with certain exceptions, were not physically harmed, but underwent extreme sovietization and elimination of traditional cultural and religious institutions and leadership. On June 22, 1941, however, the Germans started their sudden attack on the Soviet Union and Jews in eastern Poland as well as those in the Soviet Union and Baltic states, which Stalin had taken in 1940, soon experienced Nazi terror and mass killings.

CHAPTER FIVE

THE NAZI INVASION OF THE SOVIET UNION AND THE "FINAL SOLUTION"

Hitler's decision to invade the Soviet Union multiplied the terror and slaughter of the spreading war and Nazi occupation of Euope, and brought sudden death to over a million Jews, killed in mass executions by mobile killing squads, called *Einsatzgruppen*. The invasion also coincided with the period in which the decision to destroy all of European Jews was made. Hitler's plan to conquer Russia was something he had brooded on for many years. In *Mein Kampf* he says "the colossal empire in the East is ripe for dissolution and the end of Jewish domination in Russia." The plan ripened soon after the conquest of western Europe in the summer of 1940. Hitler was sure that Britain could not hold out alone and that Russia could be crushed in six weeks—two months at the most. The war was to be no mere armed conflict, but a struggle of two different ideologies. Bolshevism was to be utterly destroyed and all traditional laws of war and international conventions ignored. Special killing units were given complete independence to carry out executions against the civilian population, most particularly Jews. When necessary, the German army would be called on to hand over Jews to the *Einsatzgruppen*. (*See Reading No. 40.*)

Einsatzgruppen Actions. The German invasion found the Soviet leaders and people wholly unprepared and shocked. Stalin's purges of 1937–38 had deprived the army of its most vigorous and competent officers. The remaining leaders did not realistically guage Hitler's intentions or military build-up. Within a few days the Soviet air force in the west was wiped out, and much of its army in the south was battered to pieces. By October 1941 the capital in Moscow had to be evacuated to Kuibyshev. Jews in eastern Poland, White Russia, western Ukraine, Lithuania, Latvia, and Estonia were thus immediately vulnerable and trapped. Four *Einsatzgruppen* of battalion strength quickly began their killing actions, based on the so-called "Commissar Order" and the army agreement with Heydrich, outlining the terms under which the *Einsatzgruppen* could operate in the Soviet Union. Eleven categories of the population were marked "for execution," including "all important officials of the State and Party," Gypsies, asocials, "Asiatic inferiors," and "agitators and fanatical Communists." Category Number 10 referred to "all Jews." Certain "trustworthy" groups of Russians and non-Russians were to be excluded, but there was to be no exception made in the category "Jews."

The killing units were disposed as follows: Group A operated in the Baltic states area; Group B, in White Russia; Group C in the Ukraine; and Group D in the Crimea-Caucausus. Armed with unlimited authority, each of the four group commanders had between 500 and 900 men, many from the ranks of the security police and intelligence agents, but also from the Waffen SS, and from pools of motorcycle riders, teletype and radio operators, and clerks. Units of Ukrainians, Latvians, Lithuanians, and Estonians were added when numbers had to be filled out. At their training centers in Saxony, the men in four units were told where they were going and what they were expected to do. The training consisted largely of rifle practice and listening to lectures and pep-talks on the necessity to exterminate subhumans threatening the life of the Reich.

A few days after the invasion of Russia, the squads sped away in fast cars and trucks, armed with rifles, pistols, and submachine guns. They needed no cavalry, cannon or airplanes; there would be no reconnoitering, no surprise attacks, no armed enemy. They merely had to cover vast distances quickly and assemble their victims.

The commanders were not military men or professional soldiers, but a peculiar assortment of intellectual riffraff, from the legion of German unemployed youth and professionals, including lawyers, teachers, and artists. There were also a physician and a clergyman. They were not hoodlums, delinquents, or common criminals. Otto Ohlendorf, who commanded *Einsatzgruppe* D, was quite typical. In 1941, he was 34. He had studied at three universities and had a doctor's degree in jurisprudence. He had joined the Nazi Party in 1925, the SS in 1926, and the SD in 1936, but he regarded his main career as research economist. By the time he joined the SD, he had become research director of the Institute for Applied Economic Science at Kiel. In June 1941, he became head of *Einsatzgruppe D*, with the rank of major-general. From that murderous assignment, he slipped quietly in June 1942 into the Ministry of Economics, where he became manager of a committee on export trade. Even his chief, Walter Funk, was unaware that he had commanded the mass execution of 90,000 Jews.

Next to Göring, Ohlendorf was probably the most compelling per-

POLAND   UNDER   GERMAN   RULE   AFTER   JUNE 22, 1941

- - - - -   PREWAR   POLAND

⊚   EXTERMINATION   CAMPS

sonality of all of the defendants at the Nuremburg Trials. He was handsome, suave, and exceedingly poised. His voice was carefully modulated and his movements, graceful and self-confident. When he was on trial for his life in 1947, women spectators sent flowers to his cell. They did not know that two years earlier, when he appeared as witness in the prosecution of the SD, he had admitted to the murder of 90,000 Jews. He was interrogated by a young American naval officer, Whitney Harris, and when asked how many men, women and children were killed, Ohlendorf shrugged his shoulders and replied calmly, "90,000." The Russian judge asked why children were massacred, and Ohlendorf replied: "The order was that the Jewish population should be totally exterminated." He admitted that, "there is nothing worse for people spiritually than to have to shoot defenseless populations, but it was a matter of self-defense." The Jews posed a continuous danger for the German occupation troops and might someday attack Germany. "From my own knowledge of European history, Jews during wars regularly carried on espionage service on both sides. . . . I did not have to determine the danger, but the order said that all Jews including the children were considered to constitute a danger . . . for the children were people who would grow up and surely, being the children of parents who had been killed, would constitute a danger no smaller than that of parents." He then explained how a typical killing took place. (*See Reading No. 41.*)

The greatest murder assignment of invaded Russia was given to *Einsatzgruppen* C and D. Their areas included the Soviet Ukraine Republic and Eastern Galicia, which had been annexed by the Soviet Union from Poland in 1939. There were two million Jews in these regions. Before the end of 1941, between 150,000 and 200,000 had been killed in the Ukraine alone. At the time, a German economics expert, Professor Peter Seraphin, deplored the irrational waste of Jewish manpower in the Ukraine and the unfortunate use of army personnel in the mass shootings (*See Reading No. 42*), but his remarks were labeled "personal" rather than "official" and they did not change the destructive Nazi course.

A number of Lithuanian, Ukrainian, Latvian, and Polish auxiliaries helped in the mass executions. Among the most zealous were the Romanians who joined the Axis and joined the German forces in the invasion of the Soviet Union. Their killing zeal, which at times outpaced that of the Germans, was especially evident in the provinces of Bessarabia and Bukovina, which the Soviet Union had occupied in 1940, but which Romania regained after June 1941. There were approximately 210,000 Jews in Bessarabia, which lies between the Dniester and Prut rivers. During the first week of August 1941, the Romanians began pushing Jews across the Dniester into what was still a German military area, intending to use the killing services of *Einsatzgruppe D*. After some 15,000 Jews had been driven across the river, the German 11th Army gave orders to block traffic over the Dniester bridgehead at Mogilev-Podolsk, but the Romanians blocked the way back. Again and again, the *Einsatzgruppe* turned Jews back, but, repeatedly Jews were pushed across. In the process of being shoved back and forth, thousands of Jews died on the roadsides and ditches from exhaustion, hunger, and gunfire. The Germans, meanwhile, were straining to distinguish between ''ideological'' killing and mere killing, and complained that the Romanians were ''disorderly'' and that their ''technical preparation'' lacked ''discipline.'' In Bessarabia there were locally instigated massacres in most of the towns—in Odessa alone, without the help of the German killing units, the Romanians slaughtered 60,000 Jews. In 1944, when a visitor to Odessa asked, ''What happened to the Jews?'' a man answered: ''Oh, they bumped off an awful lot. . . . They [the Rumanian police] said if so many Jews were bumped off, it was because the Germans had demanded it. 'No dead Jews, no Odessa,' they said.''

In October 1941 the Romanians sent 110,000 Jews from Bukovina and Bessarabia into forests in the Bug River area to be killed under orders from General Ion Antonescu, the Romanian chief of state. From the fall of 1941 for a year, about 165,000 Jews from northern Bukovina and Bessarabia were deported to Transnistria. A December 1 dispatch disclosed that Romanian authorities had proclaimed the Odessa district a section of Romania proper to be known as Transnistria where 120,000–130,000 Jews perished. In Odessa, according to a November 16 broadcast from Ankara, Turkey, 25,000 Jews were herded into military barracks on October 23 and shot by Romanian machine-gunners, in reprisal for the death of 220 Romanian soldiers by a delayed action bomb. Simultaneously, it was reported that all remaining Jews were ordered to register, presumably for forced labor. Perhaps as many as 40,000 Bessarabian Jews escaped death by conversion, while about 30,000 Jews in Bukovina, considered essential to the economy, were granted exemptions. Between March 15 and April 15, 1944, the Russian Army overran all of Transnistria and a curtain of silence was lowered. Possibly 50–60,000 Jews survived, but the accurate count may never be known.

The Jewish collective farms in the Ukraine suffered almost total annihilation by the Nazis and their Ukrainian collaborators. The frequently ambivalent pro-German attitude of the native population combined with native as well as Nazi-inflamed anti-Semitism produced shattering Jewish losses in the Ukraine, Lithuania, and White Russia. In some Jewish centers such as Vilna, (*See Reading No. 43*) Kovno, Shavli, Bialystok, Riga, (*See Reading No. 44*) Minsk, Mogilev, Zhitomir, and Berdichev, ghettos were temporarily established by the Nazis and decimated in 1942–43. The Nazi advance across eastern Galicia was accompanied by pogroms in Lvov, Tarnopol, Zborow, Zloczow, and Drohobicz. Colonel Paul Blobel's Commando 4a killed masses of Jews in the main cities of the western Ukraine—Korosten, Berdichev, Uman, Vinnitsa, and Zhitomir and then went on to Kiev and Babi Yar. In Kiev and many other areas where there were Jews, mass slaughter was so swift, it precluded ghettos. In Kiev, for example, in two days, September 29–30, 1941, over 33,000 Jews were killed in the ravine Babi Yar—a greater killing rate than that of the gas chambers of Auschwitz at their murderous peak. *Einsatzgruppe C, Sonderkommando 4A* had been assigned a special function in the Kiev area. This unit, numbering 150 men, aided by several hundred from two Ukrainian police regiments, assembled in the Kiev area on September 25, under the command of Colonel Paul Blobel. Final preparations were made for a decisive action "carried out exclusively against Jews with their entire families," as a top secret report revealed. On September 28, about 2000 notices were posted throughout the city:

All Jews of the city of Kiev and its environs must appear on the corner of Melnikov and Dokhturov Streets (beside the cemetery) at 8 A.M. on September 29, 1941. They must bring with them their documents, money, valuables, warm clothing, etc.

Jews who fail to obey this order and are found elsewhere will be shot. All who enter the apartments left by Jews and take their property will be shot.[1]

These notices were printed in Russian, Ukrainian, and German. The street names were misspelled, but the designation near the cemetery

[1] Willaim Korey, "Babi Yar Remembered." *Midstream.* March 1969, p. 26.

was clear. These notices were accompanied by a rumor deliberately planted by the *Sonderkommando* that the Jews were to be evacuated and resettled elsewhere, thus giving some plausibility to the instructions. Because most of the able-bodied men were in the Red Army, the thousands of Jews who assembled were mostly women, children, and the old and sick. Ilya Ehrenburg, in his memoirs, describes how ''a procession of the doomed marched along Lvovskaya; the mothers carrying their babies; the paralyzed pulled along on hand carts.'' The victims were ordered to remove their clothing and deposit in neat piles all that they had brought with them. Before the shooting began, they had to run a gauntlet of rubber truncheons and big sticks. As described by the Soviet writer Anatoly Kuznetsov in his book *Babi Yar,* they were ''kicked, beaten with brass knuckles and clubs . . . with drunken viciousness and in a strange sadistic frenzy.'' The first persons selected for shooting were forced to lie naked face down at the bottom of the ravine and were shot with automatic rifles. Some earth was thrown over the bodies and another group had to lie on top of the others. Later, the victims were placed at the edge of the ravine, sixty yards long and eight feet wide, and shot in the back of the neck. Some, still writhing, were buried alive. For weeks afterward, the *Einsatzgruppe* continued to hunt down Jews in hiding, combing apartments and houses. In November many Russian Jewish prisoners of war were executed at Babi Yar. Later, many thousands of Russian and Ukrainian non-Jews were also slaughtered there. In August 1943, when the Red Army began its counter-offensive, Blobel was ordered to erase all traces of the Babi Yar massacres. *(See Reading No. 45.)*

The largest group *Einsatzgruppe* A with 990 men operated in the Baltic states. It entered the cities of Kaunas (Kovno), Lepaya, Yelgava, Riga, Tartu, and Tallin with advance units of the army. Local pogroms in Kaunas and Riga and other towns claimed about 10,000 Jews. Lithuanian and Latvian auxiliary police were also drawn into the killing actions. In under than three months, *Einsatzkommando 3* with Lithuanian help killed 46,692 Jews. By September 25, the figure had risen to 75,000. In the *Einsatzgruppe* A Report, as of October 15, 1941, 114,197 Jews had been killed in the three Baltic states.

White Russia was the area covered by *Einsatzgruppe* B, and included the large formerly Polish cities Pinsk, Slonim, and Baranovice. Perhaps as many as half of the 850,000 Jews in the area fled east, but were caught in later killing sweeps as the German advance drove more deeply into Russia. *Einsatzgruppe* B was commanded by Arthur

Nebe, a police detective in the Weimar Republic and a member of the *Gestapo* since 1933. Nebe's squad executed 45,000 Jews in White Russia within five months. When Himmler visited Minsk soon after the German invasion, it was Nebe who shot 100 Jews in order to let Himmler see what a mass execution looked like. Himmler apparently became sick at the stomach and very nervous during the firing. Later, he made a speech to the men in the squad admitting that theirs was a repulsive duty, but as soldiers who had to carry out orders unconditionally, they were not to feel conscience-stricken. The operations against the Jews, he said, were a necessity. They must be destroyed.

Late in October 1941, a regional commissar of Sluzk in White Russia pleaded with the local battalion commander for a postponement of the killings, pointing out that Jews were working as skilled laborers and that White Russian mechanics were non-existent. But the commander proceeded to encircle the Jewish quarter and start the massacre. Meanwhile, vehicles loaded with ammunition for the army were left standing in the streets. The aramament industry in the area gradually collapsed. Thousands of workers were "withdrawn"; ghettos were burned to the ground. Workshops that once produced candles, rope, leather, and lumber for the German army stood idle. There were no replacements at a time when German soldiers were freezing in the Russian winter for lack of shoes and clothing while Germans at home were wearing shoes with cardboard bottoms.

White Russia, or Ruthenia, and the Baltic states were incorporated into the Reich Commissariat for the Ostland, and in these areas the "extremely high percentage of [Jewish] specialized workers, who are indispensable" is admitted even in the report of *Einsatzgruppe* A, which took over the area of White Russia. (*See Reading No. 46.*)

By the end of 1941, the *Einsatzgruppen* had rolled forward six hundred miles into Russian territory in their first sweep. Five hundred thousand Jews had been killed, but two million were still alive. In order to facilitate their second sweep, the *Einsatzgruppen* were enlarged by Himmler's police and the Polish-type ghetto was introduced. Gradually, the *Einsatzgruppen* merged into the police machinery and were, in fact, directed by Higher SS and Police Leaders. Their goal was simple: to kill every Jew; none could remain alive. Himmler's machinery now was to move with a frenzied, relentless force. The SS killers had pushed aside rational arguments to protect Jewish labor for the sake of the war effort and would be further propelled by the decisions of the Wannsee Conference, January 20, 1942. (*See below, p. 58.*)

Jews Under Soviet Rule. Two questions keep recurring as one tries to comprehend the annihilation process in the Soviet Union: How much did Jews know of Nazi intentions? And, what, if anything, did Soviet authorities do to try to save Jews? There are two separate experiences of Jews under Soviet rule, and two different periods. One is the period from September 1939 to June 1941, the time of the Soviet-Nazi Pact, and the second is the period following the German invasion of Russia, after June 1941. In the first period, Jews in eastern Poland and the Baltic states came under Soviet rule. Russians identified many Jews with middle class loyalties and with capitalism, Zionism, and Bundism. In a census taken in March 1940 to determine which Jews wanted to adopt Soviet citizenship, about 250,000 or 300,000 rejected it. They were declared ''unreliable'' and were deported to Siberia and central Asia; many survived. About another 350,000 Jews fled from western Poland to eastern Poland, but many of them, for family reasons, returned to Nazi-occupied Poland, to perish with their families. Accounts of the behavior of Soviet border guards vary: some Jews say they owe their lives to the charity of Soviet guards who allowed them to move eastward deeper into Soviet territory; others witnessed scenes in which guards forced Jews back into German-controlled Poland.

After the invasion of Russia, the rescue of Jews was swallowed up by the choas and devastation over all of western Russia. The Russians were completely unprepared militarily. Evacuation plans had to be improvised hurriedly and involved mainly war-making, economic and administrative-political considerations. The most vital industrial centers—besides Riga and Minsk, which were lost during the first few days—were in central and eastern Ukraine and in Moscow and Leningrad. The gigantic industrial transplantation to the Urals, western Siberia and central Asia started in midsummer 1941—five days after the invasion—and continued into 1942, accompanied by a parallel migration of civilians.

Jews were marked by the Germans for ''special treatment,'' but there was no special Soviet effort to save them. The whole country was in grave danger. However, during the war, defenders of the Soviet Union tried to press the point that special help was indeed given. But there was no preference. If Jews were considered essential to warmaking, economic, or administrative work, they were evacuated with others likewise needed. Party members and government employees were also generally evacuated. Thus only a rough estimate of the number of Jews evacuated is possible. Perhaps as many as one million

Ukrainian and Belorussian Jews in the eastern regions of the republics were evacuated even though a considerable part of both was under German control by mid-July 1941. Possibly another half million Jews were evacuated from the western parts of the RSFSR (Russian Soviet Federative Socialist Republic). Thus, a reasonably balanced figure of the number of Jews saved by evacuation lies somewhere between one and one and a half million, out of twelve to fifteen million Russians evacuated.[2] Most Jews who were not trapped by the killing squads had no recourse but flight. Within a month, the Russians themselves had suffered nearly a million casualties and Hitler was certain that the war was virtually over.

In pamphlets intended for world Jewry, the Soviet Jewish Anti-Fascist Committee described the special efforts made by Soviet authorities to evacuate Jews, especially the weakest elements, but there is no hard evidence of such preferential treatment, nor is it reasonable to have expected it, in the light of Stalin's anti-Semitism and his policy of keeping the destructively anti-Semitic nature of the Nazi regime secret until the invasion. This last point is very significant and fraught with deepest tragedy.

During the period of the Soviet-Nazi Pact, no information about the Nazi anti-Jewish persecutions elsewhere in Europe was permitted inside the Soviet Union. Press, radio, and official statements totally ignored or evaded reporting evidence of the persecution and murder of Jews elsewhere. Soviet officials publicly toasted Hitler and other Nazis. Soviet Jews and many other Russians were, of course, sickened by these displays, particularly because the Soviet Union had taken a strong anti-Nazi line before the pact. Thus, Jewish unawareness of Nazi actions elsewhere (*See Reading No. 47*), combined with an earlier memory, made Jews utterly defenseless and unprepared after June 1941. This was the memory of the benign German occupation of many Russian towns during World War I, a memory that many Jews cherished because German soldiers had protected them and their parents from pogroms. Thus, unbelievable though it is, there are accounts of some Soviet Jews bringing flowers and candy to the invading German army in June 1941. They thought that this was another benign German

[2] Dov Levin, ''The Attitude of the Soviet Union to the Rescue of Jews,'' in *Rescue Attempts during the Holocaust: Proceedings of the Second Yad Vashem International Conference,* April 1974. Jerusalem, 1977, p. 235. Also, E. Kulisher, *The Displacement of Population in Europe.* International Labor Office, Montreal, 1943, p. 53.

army, perhaps even an army of liberation. They were totally unaware of Nazi intentions. Consequently, unprepared Jews were physically and psychologically immobilized and vulnerable to German reassurances and traps. Unarmed, they followed German orders. They were called to register and to assemble for "resettlement".

The Annihilation Process. The decision to physically eliminate the Jews of Europe crystallized at the same time that the invasion of Russia was being planned. The exterminations were carried out after the invasion began and were intensified as the war spread and lengthened. On July 31, 1941, six weeks after the invasion of Russia and the first sweep of the mobile killings squads, Göring gave Heydrich absolute power to organize the so-called Final Solution. (*See Reading No. 48.*) Heydrich knew quite well what Göring meant, for he had used the term nearly two years before, in September 1939, at a secret meeting, at which time he talked about first steps in the "final solution." Soon after Heydrich received Göring's letter, he summoned Eichmann and told him that since emigration was now impossible because of the war with Russia, Hitler had ordered the physical extermination of the Jews. Eichmann was then instructed to go to see Globocnik in Lublin. He was shown airtight chambers, disguised as farmers' huts, which were injected with exhaust gas from a Russian U-boat motor. Later that year he watched a mass execution of Jews near Minsk, and gassings of Jews from Lodz on buses.

Ohlendorf had testified that in the spring of 1942 an order came from Himmler to change the method of executing women and children. (*See Reading No. 49.*) In the future, they were to be killed in gas vans especially constructed by two Berlin firms. The purpose of the vans presumably could not be discovered from the outside. Ohlendorf explained that the vans were camouflaged to look like closed trucks and were so constructed that at the start-up of the motor, gas from the exhaust was to be piped into the van, causing death in 10 or 15 minutes.

Meanwhile, in the summer of 1941, Rudolf Hoess, commandant of the concentration camp at Auschwitz, was told by Himmler that Auschwitz would now become an important death camp because it was near rail lines, but quite isolated.

The Wannsee Conference. Heydrich wanted to act quickly after receiving Göring's order, but had to iron out certain technical matters, including the cooperation of all the government ministries. To gain this support and coordinate all preparations, on June 20, 1941, Heydrich called together a conference of thirteen men from various government ministries and party agencies at Wannsee, a suburb of Berlin. (*See Reading No. 50.*) Drinks and lunch were served while Heydrich talked of the coming "Final Solution of the Jewish Question." Eleven million Jews in Europe and England were to be eliminated. Some countries still posed difficulties, but Europe was to be combed through from west to east. A chart showed the communities to be "evacuated"—the new code word for annihilation. Jews would be brought to transit ghettos and then farther east where they would be "treated accordingly," another camouflage term. The men at the conference understood full well that an irreversible decision was being made to kill an entire people. Thirty copies of the conference record were circulated in the ministries and main offices of the SS and administrative and technical procedures were now worked out for a massive industry of death. Hundreds of thousands of Germans were now to be involved—in party and state offices, in the officers corps of the armed forces, in all businesses connected with slave labor and the vast deportation and death camp operations. These decisions actually came as no surprise to leading Nazis. For, since the invasion of Poland, Jews were considered expendable and were dying in large numbers.

The official decision to destroy all of Europe's Jews was, of course, Hitler's. No one can be sure how long he harbored the idea, but the decision crystallized during the winter of 1940–41, at the same time that the invasion of the Soviet Union was being planned. A million and a half Jews were killed there—massacres largely obscured or concealed under the murderous destructiveness of the larger war. However, reports of the killings were leaking out and photographs of massed dead were being taken by German soldiers. A faster and more efficient system of killing was needed. The new methods were suggested by the euthanasia program used in Germany itself in 1939–41. Approximately 50,000 Germans who were terminally ill or mentally defective were killed by gassing and lethal injections until the churches discovered what was happening and raised an uproar. Hitler was forced to stop the so-called mercy deaths. But the gassing of Jews were not interrupted. Gassing units using carbon monoxide or prussic acid were installed in the six death camps of Poland: Chelmno, Belzec, Sobibor, Treblinka, Maidanek, and Auschwitz, camouflaged as shower baths. Over five million human beings were gassed in these camps between 1942 and 1944, most of them Jews.

CHAPTER SIX

JEWISH RESISTANCE
AGAINST PLANNED ANNIHILATION

The question of Jewish resistance during the Holocaust has been the source of much controversy and misinformation because of the general ignorance of the conditions of Jews under Nazi control, including the Nazi deceptions regarding their fate. Many people believe that, despite the documentation available, Jews went passively to their doom. There is also the understandable tendency to compare Jewish resistance to that of other subjugated Europeans. However, among other scholars, Dr. Henri Michel, a leading authority on European resistance movements, has stated that there cannot be any fair comparison because of the profound differences between the two. Dr. Michel has defined resistance as "a patriotic fight for the liberation of a country . . . [involving] partisan or guerrilla warfare directed at liberation as well as psychological warfare, to weaken the morale of the enemy and increase the strength and numbers of the supporters of the underground. Such resistance includes passive disobedience, propaganda, and various acts of sabotage—refusing or evading the enemy's orders, calling strikes, destroying installations such as railway tracks, warehouses, bridges, etc." In short, the object of these actions was to frustrate and block the aims of the enemy.

Many Jews, of course, participated in the general European resistance movements—in France, Greece, Holland, Yugoslavia, and the Soviet Union—and they also fought in their national armies, but their identity as Jews has generally been ignored or not acknowledged. In identifying a specifically *Jewish* resistance, the central element is an understanding of the unique nature of the Jewish struggle: a struggle against physical annihilation—a fate that was concealed from the victims in all possible ways, but one which the Nazis single-mindedly planned and carried out. No other people had to decipher mass murder, disguised as "re-settlement," "transfer to the east," or "deportation to labor camps." These deceptions led many Jews to believe that they would survive, that they had a future, that their lot would be harsh, but that they would live. Thus, many Jews were never aware of the fate the Nazis had designed for them. They used their diminishing energy to battle hunger, disease, shock, slave labor, debasement, and despair.

The strategy of the general resistance movements in every country weighed the possible gains and losses of every operation, the damage inflicted on the oppressor as against the losses sustained by the general population. Dr. Michel reminds us that the non-Jewish movements were always mindful of this matter of proportion. Had resistance operations of any of the European peoples endangered the physical existence of all or most of its members, they would not have been carried out. Their fight for liberation of country and freedom was not a fight to avenge the dead but a fight for the living. In stark contrast, the Jews began to resist physically only whey they realized they were doomed and had nothing to lose. The other resistance groups fought when they believed there was something to win or gain. Jews never had a choice or chance. Others did.

Furthermore, the extermination plans were supremely important for the Nazis. They were prepared to pay any price in order to carry them out, sparing neither manpower nor transport. They even sacrificed the desperately needed manpower, which Jews filled for a time, involving shortages which certain German army commanders and civil governors fought the SS to remedy. The Nazi blueprint called for nothing less than the complete destruction of European Jewry. This fundamental fact, then, must form the basis of all discussion of the question of Jewish resistance.

Another important difference concerns external help. General resistance movements were completely dependent on outside aid, without which they would have been condemned to disappear or remain powerless. The arms, equipment, and instructions to the various undergrounds came from Washington, London, or Moscow. Moreover, military objectives did not necessarily have first priority. The general resistance movements were often armed by the Allied staffs for political and psychological reasons rather than strictly military purposes. However, Jewish resistance was not regarded by the Allies as necessary from the political, psychological, or military point of view. It never occurred to the Allies to give Jews—the prime targets of the Nazi war—any role in fighting their mortal enemy. When the Jews in British-mandated Palestine, as early as 1939, urged the British to allow them to organize a Jewish brigade within the British Army and to drop parachutists behind the German lines in the Balkans, the proposals were rejected and put on the shelf year after year. Only in September 1944, when the war was almost over, did the British consent to the creation of the Jewish Brigade and a unit of Jewish parachutists, both too late to save any Jews.

An oversimplification of the whole resistance issue during the war may also lead one to conclude that good fighters never become victims, and thus, the notion that Jews were victims because they were not good fighters. Yet, over three million Russian prisoners of war, all experienced and well-trained fighters, also perished along with Jews, victims of Nazi brutality, hunger, and gassing. We have no evidence of any organized revolts by Russian prisoners. Some escaped into the forests and joined partisan groups, as some Jews did. Possibly as many as five million non-Jews died in concentration camps, slave labor camps, and as hostages, without mounting any substantial effective resistance. Some historians have also concluded that underground resistance in general played a very small part, if any, in the final defeat of Hitler. The destructive power of the Nazis was not seriously challenged by any resistance movement in Europe, either French, Greek, Yugoslavian, Polish, Dutch, or Belgian. Only the overwhelming power of the Allied armies finally crushed the Nazi menace.

The Nazis planned one fate for all the Jews of Europe, but they were a very heterogeneous people covering a spectrum of diverse political, cultural, economic, and religious interests and attachments: Sephardic Jews as well as Ashkenazic, loyal to their respective national homes; secular, urbanized intellectuals; fervent Hasidim, praying and singing for the glory of God; Zionists; Socialists; Communists; petty shopkeepers as well as wealthy businessmen and merchants; craftsmen and professionals of every political persuasion; assimilated, converted, ambivalent, or self-aware and proud—a very diverse and often contentious people, who responded to their ordeal in different ways. For religiously observant Jews, there was a struggle to maintain a religious discipline, or symbolic commitment. (*See Reading No. 51.*) For some, submission to the horror was a form of *Kiddush Ha-Shem*, submission to death for the sanctification of God, and some Hasidic Jews danced and sang and prayed as they went to their deaths. Teachers led clandestine classes; children studied, sketched, (*See Reading No. 52*) and wrote poems; clandestine diaries and archives were kept; Socialist and Zionist youths issued underground leaflets and newspapers; factory workers sabotaged the products they made. Much resistance was thus non-physical, but was undertaken at great peril and often led to death.

Singular Problems of Jewish Resistance. The Jews of Europe belonged to many nations and were dispersed all over the continent. They were a nation in time, memory, persecution and traditions—and certainly were defined as a nation by the Nazis—but they were not a nation in space or in territory. They had no national home, no national army, no national leadership, no source of allied arms, no homeland as yet to liberate or provide support for an underground. They did not have a government-in-exile that could broadcast news and boost morale, like the French, Czechs, Poles, Norwegians, and Dutch, or resume some sort of life in their occupied country, bitter though it be.

Being dispersed and forcibly separated, Jews could not unite, nor did they face the Nazi Final Solution at the same time. The pace of destruction varied from country to country. Soviet Jews were victims of the first slaughters in June 1941, not in the gas chambers but in hundreds of execution pits such as Babi Yar and Ponary. Jews in France, Poland, and Holland began to be deported in the summer of 1942, Greek and Bulgarian Jews in 1943, Hungarian Jews in May 1944. These groups could not communicate with each other and were to a large extent unaware of what each was going through.

Partisan Resistance. Jews in the Soviet Union were the first victims of Nazi mass slaughters, but they had no time to digest the unfolding of Nazi intentions. In less than a year, over a million Jews were murdered by mobile killing units which accompanied the German invasion army. Unaware of the persecution of Jews elsewhere in Europe, Soviet Jews could not plan any substantial resistance efforts. Moreover, most Jewish men up to the age of 50 were in the Soviet army and there were no Jewish youth movements in Soviet territory to organize an anti-Nazi struggle. Yet, there were some small-scale efforts—the first forms of Jewish physical resistance during the war—in Lachva, Tuchin, Ostrog, Nieswiez, Opole, Yarmolitsy, and Mir in Nazi-occupied eastern Poland and Soviet Russia.

Much more Jewish resistance was carried on in the forests and swamps of eastern Europe. As the ghettos of western Poland were being wiped out in 1942–43, small groups of Jews escaped to the woods in a desperate bid for survival and vengeance. The guerrillas in the woods were free, but they were also alone and vulnerable. In areas controlled by Ukrainians, Poles, and Lithuanians, Jewish partisans generally did not survive. Their best chance lay in the White Russian forests, where a Russian partisan movement began to organize at the end of 1942. The vast forests, marshes and wastelands extended for hundreds of miles and created good retreats for fugitive war prisoners and soldiers. Hundreds of small Jewish bands struggled to survive in these regions. Very little value was attached to the Jew fighting in the forest, without arms, and often the butt of anti-Semitism. Good relations with the surrounding peasant population were vital, for peasants provided food and weapons, and hiding places, but they were generally hostile and often murderous toward Jews.

Many thousands of Jews fled to the forests and marshes of eastern Europe, but they existed in small scattered units stretching over huge distances. Neither a unified command nor a communications network was ever possible, yet Jewish partisans fought and killed the Nazi enemy. They attacked police stations, killed Nazi guards, exploded trains, disarmed enemy peasants, and knocked out tanks with hand grenades. Jews of all ages were involved, even children, but the decision to leave the ghettos was a very painful one. Family ties were strong, and even young Jews who had the best chance to survive did not want to leave parents, brothers, and sisters to suffer inevitable Nazi reprisal. Besides, few Jews were familiar with the forests. Their best hope lay with the Soviet partisan movement, and in time, traditional Jewish skills such as those of tailors, shoemakers, carpenters, locksmiths, doctors (*See Reading No. 53*), and nurses became very valuable to the partisans. These Jews eventually learned how to shoot, lay mines, throw grenades and kill Germans. Some Jews established family camps, especially where there were vast forests, in White Russia, Polesie, and northern Volhynia, involving Jews who survived the mass murders in the spring and summer of 1942 when Soviet partisan units were also being organized. Both operated in the same forests, faced the same enemy, and were dependent on the same sources. This situation led to some conflicts between the two groups. Nonetheless, family camps could serve as headquarters and maintenance units for the combat units. They prepared food and nursed the wounded. In this manner, several groups attained full partisan status. In addition, the family camps were organized in such a way that the armed members of the group could take active part in military actions against the Germans, as well as defending the camp members.

Perhaps the most famous was that of the Bielski brothers who brought 1,000 Jews out of the forests at the end of the war. (*See Reading No. 54.*) In 1943, when the Russian partisan movement came under an official Soviet command, all Jewish units that had grouped themselves around the Russian partisans had to give up their distinctive Jewish identity and merge with the Russian units. Some Jews who had commanded partisan brigades were decorated at the end of the war, but were not identified as Jews. By the summer of 1943, there were over 200,000 men and women in the Soviet partisan movement, of whom about 20,000 were Jews.

The most successful exodus from a ghetto in Nazi-occupied Russia occurred in the Minsk Ghetto (*See Reading No. 55*), where escape to the forests was the main strategy of the underground. Jews who worked in arms factories smuggled weapons into the ghetto when they returned from work. Two crates of sawed-off shotguns bound for Berlin formed part of the Minsk forest arsenal. Young girls were sent as couriers to study the terrain and seek out reliable elements in the population who would help. After the first large mass killings in March 1942, several bases were created. By September 1942, several thousand Jews escaped, most of them armed with weapons and ammunition sufficient to supply two companies of Jewish partisans. The fighters destroyed Nazi communications, blew up factories and stirred the local population to carry out anti-Nazi actions. Women, children, and aged Jews escaped to the Burelom forest and formed a family camp where they organized a flour mill, tailoring and shoemaking shops and a bakery which supplied nearby partisans.

For months, children like Banko (*See Reading No. 55*) led hundreds of Jews out of the ghetto, covering hundreds of miles. Later in August, when the Germans surrounded the forests of Staroje-Sielo, the resistance could not hold out against the massive attacks. Several hundred partisans died, including fifty or more Jews, among them little Banko, who had apparently been burned alive. About 5,000 Jews from Minsk survived in the forest.

One of the legendary heroes of partisan war was the Soviet Jew Misha Gildenman, who escaped from the ghetto of Koretz together with his son and 16 other Jews. Uncle Misha, as he was called, eventually got hold of some weapons and formed a partisan unit of Jewish fighters near Zhitomer. Among those who attached themselves to his unit was a little boy named Mottele, a 12-year old who was the sole survivor of his family. He eventually gained the confidence of the men, and being blue-eyed and fair-haired, he was sent on dangerous missions, including the blowing up of a German officers' club in Ovruch, an important military junction. Posing as a beggar boy soliciting alms in front of a local church while playing a violin, Mottele attracted the attention of a German commander. The German ordered him to play at a restaurant used by German soldiers and there Mottele memorized the numbers of units and the types of uniforms worn. He eavesdropped on conversations and passed information to a contact. Later, Mottele himself was given a German uniform and cap and was so well accepted he was allowed to eat in the kitchen with other employees. One day, he looked through an open door leading to storage rooms and saw a crack in the far wall. He immediately realized that if a bomb could be placed in the crack, he could blow up the club and all the German officers in it.

He discussed all the details of such a project with the partisans and for several days transported explosive material in his empty violin case. He also set up a bomb wick. One night, after playing for a large crowd of SS officers, he slipped down to the cellar, ignited the wick and left. After running about 200 yards, he heard a powerful explosion and saw red rockets lighting up the sky. Frightened and elated, he ran to a pre-arranged spot where he was picked up in a wagon. With clenched fists raised upward, he shouted, ''This is for my parents and little Bashiale, my sister.'' Shortly before liberation, Mottele was killed. He was crawling to a new position to warn Soviet officers of danger when he was struck by a German bullet.

Elsewhere in Europe, Jewish youths were involved in many different kinds of anti-Nazi activity. In France, for example, there was the Jewish scout movement—*Eclaireurs Israélites*—which evacuated Jewish children from the cities to the countryside. In the summer of 1942, when deportations to Auschwitz began, foreign Jews were the first to be seized by Nazis and French police. It became especially important to try to hide Orthodox Jews, who were conspicuous because of their dress and speech. The scouts obtained forged identity papers, ration books, and hiding places in the countryside. At great peril, they rode the Paris subways all night long with their frightened charges, taking them out of the city to farms. Of the original 88 youths in the most daring section of the scouts called ''The Sixth,'' four were shot to death and 26 were deported, never to be heard from again. When the scouts moved to armed resistance, their losses were heavier. (*See Reading No. 56.*)

In Hungary, Jews were in extreme physical danger after the occupation of the country by the Germans in March 1944. Again, it was Zionist youths who first saw the coming crisis. Their ranks had been strengthened by young refugees from Poland who were able to escape in 1943. Their chief task was to get Aryan papers and then cross the border to Romania. They also tried to warn Jews in the countryside of the deportations, which started in May. Some were arrested; others were betrayed by smugglers. Several groups were aided by Seventh Day Adventists. As many as 6,000 Jews were saved from death by these border crossings, a remarkable figure when we realize that there was not a single anti-Nazi underground in Hungary at the time. Even in Germany, where there was little political or physical resistance, there was a Jewish group of youthful resisters called the Baum Group. (*See Reading No. 57.*) Most of them were from eleven to fourteen. This group, at great risk, monitored radio broadcasts from London, distributed anti-Fascist leaflets in factories and offices, and painted anti-Hitler signs on the walls of Berlin at night. Their most daring act was the destruction of an anti-Soviet exhibit in Berlin in May 1942, to demonstrate the activity of Jewish anti-Fascists. All but two of the Baum Group were eventually executed or perished in the camps.

Resistance in Polish Ghettos. More direct and active resistance was organized by Jewish youths in the ghettos of Poland. The decision to resist was taken only after long, agonizing discussions and debates. To stay and fight inside the ghettos would risk thousands of lives. To leave and fight in the forests meant leaving families to face Nazi reprisals and the destruction of the ghettos.

It must be remembered that Jews in the ghettos were cut off from all outside sources of information except for a few secret radios and couriers who disguised themselves and went from ghetto to ghetto bringing news, messages, and occasionally arms. It was impossible for most Jews to grasp the Nazi master plan to annihilate them. Jewish youths were the first to understand the truth of the Nazi annihilation plan, especially Zionist and Socialist youths.

At first, there were underground handbills and crudely mimeographed newspapers. Political issues were analyzed and educational tasks outlined in Yiddish, Polish, and Hebrew. There were dozens of such papers, dailies, weeklies, and monthlies, aimed at keeping up Jewish morale in the ghettos and urging passive resistance to the Nazis. The papers also reported news from the war fronts, the struggle in Palestine, life in the labor camps, and acts of sabotage. They countered rumors, tried to calm false hopes, and prevent demoralization. "The very expression of apathy," wrote the *Yugend Shtimme* (Voice of Youth), "indicates submission to the enemy, which can cause our collapse morally, and root out of our hearts our hatred for the invader. It can destroy within us the will to fight—And because our position is so bitterly desperate, our will to give up our lives for a purpose more sublime than our daily existence must be reinforced. . . . Our young people must walk with heads erect.''

Toward the end of 1942, these youths in the Polish ghettos planned and mobilized for an armed struggle. In setting this course, they had to overcome not only general opposition in the ghettos but inner conflicts and uncertainty about their decisions. They made agonizing choices which most adults shunned.

The spark to resistance in the Polish ghettos was ignited by news of mass murder in the Vilna area in the autumn of 1941. At the end of October, a *Hechalutz* courier was sent from Warsaw to Vilna and other parts of Lithuania. He returned in the middle of November with the news that Germans were murdering Jews in the tens of thousands and burying them in mass graves in Ponary. In January 1942 Frumka Plotnicka reported similar actions in Wolyn. A few refugees who had escaped from Chelmno reached Warsaw and told of Jews being gassed in trucks. In the middle of March, *Hechalutz* representatives held a meeting and decided to create a general Jewish fighting organization. Later, an Anti-Fascist Bloc was formed. A few hundred youths and workers began to train—without arms—in groups of ''fighting fives,'' but the first massive deportations, beginning July 22, 1942, slashed into their ranks.

Each day thereafter, thousands of Jews were herded into deportation columns and put on trains to the death camp at Treblinka. On July 28, Zionist youth groups in Warsaw created a Jewish Fighting Organization (JFO) and sent agents to contact the Polish underground for arms. A proclamation was issued to the ghetto, warning that ''resettlement'' meant death and urging men to hide their wives and children. The ghetto residents did not believe the report. Faked cards had been received from the deported Jews saying they were working hard but were alive. There was nothing to fear. Famishing victims were lured to the trains by marmalade and bread. Meanwhile, the young fighters were struggling to obtain arms. By August 1942 there were ten revolvers and powder for explosives smuggled over the ghetto wall where guards could be bribed. The youths in the JFO gathered in closets and talked with burning eyes about revenge. They stored up bread, mimeographed instructions on guerrilla fighting and created underground bunkers.

Meanwhile, massive deportations in September 1942 further disrupted the underground network. Systems of communication were broken and sections of the ghetto that had been linked were torn apart.

All of the units had to reform. Frantic appeals for arms went out. The Jewish Socialist Bund finally realized that the Poles were not going to make a common anti-Nazi front with Jews and joined the JFO. Mordecai Anielewicz, the modest, popular leader of *Hashomer Hatzair*, became commander-in-chief. He realized that neither the Jewish masses nor the fighters could escape from the ghetto and fight outside of it. "Antek" Zuckerman, second in command, had taken part in attacks on cafes in Crakow, in December 1942, in which German officers had been killed and wounded. He shared this effort at armed resistance in the capital of the General Government and the lessons to be learned.

Although most Poles were hostile or indifferent, several who were friends of the ghetto fighters or shocked by the atrocities, offered help. For example, Irina Adamowicz, a good friend of the commander, Mordechai Anielewicz, risked her life daily to maintain contacts between the ghettos of Warsaw, Vilna, Kovno, Shavli, and Bialystok. Other Poles in the People's Guard, a Polish underground movement, bombed German clubs and artillery emplacements in the ghetto. Secret workshops were set up inside the ghetto for the production of Molotov cocktails and hand grenades. Polish contacts smuggled in textbooks on chemistry and helped to make explosives.

The JFO soon displaced the Jewish Council as the main force in the ghetto and levied heavy taxes on Jews who still had money. By January 1943, when the fighters had their first baptism of fire, they had a store of 143 revolvers, one machine pistol, and seven rounds of ammunition per weapon. They became known as "the people's avengers" and planned their first attack on January 22, but the Germans acted first. On January 18, German troops suddenly surrounded the ghetto and seized workers for deportation. The fighters put out an emergency leaflet: "Jews! The enemy has moved on to the second phase of your extermination! Do not resign yourselves to death! Defend yourselves! Grab an axe, an iron bar, a knife! Let them take you in this way, if they can!"

Fifty fighter groups were ready, but most of them could not reach ammunition stores in time. Four battle groups fought like guerrillas— from rooftops, cellars and attics, moving from street to street through underground passages without leaving houses. In several encounters, Germans were killed or forced to retreat. Jews also fought guards at the *Umschlagplatz*, where victims were loaded onto trains to Treblinka. The January action lasted four days. The fighters killed twenty Germans and wounded fifty more, but their own losses were very heavy.

However, the action electrified the ghetto. These first shots of revolt showed Jews that they could kill Germans. For the thousands still left in the ghetto but unarmed, the thought that Jews were avenging Germans made death more bearable. The attitude of some Poles now changed as well. The ''power'' of the JFO now began to spread in Warsaw; Poles were now more eager to sell arms.

During the period between the January 1943 action and April 19, when the large uprising began, the JFO took stock, regrouped, and managed to increase its number to 650, divided into 22 fighting groups. Jews left in the ghetto worked in a frenzy digging tunnels, underground bunkers, and attic hideouts. Mines were laid. Trenches and ditches were dug under pavements and behind walls. Couriers met agents in deserted houses and exchanged money for dynamite.

The Germans, meanwhile, determined to liquidate the ghetto through deportations. The end of the Warsaw Ghetto was to come on April 18 as a birthday gift to Hitler, but German plans were thwarted. At 2 A.M. the following day—the day before Passover—the fighters learned that patrols of Germans, Ukrainians and Letts had circled the ghetto at 30-yard intervals. Fifteen minutes later all were at their battle stations and all other Jews were told to go to prepared hideouts. At 6 A.M. a contingent of 2,000 heavily armed SS men entered the Central Ghetto with tanks, rapid-fire guns, trailers loaded with ammunition, and ambulances. Jews were nowhere to be seen. The first main onslaught took place at the corner of Mila and Zamenhof where the fighters attacked a German column. A tank was set on fire and the whole crew was burned alive. Altogether the Germans lost 200 in dead and wounded; one Jewish fighter was killed. After several other actions, the Germans withdrew to the uninhabited areas and flooded the sewers, but the fighters shut off the water by turning the valves of an auxiliary system.

On the second day, the Germans tried to storm the brushmakers' area, but the fighters exploded an electrically-operated mine. Again the Germans fled, leaving 80 or more dead. German blood was in the streets. Ambulances came for their wounded. When they returned in two hours, they were attacked with grenades and incendiary bottles and again driven away. (*See Reading No. 58.*) Then something extraordinary happened: Three German officers carrying machine pistols and the German director of the brushmakers' factory asked for a truce so that the dead could be removed. Germans were asking Jews to agree on rules! The only reply was more firing. Even after three light howitzers and a large field gun pounded the buildings in the area, the Germans had to fall back.

The ghetto defenders were elated. "What we have lived through," Anielewicz told Zuckerman, "after two days of defense, defies description in words. We must realize that what has happened exceeds our most audacious dreams. Germans twice fled the ghetto. One of our sectors held out for forty minutes; another, six hours. . . . Our losses in men are very small. . . . I have the feeling that what we have dared is of great significance."

Stroop had 2,090 men, about half of them regular army or Waffen SS troops, and the rest SS police, reinforced by 335 Lithuanian militia and Polish troops. Shocked by the success of the Jewish fighters, he called for tanks, armored cars, artillery, flamethrowers, and aerial support. Superior firepower could easily crush the poorly armed youths. Stroop's main problem, however, was that tens of thousands of Jews were hiding in bunkers. They would have to be dug out or burnt out, block by block, house to house. Only fire could destroy the ghetto.

On the third day of the rebellion, Stroop bombed the brushmakers' block continuously but the resistance was still stubborn. In the afternoon, fires were started and flames raged fiercely. (*See Reading No. 59.*) The fire spread to the central ghetto area, but sporadic gunfire and grenades showered the moving truckloads of SS forces from balconies, windows, and rooftops. Every house now became a battleground.

The Germans had planned to destroy the ghetto in three days, but resistance continued. Stroop admitted that it was hard to capture Jews and that young women were conspicuous among the fighters: "They belonged to the *Chalutzim* (pioneers)," he said, "and fired pistols with both hands. They also threw hand grenades concealed in their bloomers." Meanwhile, the Germans called for voluntary conscripts to be "evacuated" (deported to Treblinka), but no one showed up. Police dogs and listening devices were now used to force Jews out of their hideouts. Bunkers were dynamited and smoke candles were lowered into sewer entrances. Fighters joined Jews in shelters and tried to defend them.

On the fifth day of battle, the Jewish fighters published a manifesto and a message of solidarity to the Poles: "We, as well as you, are burning with the desire to punish the enemy for all his crimes. . . . It is a fight for our freedom as well as yours; for our human dignity and national honor, as well as yours." There were a few messages of fraternity and admiration, and a few scattered actions by the People's Guard, but no armed help from the official Polish army. The next day, the fighters destroyed a huge tannery, German storehouses, and the military cannery. "Struggling grimly," they reported, "the fighters continue to pound the enemy." Through the spreading fire, smoke, and explosions, some civilians were moved to safer bunkers, and Jews in houses on Niska Street, which the Germans had drenched with kerosene, were moved through holes in the walls. Some fighters, dressed in German uniforms and helmets, wrapped their feet in rags and attacked German patrols in ambushes. Urgent calls for help were sent to the Polish National Council in London and Allies through underground channels, but no help came.

On April 26, a final communiqué was issued:

> We are now in the eighth day of our fight to the death. . . . The Germans have suffered heavy losses . . . [but] the number of Jewish losses is enormous. Our days are numbered. . . . We have rejected the German ultimatum calling upon us to capitulate. Since we see our end drawing near we beg of you: Do not forget!

> The day shall come when the innocent blood spilled will be revenged. Help those who manage to escape from the enemy so that they may continue the fight.

Pockets of resistance flared from bunkers and tunnels, but Stroop attached pneumatic boring machines to flamethrowers and gasoline and poison gas were thrust into openings. Scattered remnants of fighters tried to flee to the forests, but almost all were killed or captured.

Meanwhile, several blond Jewish youths had gone to the so-called Aryan side of Warsaw to investigate the possibility of an escape route through the sewers. Several Polish comrades had arranged hideouts for them. A mass exodus through this route was clearly impossible. When the manhole cover of the sewer exit was raised, the Germans opened fire.

On May 8, Germans attacked the command center at Mila 18. This was a large bunker sheltering 300 civilians and 80 fighters, including Anielewicz. Resistance lasted for two hours. The Germans blew up entrances with hand grenades, but the fighters would not surrender. Finally, the Germans sealed up all the exits and sent down smoke bombs. Choking from the gas, most of the fighters died. Others, including Anielewicz, committed suicide rather that be taken alive. A few survivors stumbled to a nearby bunker and joined others. This remnant was then led by two Jewish youths from the Aryan side to the sewers. (*See Reading No. 60.*) Several lost consciousness. Some drank the thick slimy water. Some begged to be left, but no one was abandoned. On the morning of May 10, the manhole on the Aryan side was opened briefly and a few Jews climbed out. The rest had to wait until midnight for the cover to be opened again, but they were quickly captured. Among the first group, most perished in the woods or in the Polish Warsaw uprising of August 1944. By May 16, Stroop claimed that the Warsaw Ghetto no longer existed, but there are eyewitness accounts of clashes between Jews and Germans in June and July.

The Warsaw Ghetto fighters were overwhelmed but they, indeed, died with honor. Their resistance lasted longer than the Polish resistance to the German invasion in September 1939 and was, in fact, the very first open armed confrontation of an underground with the Nazis.

After the doomed revolt in the Warsaw Ghetto, the ghettos of Bialystok (*See Reading No. 61.*) Czestochowa, Bedzin, Tarnow, Riga, Grodno, and Lvov also rose up against the Nazis. Jews were also involved in uprisings in the death camps themselves—Treblinka, Auschwitz, and Sobibor. In Bialystok, from August 16 to 20, 1943, Jewish youths organized armed resistance as in Warsaw, largely on the iniative of left-wing Zionist groups. In Bialystok, Jewish Communists were also very active. An Anti-Fascist Fighting Bloc was formed in July 1943, and it was finally decided that resistance should be organized both within the ghetto and in the forests. Obtaining arms was a major problem. The Polish Home army refused to help and the Polish left-wing underground could only send token supplies. The ghetto fighters stole some arms from German barracks and bought some from Polish peasants at great cost. They also made hand grenades and Molotov cocktails inside the ghetto. When the fighting began, the fighters had only 25 German rifles, about 100 revolvers and pistols, a few hand grenades, a few tommy guns and one machine gun. They also had a few sticks of dynamite, bottles filled with vitriol, and axes, knives, and bayonets.

On August 16, 1943, Bialystok Jews were told they would be "evacuated" to Lublin, the code for liquidation. The fighters warned the ghetto of its fate in proclamation:

Five million Jews in Europe have already been murdered by Hitler. Of Polish Jewry no more than a tenth remains. You must know that all Jews driven

away are led to their deaths. Do not believe the Gestapo propaganda. . . .
Each of us in under a sentence of death. We are being driven to Treblinka!
Do not go freely to your death! Fight for your life until your last breath. With
tooth and nail, with axe and knife, with vitriol and iron, greet your execu-
tioners. Make your enemy pay with blood.

The Nazi commander of the action brought in one German battalion
and two battalions of Galician Ukrainians. Forty thousand Jews in the
ghetto were driven into narrow alleys close to the ghetto fence. Tenenbaum and 500 ghetto fighters tried to storm the fence and lead at least
some of the Jews into the surrounding forests where Jewish partisans,
who had left the ghetto earlier, were waiting. At 10 a.m. a group of
girls fired on a number of houses and factories and several German par-
tols were forced to retreat. A German SS officer was killed, but German heavy machine-gun fire and tanks felled thousands trying to break
through the fence. Some managed to break free, however, and take
cover in an underground bunker. Short but desperate resistance was
put up by a group of fighters in the Jewish hospital. Many of the sick
were murdered in their beds; children and babies were flung out of windows. The unequal battle lasted for four days. After August 20, thousands of Jews refused to report for deportation, but they were trapped
in manhunts. Some fighters dug a tunnel leading to the forest but were
ambushed. Several were forced onto the trains going to Treblinka but
jumped off only to be killed by Ukrainian guards. A remnant of fighters
did escape to the forests and joined Russian partisans, continuing the
struggle after the ghetto was destroyed.

Other resistance efforts flared briefly, but were doomed by absence
of outside help, lack of arms, physical attrition, and by the massive deportations that began in the summer of 1942.

Annihilation. The most murderous destruction took place in the
ghettos and camps of Poland, the heartland of European Jewry, where
three million Jews in what had been prewar Poland perished. During
their short life, the ghettos accounted for the death of one-fifth of Polish
Jewry, a very high rate of mortality but not fast enough for the Nazis.
The industrialization of killing through gassing had undergone several
stages, starting with the "euthanasia" program in Germany, the
primitive gassings in Lublin (*See Reading No. 63*), the gas vans, and
the high pitch of efficiency at Auschwitz. (*See Reading No. 64.*)

Beginning in March 1942, Jews in the Lublin region were deported to and then gassed at Belzec. The deportation agony for Warsaw Jews began July 22, 1942. (*See Reading 65.*) One of the most poignant of the many accounts of these deportations is the one describing the "evacuation" of the Janusz Korczak orphanage. (*See Reading No. 66.*)

All of the other ghettos in Poland except Lodz were extinguished in 1942–43. (Lodz survived until August 1944, when the last of its workers—70,000—were deported.) Orders had come form Himmler on July 19 to wipe out all of the ghettos in the Government-General as a fitting memorial to Heydrich, who had been assassinated near Prague on May 29. The code name for this massive killing was "Operation Reinhard," which yielded for the Nazis not only hundreds of thousands of dead Jews, but their assets. Globocnik did a detailed inventory of the confiscated wealth, including money, jewelry (including 67,000 watches), clothing, bed feathers, and 1,000 wagonloads of textiles tentatively valued at 100,047,983.91 RM, as of February 3, 1943. In Himmler's speech to SS leaders later that year, he noted this wealth, threatened punishment to any men who took any of it for private gain, and congratulated them on writing "a page of glory" in German history in the difficult task of the "extermination of the Jewish race." (*See Reading No. 67.*)

It was against this planned, systematic, and relentless end-goal that Jews struggled to resist.

CHAPTER SEVEN

DEPORTATIONS FROM WESTERN EUROPE

Some of the problems confronting Jews who wanted to resist physically will come into sharper focus as we analyze the political and military relations between Nazi Germany and the countries from which Jews were deported. Among the elements to be considered are the degree of native anti-Semitism and its intensification by Nazi infiltration or Nazi support for indigenous fascist movements; the power of the Nazi presence in an occupied country; the degree of sovereignty permitted in the political and military arrangements—whether a country was occupied, had satellite status, or was technically independent, as in the case of Italy. The territorial ambitions of a nation also were significant, if Hitler could satisfy them, in determining its collaboration in the deportations, as in the case of Romania and Hungary. In other situations, such as in Holland, the presence of a huge Nazi police force and the character of the terrain made it impossible for Jews to escape, despite the widespread good-will among the Dutch. German control inside the country was total, in contrast with the situation in France, where German police forces were thinned out, thus requiring French police help in the round-ups. In countries that owed their existence to Hitler, for example, Slovakia and Croatia, Jews were killed off readily.

Scandinavian Countries. Before Hitler came to power in 1933, Jews in the Scandinavian countries lived in peace and comfort and were well integrated. Anti-Semitism was virtually non-existent, but there were small native pro-Nazi parties in each country. There were about 8,000 Jews each in Sweden and Denmark, 1700 in Norway, and 2000 in Finland, with most concentrated in the capitals. Until 1939, public opinion and government policy in all three countries on the question of absorbing Jewish refugees from Germany were affected mainly by fears that Jewish immigrants would increase unemployment and provoke Hitler. Traditional respect for German culture was widespread and many Scandinavians, at first, refused to believe that German Jews had actually been deprived of their rights. Jewish and non-Jewish relief committees worked hard to obtain transit visas for refugees, especially children, who needed a temporary asylum en route to Palestine. The work of N. Ch. Ditleff, who set up a rescue committee in Stockholm, is particularly noteworthy.

Norway. Sweden remained neutral, a status which was beneficial to the Allies as well as to Germany. Norway and Denmark were invaded on April 9, 1940. Norway offered resistance, but was forced to capitulate within two months. The country became a Reich Commissariat, under Josef Terboven, who was directly responsible to Hitler. The monarchy, the constitution, and all political parties, except the pro-Nazi party headed by Vidkun Quisling, were abolished. Quisling later became Minister-President. The early months of Nazification were bearable for Jews, but in June 1941, soon after the invasion of Russia, Jews in northern Norway were rounded up and deported to Germany. Early in 1942, passports and identity cards were marked with a "J." Property of Jews was confiscated. On October 25, 1942, male Jews over 16 throughout Norway were arrested, but some fled to Sweden. A month later, 531 Jews, including women and children, were shipped to Stettin and then deported to Auschwitz. In February, 1943, another group was deported to Auschwitz, making a total of 770 Jews deported from Norway. All but 23 perished.

Another 900 managed to avoid arrest and crossed into Sweden. They walked for days through thick forests and wild country, generously helped by Norwegians who gave them food and shelter until guides took them past German border patrols. Later, they were looked after by Jewish refugee committees.

Denmark. The story of the Danish Jews is unique in the annals of the Holocaust and is perhaps the most inspiring of all episodes in its expression of simple decency and humanity. From the old King Christian to the humblest fisherman, the entire people resisted the deportation of its Jews and succeeded in saving most of them. In the early period of the occupation, the Danes seemed compliant. This absence of resistance and the German view of the Danes as ethnic cousins resulted initially in an indulgent German policy. However, the threat of anti-Jewish measures brought an unexpected protest. When the Nazis threatened to impose the Nuremberg Laws in Denmark, the king threatened to abdicate, and in 1942, when an attempt was made to set fire to the synagogue in Copenhagen, the Danish police stopped the action. In January 1942, at a student festival, when Danish students asked the audience to sing two songs dear to the Danish people, they

AXIS EUROPE - 1942

⧄	Occupied, Annexed, Created, or Controlled by Germany
▓	Controlled by Italy

sang the Danish and then the Jewish national anthem, *Hatikvah* (Hope).

For several years, Denmark was able to retain a large measure of autonomy. The monarchy, constitution, government, courts, and even the press were allowed a surprising degree of freedom. The Reich Minister to Denmark, Karl Werner Best, himself enjoying the relative quiet in a quasi-free society, warned Berlin that anti-Jewish measures would create a constitutional crisis in Denmark. He suggested taking action against the 1,350 stateless Jewish refugees in the country, but the Danish government, unlike other governments, protected them. It refused to make any distinction between native Jews and foreign Jews.

In the summer of 1943, however, the situation radically changed. The war was going badly for the Germans and an underground resistance movement, largely guided by British agents and communications, began to engage in acts of sabotage. Danish dock workers refused to repair German ships and went on strike. The Danish prime minister threatened to resign if the strikers were tried in Danish courts. The Germans declared martial law, and the German army entered Copenhagen. On September 18, 1943, Rolf Günther arrived in the city with a special commando from Eichmann's office. Himmler was now sure that the time had come to enforce the Final Solution in Denmark, but he had not reckoned on the popular resolve to resist (*See Reading No. 68*), nor on the refusal of the German military commander, General Hermann von Hannecken, to help the Nazi police with round-ups.

Deportations were scheduled for October 1, but a few days earlier, a German shipping expert, Georg Duckwitz, who was employed as attaché of the German merchant marine, revealed these plans to an acquaintance, Hans Hedtoft (later prime minister). Hedtoft, in turn, spread the news to his friends and the president of the Jewish community. On the morning of September 29, Rabbi Marcus Melchior, the chief rabbi of Copenhagen, warned his congregation to leave their homes. Throughout the day, Danish policemen, mail carriers, taxi drivers, shopkeepers, and students spread the word. Some Jews who had no place to go were piled into an ambulance and taken to the Bispejerg Hospital, where they were sheltered. *Gestapo* squads roamed the streets, broke into homes and made arrests. Some 1,600 were captured and interned. The Germans declared that Jews had been eliminated from Danish life, but a deluge of protests poured in and sabotage of German property increased. Students, teachers and church officials were particularly active. (*See Reading No. 69.*)

On October 1, the Swedish government offered refuge to all Danish Jews, but hiding places in Denmark had to be found first. Ingenious escape routes were created across the Kattegat Sound between Denmark and Sweden. Out of Copenhagen, there were mock funeral processions of Jews dressed in black, stopping at a cemetery, and then disappearing into the Bispebjerg Hospital where they were hidden and then driven away in ambulances to a rendezvous with fishermen on the coast.

A whole mobilization of fishermen and helpers was needed to effect the rescue and many boats were boarded by Germans with their police dogs, but when the exodus was over, the number of those saved was quite spectacular: 6,000 full Jews, 1,310 half-Jews, and 686 non-Jews married to Jews. The operation had taken less than a month. In the arrests earlier, between 400 and 500 Jews had been deported to Theresienstadt in Czechoslovakia. Through the special efforts of private funds, the Danish Red Cross and the Danish Ministry of Welfare, special food parcels, letters, and vitamins were sent to these Jews. (*See Reading No. 68.*) Fifty-three perished, including two still-born babies; the rest survived, an exceptional statistic in the context of the near total annihilation of Jews in Theresienstadt, and another tribute to the dogged efforts of the Danes to protect their Jews.

Finland. Finland had been invaded by the Soviet Union in November 1939, and became Germany's ally in the war against Russia. The north of Finland was occupied by German troops and Nazi ideological pressure soon made itself felt. The *Gestapo* gained a foothold in the pro-Nazi elements among the Finnish police and demanded the surrender of 300 Jewish refugees, but they were hastily packed off to Sweden. Himmler, himself, went to Helsingfors in July 1942 to demand the deportation of Finnish Jews, taking with him his personal physician and physical therapist Dr. Felix Kersten, who was a Finn. Kersten alerted political leaders of Himmler's intentions and they resorted to a variety of delaying tactics. The Finnish Foreign Minister, Rolf Witting, told Himmler that the Finnish people had no sympathy with the German anti-Jewish policy and that a number of Jews had died in the war against Russia. ''Finland is a decent nation,'' he said. ''We would rather perish together with the Jews . . . We will not surrender them.'' Even the dangerous food situation did not change this attitude. From the German point of view, Finnish nickel and timber were necessary, and Finland was needed for the coming German advance on

Leningrad. Ultimately, only four Jews were seized and deported. The Finnish police and government refused continued threats and pressures. In September 1944, when Finland surrendered to the Russians, its Jews were intact.

Scandinavia admittedly had few Jews for the Nazi death mills, but in Holland, Belgium, and France, their numbers were much greater, the Nazi persecutions commensurately more ruthless, and the destructive results, much more devastating.

In the six weeks between May 10 and June 25, 1940, a half-million Jews of western Europe came under German control in France, Holland, and Belgium. Most were from old and largely integrated communities where they had lived for hundreds of years. In contrast with the Jews of eastern Europe, western Jews were considered by their non-Jewish neighbors as nationals having all of the rights and obligations of first-class citizens. They posed a more difficult problem for the Germans, but when the machinery of death began to operate, it drove on as relentlessly as in the East. There were no massed executions as at Babi Yar, and no ghettos, but Nazi plans and goals were the same: the physical annihilation of every Jew. The Germans were frustrated somewhat where their military and police control were limited, as in France and Belgium, but in Holland, their grip was absolute, and most Jews perished, more than 100,000.

The Netherlands. The Germans suddenly invaded Holland on May 10, 1940 and within four days the country's resistance crumbled. While surrender negotiations were under way, the city of Rotterdam was bombed and almost wiped out. The Queen and government fled to London and set up a government-in-exile. A Reichkommissar, Artur Seyss-Inquart, was installed and anti-Jewish measures were imposed quickly: confiscation of Jewish property, registration of all Jews, and the setting up of a Jewish Council (*Joodse Raad*). Jews were dismissed from public office, jobs, and professions. Of the 140,000 Jews in Holland at the time, about 30,000 were refugees, mostly from Germany and Austria. Another 20,000 were *Mischlinge,* Jews in mixed marriages and those having varying degrees of "Jewish blood," involving Nazi racial specialists in specious physical examinations to determine whether they were Jews or Aryans. In February 1941, the Germans tried to provoke a pogrom by sending Dutch Nazis into the old Jewish quarter of Amsterdam where they attacked Jews and set fire to several synagogues. Jews and their Christian neighbors fought back and resisted several waves. The Germans, themselves, finally had to come in with automatic weapons and tanks.

They inflicted heavy casualties and cordoned off the Jewish section. At this point, Hans Rauter, Higher SS and Police Leader, summoned several of Amsterdam's Jewish leaders and forced them to set up the *Joodse Raad,* warning that all signs of disobedience would be severely punished. Some Jews protested any dealings with the Germans, fearing that the Raad would eventually become a tool of the Germans, but no one could grasp the ultimate Nazi design.

A new outbreak of violence drew frightening consequences. A German police unit entered the apartment of a Dutch Jew and was attacked by bullets and acid. In reprisal, 425 young Jews were seized on the streets and sent first to Buchenwald, then to Mauthausen, a dread camp in Austria, where they perished. The Dutch answered on February 25 with a wave of strikes in shipyards, armament industries, sanitation, and transport *(See Reading No. 70)*, the only such expression in Europe. The Germans were stunned, but the strikes were soon crushed, workers sent to concentration camps, and martial law declared. In the spring of 1941, a ''Central Office for Jewish Emigration'' was established in Amsterdam, headed by one of Eichmann's agents, Ferdinand Aus der Funten. This was the mechanism to process the deportations. Labor camps were established in January 1942 in Vught and Westerbork, which became way stations to Auschwitz. By the end of April, all Jews had to wear a Jewish star.

These anti-Jewish decrees aroused deep resentment among the Dutch. Students went on strike to protest the dismissal of Jewish teachers and to express their sympathy. Many Dutch citizens wore yellow flowers in their lapels. Church leaders urged resistance. A typical pastoral letter read: ''We know what conflicts of conscience result for those concerned. In order, therefore, to eliminate all doubts and uncertainties that you may have in this respect, we hereby declare most explicitly that no compromise in this domain of conscience is allowed . . . remain steadfast in the certainty that you are fulfilling your duty toward God and man.''

But the enemy was too powerful. There were more German police forces in Holland than in France. Moreover, the country's geography conspired against escape or rescue. Holland is flat and has no forests. On the east was Germany; on the south, occupied Belgium; and on the north, the open sea. The small, trim Dutch homes and gardens could not easily accommodate underground bunkers or tunnels. Yet, when the deportations started in July 1942, many thousands of Dutch Christians hid Jews in attics, ceiling spaces, cellars, cloisters, and orphanages. The experience of Anne Frank and her family was not exceptional. It is estimated that 20,000 Dutch Christians perished, many of whom were shot trying to save Jews, as well as those who were charged with sabotage and underground resistance.

Foreign Jews were the first to be called up to serve in so-called "guarded communal work camps" in Germany. The *Joodse Raad*, ordered to provide 4,000 Jews between 16 and 40, had to inform them by letter on July 4. About 400 who did not report received help from the Dutch underground. Seven hundred other Jews were kept as hostages and threatened with Mauthausen if the quota was not filled. The deportees were instructed to take along work clothes and an eight-day food supply. For a time, it was believed that deportations were a true resettlement, especially since the first deportations involved Jewish men who worked in Dutch-supervised camps under fairly tolerable conditions while their families received their wages. But these snares were typical of Nazi deceptions. From the Dutch camps Jews were transported to Auschwitz.

On August 13, the *Joodse Raad* received the first batch of letters from the deportees, postmarked Birkenau. (*See Reading No. 71.*) It took the *Raad* five days of searching the best available maps to discover that Birkenau lay in Upper Silesia. But no one knew that Jews were being gassed there. The letters reported that the work was hard but tolerable, and the food and sleeping arrangements adequate. Questions and disquiet grew. Only fifty-two letters came while 16,000 Jews had already been deported. What had happened to the others?

A short time before the letters came, Seyss-Inquart's political advisor Schmidt had said that the deportees would work at "making a start with clearing the rubble in the empty towns of the devastated East," one of the numerous camouflages that led many Dutch Jews to conclude that although some might not survive the rigors, most would return to Holland. Had Jews been able to keep their radios, some may have heard BBC reports on June 26, 1942, of mass murders of Polish Jews, but they had been forced to turn them in early in 1941. Other reports which were heard were dismissed as exaggerated anti-German war propaganda. Moreover, the Allied reports made no mention of Auschwitz-Birkenau or any of the other death camps. Furthermore, not a single Dutch victim escaped from Auschwitz to bear witness to the awful reality.

This widespread ignorance of the true nature of these camps and the refusal or inability of most Europeans to give credence to the truth have been noted frequently by many survivors and contemporary witnesses. As the historian, Louis de Jong, who was also a teacher at the Amsterdam Jewish Lyceum in 1942–43 (where Anne Frank was a pupil) has said, ''During all the years that European Jews were being driven into the gas chambers, the very idea of mechanized mass murder struck most people . . . as utterly inconceivable.'' Among many others, the *Joodse Raad* could not face the unbearable truth. The Nazis cunningly lulled any suspicions that may have arisen.

By the end of 1942, 38,500 Jews had been deported from Holland, but the round-ups fell behind Rauter's timetable. In the spring and summer of 1943, there were large-scale seizures of Jews at the rate of 2,000 per week. Because the Auschwitz crematoria were overworked at the time, thousands were sent to Sobibor instead, a killing center where no selections took place. The temporary exemptions for most of the employees of the Raad ended in May-June 1943, and for the rest, in 1944. The deportations lasted until September 1944 when Allied patrols reached the Dutch border.

Belgium. The Germans invaded Belgium on May 10, 1940, and by May 16, the German army had entered Brussels. The government had fled to London, although King Leopold III remained in the country. Of the 90,000 Jews in Belgium, many were foreign or stateless, mainly east European and German refugees, an index of the liberal immigration policy of the Belgians. Thousands of Belgians, including Jews, fled to France during the invasion, but some Jews returned in the summer of 1940 after France itself was occupied.

Belgium, like France, was placed under a military administration headed by General Alexander von Falkenhausen, but the actual administration of the country was handed over to the pre-war civil service. Falkenhausen was chiefly interested in strengthening German military security and exploiting the economy of Belgium and wanted to avoid any entanglement in the ''Jewish Question.'' He also opposed Nazi excesses and until his arrest for involvement in the July 20, 1944, conspiracy against Hitler, he resisted SS pressure to help in the round-up of Jews.

Anti-Jewish laws were introduced beginning in October 1940, including a registration decree. However, only 42,000 registered. Another 20,000 or more remained in hiding and a Jewish underground organization, *Comité de Défense des Juifs,* affiliated with the Belgian resistance movement and recognized by the Belgian Government-in-Exile, struggled to blunt or defy the anti-Jewish laws. It included non-Jews as well as Jews and viewed rescue as part of resistance. This organization also opposed the activity of the *Association des Juifs de Belgique* (AJB) which had been appointed by the Germans in November 1941. At first, the AJB provided schooling for children who had been expelled from Belgian schools and varied social services, but was intended to transmit Nazi orders. In the spring of 1942 it notified Jews of the Nazi order to report to the Dossin barracks in the camp at Malines, and in June, of the order to wear the Jewish star. Men and women over 16 were sent to forced labor at Audinghem.

Many Belgians as well as Jews were opposed to the star decree. On the first Sunday after the decree, the streets in Brussels were filled with Belgians wearing Jewish stars. Shopkeepers sold them in the Belgian national colors. A conference of Belgian mayors met and denounced the order. The German military command consistently refused to help enforce the order and the inadequate number of German police made it generally difficult to implement. Meanwhile, the AJB, under the illusion that Jews were being sent for labor, passed on the orders in the summer of 1942, at first directed to foreign Jews. However, within a few months, Jews did not report voluntarily and had to be forcibly seized. A Belgian partisan group also helped to sabotage the deportations by setting fire to the files in the AJB building. Belgian police were also helpful, losing and misplacing files on Jews and forging documents for them. Belgian railway workers left doors of deportation trains open to facilitate escape. Other railway workers held up trains to enable the Belgian underground to carry out ambushes.

Belgian clergymen were among the most active in Europe in aiding and rescuing Jews, particularly children, while the people as a whole were strengthened in their resistance by the strong denunciation of the Nazi occupation by the Primate of Belgium, Joseph-Ernest Cardinal van Roey. Cardinal Roey believed he might even be able to save Belgian nationals from deportations. A pledge to this effect had been extracted from the military administration, but, as happened elsewhere, Eichmann overrode this promise. In August and September 1944, about 1000 Belgian native Jews were deported to Malines, and from there to Auschwitz. A much larger number of foreign Jews, almost

25,000, had also been deported. Most who had fled to France were caught up in the deportations there. At liberation, about 20,000 Jews were found in Belgium.

In Belgium, no distinctions had been made between native and foreign Jews. The Belgians had tried to help them all. This was, however, not the case in France.

France. On the eve of the German invasion, France was a sorely divided nation. There were many conservative and right-wing, anti-Semitic forces in the country which secretly and publicly were in sympathy with Hitler, while the left-wing groups were fighting a weak capitalism at home and only dimly saw the danger of Nazism, concentrating mainly on scoring the French and British ruling classes for refusing a collective security arrangement with Russia before the Soviet-Nazi Pact of August 1939. All classes painfully remembered the great French losses in World War I and dreaded the prospect of another war. After the German invasion of Poland, the French believed that Poland would offer long and stubborn resistance and did nothing to threaten the Germans in the west. At the time of the German invasion of France on May 1940, the French forces were ill-prepared for the swift, high-powered German advance and collapsed quickly in a mood of defeatism. As early as May 17, the aged commander-in-chief, Maxime Weygand, believed that the war was over. No utilization was made of the French navy or the resources of the French empire. On June 16, the 80-year old Marshal Henri Pétain, who would soon become head of state, surrendered. Three-fifths of France to the north and west came under German military control, while in the south, in the so-called Free Zone, Pétain set up an authoritarian regime in Vichy. The arch collaborator, Pierre Laval, who had helped pave the way for French submission, became vice-premier and the real power.

There were about 310,000 Jews in France at the time, about half of them refugees from Germany, Austria, Belgium, and central and eastern Europe. These foreign Jews, many of whom were stateless, were fated to be destroyed, while native and naturalized Jews in the main survived. To the Vichy government, the German victory was decisive and German demands were not opposed at first. In fact, the early Vichy collaboration exceeded Nazi hopes. In October 1940, without any German prodding, a severe *Statut des Juifs* was passed which affected Jews in both zones. They were ousted from all public and administrative work, forbidden to teach, defined in accordance with the Nuremberg principle, and required to register. (Fortunately, there was no central register of Jewish names in France, but some lists were obtained through the French police and among records of Jewish organizations.) In April 1941, Xavier Vallat, a notorious anti-Semite, became the first head of the *Commissariat Général aux Questions*, set up to carry out the anti-Jewish measures and prepare the way for deportations.

Drastic actions against foreign Jews came even earlier. Beginning in July 1940, 22,000 French Jews from Alsace-Lorraine (in the occupied zone) were piled into trucks and driven across the demarcation line into Vichy France and dumped on country roads. By November, an additional 47,000 were deported to Lyon. With the connivance of local German administrators and on instructions from Heydrich, 7,450 Jews from the Baden-Saar area in Germany were also dumped into the Vichy zone and sent to French camps, Les Milles near Aix-en-Provence and Gurs and Rivesaltes in the Pyrenees. Later, there were brutal round-ups of all foreign and stateless Jews in the Vichy zone as well as the occupied zone and forced transfer to these camps and Noé, Récébédon, and Le Vernet.

The concentration camps in France, operated by French personnel, represented a victory for Nazi doctrines. At first they provided neither food nor shelter for the victims, many of whom died of hunger, cold, cruel treatment, and disease. They were systematically dehumanized by officials using methods starkly described in Arthur Koestler's book *Scum of the Earth*. By the end of 1942, officials in these camps had sent 42,000 of the interned Jews to the east—to death—in cattle trains. Jewish and non-Jewish relief agencies worked heroically to improve camp conditions and help some of the inmates escape. Teams of social workers tried especially to improve living conditions for children, but few were saved from the camps.

For the Jews in France, the persecutions were a nightmare. Letters of bewilderment and protest were sent to Marshal Pétain and Vallat. (*See Reading No. 72.*) Pétain, himself, sent a letter of inquiry to the French ambassador at the Vatican, but he was reassured that there was no disapproval or criticism of the anti-Jewish legislation. Aquinas's recommendations on restricting Jewish activity, but barring oppression, were noted. Nor did the Vatican intend "quarreling with us over the Jewish statute." However, Vichy was faced with considerable opposition from the French Christian clergy. There were strong letters of protest, urgent messages and instructions read to congregations, and calls to help Jews. (*See Reading No. 73.*) The Archbishop of Toulouse, Jules-Gérard Saliège; the Archbishop of Lyon, Pierre Cardinal Gerlier; and Pierre-Marie Théas, Bishop of Montauban, were especially vigorous in their denunciations of anti-Jewish brutalities and made pleas to help out of the demands of Christian conscience. These calls intensified in the summer of 1942.

By this time, the camp at Drancy, in a suburb northeast of Paris, had been established as a transit to Auschwitz. The first transport consisted of almost 1000 Jews seized in Paris in December 1941 and taken from Drancy to Auschwitz in March 1942. SS headquarters were set up in Paris and in May, Heydrich, himself, went to the city to prod the French police and accelerate the deportations, and to include French as well as foreign Jews. A decree requiring all Jews in both zones to wear a Jewish star went into effect June 7, but had only limited success. A few days later, Eichmann met in Paris with his agents from France, Belgium, and Holland and set a quota of 100,000 deportees form France for the subsequent three months. The French police were to help in the seizures. The first trainload was to leave Bordeaux on July 13. Ironically, Eichmann's agents were not able to find enough victims to fill up a train from Bordeaux—a failure which infuriated Eichmann. But a few days later, the focus shifted to Paris.

Beginning at 4 A.M. on July 16, 1942, and continuing for two days, almost 13,000 stateless Jews were seized, including 4,051 children. Men without families were sent directly to Drancy. Families and all women and children were taken to the bleak spaces of the Vélodrôme d'Hiver, where they were penned up without food for several days. A single street hydrant supplied water, and 10 latrines, the lavoratory facilities. Several women gave birth to children; 30 people died. A triple epidemic of scarlet fever, measles, and diphtheria broke out. On the fifth day, the mothers and fathers were separated from the children, never to see them again. The parents were sent to Drancy, the children to camps at Pithiviers and Beaune-la-Rolande. Frantic efforts to obtain the release of the children were made but failed. The children, many of them infants, were taken to Drancy and from there to Auschwitz. Thirty adults survived, but all of the children perished. In the boxcars returning empty from Auschwitz, railwaymen found 25 bodies of children from two to four.

Beginning in September 1942, foreign and stateless Jews were deported from the Vichy zone, but the Council of Ministers at Vichy decided to protect French Jews from deportation. In November, the

Allies landed in North Africa and the Germans occupied most of the Vichy zone except the south. Thousands of foreign Jews now streamed into the south, in the Italian zone, from the Alpes-Maritimes to Savoie, where they were temporarily protected by Italian soldiers and police who refused to deport them. This safety zone, however, lasted only until September 1943, when a pro-Allied Italian government surrendered to the Allies. The humane blocking of Nazi pressures by the Italians and the rescue efforts of the Italian police inspector, Guido Lospinoso, a French Capuchin monk, Father Marie-Benoit, and Angelo Donati, an Italian Jew, gave Jews in the south an interlude of security and hope, but it was a brief interlude. (*See Reading No. 74.*) After the Italian surrender, the Germans swept into the Italian zone, dooming the Jews left there. German police raided hotels, homes and rooms day and night. By then, the French police did not offer their help, nor did the German army, and the Germans were reduced to street manhunts. Thousands of Jews tried to flee across the Alps, attempting to reach the frontiers of Switzerland or Italy. By the time of the Italian surrender, it is estimated that 52,000 Jews had been deported from France (about 6,000 of whom were French nationals). From that time to liberation in the summer of 1943, eighteen more transports left France, some of them carrying 1,000 Jews to Auschwitz. In the last months, Germans made sudden raids on children's homes, labor camps, prisons, homes for the aged, and other institutions run by a Jewish Council called *Union Générale des Israélites de France* (UGIF). Among these raids was the one of April 6, 1944, ordered by *Gestapo* chief in Lyon, Klaus Barbie, against the children's home at Izieux.

The Allied invasion of Europe in Normandy in June, 1944, created new dangers for some Jews as well as salvation for others. As the Germans retreated, Jews were killed at random. In July, the Paris orphanages and the Rothschild Home for the Aged were attacked, but the bombing of French railways finally stopped the transports. The evacuation of Drancy, which the Germans had planned for August 10, had to be canceled. When the Allies arrived, they found 700 Jews there. The Normandy invasion also sent a surge of hope and life into the French underground movements and compounded the problems of the German forces.

During the first phase of the German occupation, French resistance was weak. The Pétain regime was widely accepted and left-wing and Communist groups generally opposed any underground activity during the life of the Stalin-Hitler Pact, but resistance gathered strength after the German invasion of Russia. However, there could be no national, united resistance movement under the conditions of the German occupation and Vichy control. Separate groups formed, among them: *Libération, Combat, Franc-Tireur, Liberté,* and *France Combattante.* It is estimated that Jews constituted 15 to 20 percent of the active membership of these groups. Separate Jewish groups were also formed by those who believed that since Jews had been singled out, there should be autonomous Jewish fighting groups. These were drawn from the ranks of the French Jewish Scouts (EIF—*Éclaireurs Israélites de France*), *Combattants Zionistes, Rue Amelot, Combattants Juifs,* and *Main Forte,* among others, and engaged in sabotage, ambushes, and other military operations as well as the placement of children in the countryside, convents and homes of sympathetic Frenchmen, forging documents, and rescue efforts in Spain and Switzerland. The General Union of French Jews (UGIF), although it was often attacked for seeming compliance with Nazi orders, combined all of the diverse Jewish agencies that had been forced to dissolve, including the Jewish Scouts, and carried on underground assistance for refugees, Jews in camps, and children, under a legal facade.

Himmler considered the German record in France a failure, even a source of embarrassment, yet 80,000 to 90,000 Jews perished, a very heavy toll.

Germany and Austria. The first transports to "the east" from Germany were made in the fall of 1941 between October 15 and 31—when 20,000 German Jews, mostly old persons, were shipped off to Lodz in Poland. Later, in November, 50,000 German and Czech Jews were deported to occupied Russia, chiefly Riga and Minsk. The deportees to Lodz were killed within a few weeks; those to Russia survived for a few months, after being worked to death in the icy cold, or starved, or marched to execution pits. For many months, German bureaucrats labored over technical definitions of half-Jews and quarter-Jews. Should they be considered German or Jewish? What should be done with war veterans? For such Jews and many Jews from Austria and Czechoslovakia, a special ghetto in Czechoslovakia, called Theresienstadt, was created, which will be described in the next chapter.

In Austria, which had a Jewish population of 185,000 in March 1938, at the time of the *Anschluss,* within one year Eichmann had expelled 100,000 Jews. Some fled to England, France, Yugoslavia, and

Czechoslovakia. After the November 1938 pogrom, 5,000 Jews were deported to Dachau. Many Jews struggled to emigrate to Palestine, but the British permitted only 4,146 certificates. As a result of the Jewish expulsion from economic life, pauperization increased. Many Jews were turned out of their flats and had to find shelter in vermin-infested barracks in Simmering. Jews attempting to cross into Belgium and Poland in March 1939 were turned back. Most Central and South American countries closed their borders to Jews in June 1939. On July 6, 1939, all Jewish community offices in Germany officially became branches of the *Reichsvereinigung der Juden in Deutschland* (Reich Association of Jews in Germany), totally controlled by the *Gestapo* to force the pace of deportations. Membership was compulsory. On September 9, membership was enforced in Austria.

Later in the year, Eichmann fabricated reports about ''colonization work'' in the Lublin Province in Poland. The ''Lublin Reservation'' was widely publicized in the German press and the first groups numbering 1,672 left from Vienna in October. Later, German as well as Austrian Jews, some Poles and Gypsies were transported to Lublin. However, nothing was done to prepare the area for human settlement. The population transfers were controlled by Globocnik, whose aim was not resettlement but death to the victims. He experimented with primitive gassing installations in huts for laborers and more efficient equipment in all of the death camps in the General Government: Treblinka, and the three camps in the Lublin district: Belzec, Maidanek, and Sobibor. The ''plan'' for Lublin was officially dropped in March 1940, but the myth of resettlement there lived on. In 1942 and 1943, many Jews in Poland still believed that Germans were creating a Jewish reservation in Lublin. Another German deception also masked the truth about what would happen to Jews, namely, the publicity surrounding the so-called ''Madagascar Plan,'' which aroused international interest and some support, but which was merely another Nazi cover to deceive Jews and others as to their real intentions. These snares and delusions overlapped yet another myth—the myth of the ''model ghetto'' in Theresienstadt.

CHAPTER EIGHT

DEPORTATIONS FROM CENTRAL AND SOUTHERN EUROPE

Protectorate of Bohemia-Moravia. Theresienstadt was about 35 miles from Prague, but the capital and nation of Czechoslovakia disappeared in March 1939. The western areas of Moravia and Bohemia were absorbed into the Third Reich as a ''protectorate'' and the eastern part was created as a puppet state called Slovakia. The protectorate contained about 120,000 Jews. Within six months, 35,000 were expelled and many Jews were put aboard German ships with bogus Latin American visas. Eichmann threatened imprisonment at Dachau if Jews did not leave the country quickly—70,000 per year. The first transports to Lublin left in October 1939, and in March 1940, the *Gestapo* was in complete charge of ''emigration.'' By May 1941, 83 Czech towns had expelled their Jews. The pre-war Czech leaders and public figures who had had good relations with Jews went into exile; the new Czech leadership, anti-Semitic and pro-Nazi, collaborated in these measures and severed connections between Jews and the Czech people. Efforts to mitigate these measures were crushed when Heydrich became Acting Protector of Bohemia-Moravia in September 1941 and a reign of terror swept over the country.

Theresienstadt. Theresienstadt was created in October 1941 as a transit camp, but was promoted as a model ghetto, especially designed for old people and war veterans who, as Heydrich said, ''could not stand the strain of resettlement,'' and who paid a heavy price to go there. In return for all his assets, a Jew bought a place in the ghetto and was guaranteed food, clothing, housing, and medical care for life. Soon the inmates realized that it was a transit to the dreaded east. Terezin, as it had been known under Czech rule, had been a fortress town of several thousands soldiers and peasants. By the end of 1942, over 85,000 Jews from Germany, Austria, and Czechoslovakia were crowded into its ugly barracks, wasting away from disease and hunger, or dead in the gassings at Auschwitz. By 1945, 135,000 Jews had passed through the ghetto; only 17,000 survived. Of the 15,000 children who were sent there, only 100 survived. (*See Reading No. 75.*)

Czech Jews, when the Nazis announced that an ''autonomous ghetto'' would be set up on German territory, received the announcement with a certain feeling of relief. Community leaders, some of whom had seen Lublin, looked upon Theresienstadt as a way of saving Jews from the horrors of transfer to Poland. They also believed they could maintain contact with fellow Czech Jews and build some sort of Jewish community as a temporary refuge. Zionist leaders even hoped that Jewish youth there could be trained to serve the Jewish people after the war.

The first Czech Jews arrived in Theresienstadt late in November 1941, made up of 342 young men who worked hard to rebuild the dilapidated houses and barracks. They smuggled in books, medicines, building materials, and straw. The harsh realities of the place were soon evident once later transports came in: men and women were separated and children were separated from their parents. No contact with Czechs was permitted. There was little water, or food, or fuel. Beatings and hangings became commonplace. Life was hardest on the old people. (*See Reading No. 76.*) Many had traveled in sealed trains for 20 hours, carrying with them top hats, lace dresses, and parasols. Their old world quickly evaporated. They had to sleep on barracks floors, suffer indignities because of the absence of toilets, beg for food, and endure or succumb to pneumonia, hunger, dysentery. Sixteen thousand aged died in 1942; another 13,000 in 1943. The rest were scheduled to be transported to the east, but the exact nature of the east was, as elsewhere, disguised.

The ghetto had its own SS command and under its control was a Council of Elders who were to carry out its orders, including orders for deportations. Deportations started in January 1942 and continued until October 1944, but knowledge of the exact nature of Auschwitz— ''the East''—was not fathomed until April 1944, and then, only by some, when a Czech Jew, Vitezlav Lederer, escaped from Auschwitz dressed in an SS uniform, made his way back to the ghetto and tried to warn the prisoners about the gas chambers. Although deportation ''to the east'' caused panic and fright, most refused to believe him. Again, the deception of the Nazis thwarted acknowledgment of the reality. From early 1942 until October 1944, soothing postcards, written at Nazi order, were sent from a so-called family camp at Auschwitz, to reassure those still in the ghetto. Many volunteers signed up for the transports, hoping to rejoin family members who had already left.

In this gateway to death at Theresienstadt, there was a remarkable array of talent combed from the cultural richness of writers, artists, and musicians from central Europe. We have evidence of their creative work in the stark drawings of Leo Haas, Karl Fleischmann, and Bedrich Taussig (known as Fritta in the ghetto); the astonishing poetry and drawings of children; memoirs of the grim performances of Verdi's *Requiem;* and secret performances of the children's opera *Brundibar.* The pioneering Zionist youth movement called *Hechalutz* organized classes, games, and work details for Jewish youth and children, creating an orderly daily routine for them and strengthening morale under the appalling conditions in the ghetto. Often children could be seen tending the old people and sharing their own miserable rations.

In order to maintain the fiction that Theresienstadt was a model ghetto, the Nazis spent nine months stage-managing a beautification program for the Danish Red Cross, which visited the ghetto in the summer of 1944. *(See Reading No. 77.)* Tablecloths, silverware, and flowers were placed on dining tables in a specially created dining room. Waiters suddenly appeared in fresh uniforms, new barracks were built, and new clothing given to certain prisoners. A special children's pavilion was set up and stocked with toys. The head of the Jewish Council was given his own apartment and a chauffered car. All SS men were dressed in mufti. The Czech police suddenly disappeared. Only the lower floors were redecorated. The visitors could not go upstairs, and only the old inmates were to be seen to maintain the myth of Theresienstadt as a model ghetto for the aged. Some 3,000 youths were sent to Auschwitz just before the delegation arrived. For the Nazis the visit was a great success. The prisoners, however, were crushed. Rabbi Baeck, one of the inmates, said: "Perhaps they knew the real truth. But it looked as if they didn't want to know it. The effect on our morale was devastating. We felt forgotten and abandoned." After this fraud, the Nazis then made a propaganda film of Theresienstadt while SS forces stood over the camera crew. Jews were taken to SS swimming pools and to a meadow outside the ghetto where they were entertained at an open air cabaret. Shops were opened. A genuine Bechstein piano appeared, and SS guards were seen tenderly lifting up Jewish children. Worthless money was printed to show that the inmates were paid for their labor. Did the visitors really believe in this facade? Not likely. But they published a favorable report soon after their visit. After the war they admitted that they feared that adverse publicity would have endangered special package privileges for Danish Jews and would have caused brutal reprisals on others.

Toward the end of 1944, with the war clearly lost, the Germans continued their deceptions. They were so sure the prisoners did not know where they were going, that they threatened anyone who did not leave when called up. One transport of Jews was actually sent to Germany and returned to Theresienstadt so that they could report on their hard work. One of the last transports left for Auschwitz on September 28, 1944, consisting of 2,300 volunteers who thought they were going to German factories. Nine hundred were gassed immediately at Birkenau. Wives and children received postcards from some of the survivors and subsequently formed another transport. Dr. Miklos Nyiszli found the dressing-room of Crematorium no. 1 strewn with permits that had been given to this transport. Eichmann had apparently planned to gas any survivors left in the ghetto and asked his subordinate Hans Günther how much Zyklon B would be needed, but on May 11, 1945, Theresienstadt was delivered to the Russians.

Slovakia. Slovakians in the eastern part of Czechoslovakia had been frustrated in their ambitions to establish their own state. A nationalist/Catholic party was established in 1918 under the leadership of Andrej Hlinka, a Catholic priest, and agitated for independence. Their grievances fit in perfectly with Hitler's designs. Not only would he have a pro-Nazi, collaborative state, but he would have free access to roads, railways, and airfields needed for the coming invasion of Poland. The Jewish population of 90,000 in the new-state, created in March 1939, soon felt the lash of anti-Jewish legislation. Besides the social and economic persecution, Jews were accused of spreading Hungarian culture and causing the loss of some Slovakian territory (Kosice province). About 42,000 Slovakian Jews came under Hungarian rule in November 1938, most of whom were later deported to Auschwitz.

A heavy barrage of anti-Jewish propaganda ushered in the new regime of Vojtech Tuka, prime minister. A German expert was assigned to organize the Hlinka Guards on the model of the Nazi Storm Troops, and Dieter Wisliceny, Eichmann's representative from the Reich Security Main Office, arrived in Bratislava as "adviser on Jewish Affairs." A Jewish Council (*Ústredňa Židov*) was formed to organize Jewish life after the liquidation of all other Jewish agencies and carry out state orders. Emigration was, at first, encouraged and the emigration department was directed by Gisi Fleischmann, who later became the center of a daring ransom scheme, the *Europa Plan*. A severe Jewish Code was passed in September 1941, affecting 15,000 converted as well as so-called full Jews. Jews were required to wear the yellow badge and serve in forced labor camps within Slovakia. Ten thousand Jews were evicted from Bratislava, a deliberate preparation for the herding of Jews at assembly points. Slovakian officials eagerly began to negotiate with the Germans for the complete removal of Jews from Slovakia. Early in 1942, 20,000 Jews from 16 to 35 were sent to Germany; in March, the government paid Germany 500 Reichsmarks for every additional Slovakian Jew deported. Concentration points were set up and by the end of May, 40,000 Slovakian Jews were deported to Auschwitz or Lublin. By the end of June, the figure reached 52,000.

The Vatican was particularly embarrassed by these actions because Slovakia was a Catholic state, ruled by Catholic priests. Through its papal nuncio in Bratislava and certain local clergy, the Vatican learned that Jews were going "to the east" and sent no fewer than six notes protesting the deportations, the first dated March 14, 1942. In them, the Vatican openly declared that Jews were not being sent to the east for labor, but to "certain death." Reports of the gassings also began to spread as a result of some escapes from Auschwitz, but the deportations continued until the summer. In desperation, as many as 7,000 Slovakian Jews fled to Hungary to seek refuge. Pressures from the Vatican and a few Slovakian bishops to inspect the "camps" in Poland were put off and then rebuffed by Eichmann. The uneasiness surrounding the deportations was countered by propaganda which the Germans had prepared. Articles were planted in newspapers presenting in great detail the pleasant life of Slovakian Jews in exile. They were said to have everything they needed: work, sufficient food and shelter, rabbis, doctors, self-government, and other attractive services. The postcard ruse was also used to calm anxieties and refute reports and rumors, but transports continued through the fall of 1942. About 25,000 remained, temporarily safe from deportation while Gisi Fleischmann and Wisliceny negotiated over a possible ransom scheme (*See Reading No. 78.*) which later developed into the so-called Europa Plan.

During the summer of 1944, as the Red Army advanced closer to Slovakia, a left-wing revolt erupted. The Germans then invaded the country, dooming most of the remaining Jews. After the revolt was put down, Slovak Fascist leaders exaggerated the involvement of Jews in the resistance. Germans renewed the deportations, and from October 1944 to March 1945, 13,500 Jews were deported to Auschwitz, Ravensbrück, Bergen-Belsen, and Theresienstadt, many of whom perished. About 5,000 Jews lived clandestinely with false papers or in hiding. Thus, the chapter of Slovakian Jewry in Holocaust history caused one of the most shattering destructions in Europe.

Italy. Reference has already been made to the benign, humane attitude of Italians toward Jews in southern France. This attitude also prevailed in every other area occupied by the Italians and, to a large extent, within Italy itself. In 1938, there were about 47,000 Italian Jews and 10,000 or so refugees from Germany and Austria. From the time of the abolition of the papal ghetto in Rome in 1870, Jews had been rapidly absorbed into the cultural and economic life of the country. Jews lived comfortably with their Christian neighbors and there was little anti-Semitism. Frequently between 1922, when Mussolini came to power, and 1936, he and other Fascist leaders repeated the same phrase: "The Jewish problem does not exist in Italy." Privately, however, Mussolini's attitude was more ambivalent and changeable. He believed that "international Jewry" was hostile to his Ethiopian campaign and, when he sought a rapprochement with the Vatican, which was opposed to Zionism, he opposed any expression of Jewish "separatism." Yet, he could also speak fulsomely about Jews and often expressed distaste for Nazi anti-Jewish racist ideas and excesses. His anti-Jewish measures, when they were introduced, were largely inspired by political expediency, (*See Reading No. 79.*) mainly to achieve foreign policy objectives.

Possible advantages in such a policy were evident in Hitler's triumphs. Beginning in 1936, with Italian-German collaboration in Spain, an anti-Semitic campaign was launched in the press, and anti-Jewish legislation was passed in November 1938. Jews were expressly defined and excluded from the armed services, civil service, and from large businesses. Their property holdings were limited. However, they could still work. There were no ghettos or large-scale deportations. The anti-Jewish code was not mild, but was much more moderate than measures elsewhere. Besides, it was often circumvented or loosely enforced. There are countless stories of Italian kindness and compassion. Even so, about 7,000 Italian and foreign-born Jews had to leave the country. For his part, Hitler considered Mussolini the senior Fascist and overestimated Italian power. German officials were not permitted to interfere in Italian matters, including the Jewish question, as long as Mussolini remained in power. When he was overthrown in July 1943, however, the Germans acted swiftly, overruning most of the country and ordering deportations to begin in Rome.

There were about 8,000 Jews in the capital, but most were sheltered in convents, monasteries, private homes, and in the Vatican itself. The rector of the German church in Rome, believing that Pope Pius XII would make an open stand against the deportations, urged German officials to stop the arrests (*See Reading No. 80*), but the Pope was silent, and the deportation on October 15–16, 1943, trapped 1,000 Jews, who were sent to Auschwitz. From October until June 4, 1944, when the Allies entered Rome, the Jews there led hunted lives. The chief German target, however, was northern Italy, where 35,000 Jews were concentrated. Mussolini had been set up by the Germans in Verona and was now the prisoner of their policies. An *Einsatzgruppe* commander and Theodore Dannecker, fresh from France, were sent to Verona to organize a systematic deportation. Empty prisoner-of-war camps were found for Jews, Yugoslavian partisans and opponents of the new "Fascist republic." A new law on December 1 branded Jews as "enemy foreigners" and ordered them transferred to the camps. In March 1944, the main camp at Fossoli, near Modena, was turned over to the Germans and deportations to Auschwitz began. Transports also left from a camp at Gries, near Bolzano, and La Risiera di San Sabba, near Trieste. Roundups of Jews in Genoa, Florence, and Bologna pushed the total deported from northern Italy to over 10,000 during the 20 months of the "fascist republic", most of whom perished in Auschwitz and Mauthausen.

Yugoslavia. Italy and Germany were also involved in southeastern Europe very early in the war, specifically in Yugoslavia and Greece. Mussolini, chafing under Hitler's impressive, unshared victories, tried a solo venture in Greece in October 1940, but failed dismally. The Italian defeat threatened Germany's plans in the Balkans and strengthened Britain's strategic position in the Mediterranean. Germany moved troops into Greece and crushed Greek resistance in February-March 1941. The Yugoslavians, especially the Serbs, were unwilling to submit to German pressure and overthrew the government of Prince Paul that was ready to capitulate. They gallantly resisted the German invasion, but all resistance was smashed in a few days in April 1941. Hitler's victory, however, as was later realized, was won at a very great price. The German actions in Greece and Yugoslavia delayed the invasion of Russia by five crucial weeks and caused the German army to be immobilized there by deep snow and sub-zero temperatures.

After the German conquest, Yugoslavia ceased to exist as a nation and its Jewish population of 75,000 was redistributed. Macedonia was given to Bulgaria. Another slice in the north, Bačka, was annexed by Hungary. A new puppet state, Croatia, was created in the northwest, and to the south, Old Serbia, with Belgrade as its capital, came under German military rule. It was the Serbian Jews who were the first in southeastern Europe to suffer the Nazi onslaught and mass murder.

On May 31, 1941 in Serbia, the military administration issued a definition of Jews, removed them from public life and the professions, registered their property, and introduced compulsory labor and the wearing of the Jewish star. Serbia was densely occupied by German troops who carried out murderous reprisals against Jews and Serbs as a way of dealing with a powerful partisan movement. For every dead German soldier or civilian, a hundred Jews and/or Serbs were killed. (*See Reading No. 81.*) In the fall and winter of 1941, Serbian Jews were herded into camps and the Belgrade Ghetto. About 6,000 men were killed in mass shootings by army troops, and the women and children in the ghetto, swollen by Jews from the Hungarian Bačka, were destined for "resettlement" in the east. However, outside of Yugoslavia, the ruthless shooting of hostages was causing disquiet and protests. The German Foreign Office was being deluged with complaints, but they were cleverly fobbed off. The removal of 7,500 women, children, and old persons was finally resolved: they were "resettled" at a camp in Semlin under Croatian jurisdiction. The Foreign Office urged the deportation of these Jews to Romania. Instead, because the death camps were not yet ready, gas vans, using gas exhaust instead of bottled carbon monoxide (as in the euthanasia program), were used, beginning in March 1942. Each van was loaded with women and children while a second vehicle, an open truck, picked up baggage. Children were given candy and a Jewish doctor or nurse was selected to accompany each transport. The deception was complete. The sealed vans crossed the Sava River bridge and drove through the center of Belgrade to a shooting range a few miles outside of the city where the corpses were unloaded.

The puppet state of Croatia contained about 30,000 Jews, of whom 5,000 lived in the Italian-occupied zone. The rest of Croatia was occupied by German troops and ruled by Ante Pavelic, the founder of the killer-terrorist group called Ustashi. The Jews under Pavelic were quickly subject to anti-Jewish laws, forced labor, and deportations, beginning in August 1942. In the Italian zone, the Germans tried to goad the Italians to cooperate, but the Italian commanding general Mario Roatta rejected any anti-Jewish measures, saying "they were incompatible with the honor of the Italian army." (*See Reading No. 82*) After the Italian surrender to the Allies in September 1943, the Italian zone disappeared. Some Jews went into hiding; others joined Tito's partisans. (*See Reading No. 83*) Most were sent to the labor camps: Loborgrad, Jasenovac, and Djakovo, or to the salt mines at Karlovac and Yudovo, where they were tortured, starved, and shot. About 2,000 were deported to Auschwitz by way of Austria. In April 1944, the German Foreign Minister in Croatia, Siegfried Kasche, declared in his final report to Berlin that the "Jewish question" in Croatia had been solved except for three categories: "Honorary Aryans," Jews in mixed marriages, and *Mischlinge*. Fewer than 2,000 survived.

Greece. In Greece, too, the destruction was almost total. The German military Organization *Südost* controlled part of Greece as well as Serbia after the Germans over-powered the stiff Greek resistance and swept into full control of the Balkans in April 1941. In Greece, as in Croatia, control was divided between Germany and Italy. The Germans occupied eastern Thrace, Salonika, and the island of Crete. The Italians, until September 1943, occupied "old" Greece, including the capital Athens. The Ionian islands, western Thrace and Macedonia were annexed by Bulgaria.

Of the 70,000 Jews in prewar Greece, more than 50,000 lived in Salonica, the great historic center of Sephardic Jewry. About 13,000 were under Italian jurisdiction, and 6,000 fell under Bulgarian control. In the Nazi-occupied area, Jewish homes and community property were confiscated and the Chief Rabbi, Dr. Zevi Koretz, was arrested. Jews had to give up their radios and were forbidden to enter cafes, but for over a year there were no other specific anti-Jewish measures. Jews shared the suffering of all Greeks, including widespread hunger and an outbreak of spotted typhus. The beginning of the massive persecution started in the summer of 1942, in a disguised form. Orders were issued for all adult male Jews between 18 and 45 to register for forced labor, but only a few thousand were considered fit enough for railway construction required by the military command. Many of these perished in malarial swamps. For a time, the German army agreed to exempt Jews from forced labor for a ransom, which was paid, giving rise to a false sense of security. The Prime Minister of Greece, General Tsolacoglou, also made reassuring statements. Further seizures of Jewish property and synagogues soon followed, and in February, 1943, Eichmann's agents arrived in Salonica to implement the deportations. (*See Reading No. 84.*)

All Jews five years and older had to wear a Jewish star and all Jews were ghettoized in an area called the Baron de Hirsch quarter, near the railway station in Salonika. This ghetto was to be the funnel to Auschwitz, 1,000 miles away. Outside the ghetto, behind a high fence were 300 empty railway cars lined up along railway sidings. The Nazis used their customary deceptions: they brought in documents of grants of land in the Ukraine and picture postcards of a fictitious place called Waldsee, where Jews had been sent. This ploy further lulled Jews as to Nazi intentions. Meanwhile, Rabbi Koretz, who had been released, was appointed president of the Jewish community. Together with six other Jews, he was now responsible to the German authorities. By the end of February, German orders were issued in the form of commands to Rabbi Koretz. The soothing deceptions, the impoverishment of most Jews, making escape or hiding impossible, the occasional concessions which Koretz gained, and the ignorance of Nazi intentions created a "wait and see" attitude on the part of Koretz and his associates. They believed that by persuasion and negotiation, they could gain time and thus save Jews. One important element in their unawareness lay in the fact that when 5,000 Greek Jews living in Paris were captured and sent to Drancy November 8–9, 1942, for transport to Auschwitz, not a word of this capture reached the Jews of Greece, although this occurred four months before the deportations from Salonica started.

Dr. Max Merten, German adviser to the military, who negotiated some of the concessions with Koretz, played on this unawareness. He said that the de Hirsch quarter would have to be emptied because Communists were threatening the security of the occupation army. Jews would not be harmed, he said, but would be sent to Crakow, Poland, where they could take up a new life. To complete the deception, Polish paper money was distributed. No one in Salonica seems to have suspected what deportations meant—even as late as March 1945, after

Greece was liberated, knowledge of the death camps was virtually unknown. When a survivor of Auschwitz returned to Salonica and told the handful of Jews remaining these facts, he was thought to be insane.

At first Rabbi Koretz urged Jews to make the best of things in preparing to go to Poland. "There is no way out," he said. We know he also tried all sorts of schemes to keep Jews inside Greece, believing that forced labor in Greece was preferable to deportation to Poland. He sought to have Jews sent to the Greek islands. But nothing availed and he, himself, was arrested on April 10, confined to the ghetto and then sent to Bergen-Belsen, where he died of typhus. Meanwhile, the first transport of 2,800 Jews had left on March 15, 1943; others continued until August, by which time almost 46,000 Jews had been deported. Virtually all perished. Hoess later told Wisliceny that the Salonika Jews were "all of such poor quality" that they had to be exterminated quickly.

Until September 1943, the Italians in their zone of Greece adroitly sidestepped Nazi pressure. They refused to persecute or deport Jews in their area. In Salonica, they handed out Italian naturalization papers to 500 Jews and sent others off in their own military convoys, but after September 1943, all Greek Jews were trapped, even those on the islands of Corfu, Crete, and Rhodes, almost 2,000 miles from Auschwitz. At a time when the Germans were abandoning great quantities of supplies to Greek partisans and cluttering up evacuation routes with transports of Jews, violating every military consideration, the cars rolled blindly on. Almost all of Greek Jewry perished; a scant 1,500 survived the deportations.

In Athens, on September 21, 1943, Rabbi Eliyahu Barzilai was summoned to appear before Wisliceny and was commanded to compile a list of all Jews in the city. Barzilai already knew what had happened to Salonika Jews and tried to obtain permission from Metropolitan Damaskinos to hide Jews in the churches. The Prime Minister assured him that the Jews of Athens would not be harmed. Nevertheless, Barzilai told Wisliceny that the archives had been destroyed, making it impossible for him to provide the lists demanded. By the end of September, however, all of Greece came under German control and the destroyer of the Warsaw ghetto, Jürgen Stroop, took over the SS command in Athens, where there were about 3,500 Jews. All Jews were ordered to register, but only 1,200 reported. Resistance groups tried to organize an evacuation, but only a few hundred were removed to remote villages. About 900 Jews attending services in synagogues were seized; another 500 were dragged from hiding places. In March 1944, over 5,000 were deported after round-ups of all Jews on the mainland outside of Athens, and another 5,000 were deported from the islands.

Several hundred Jews survived in partisan groups, either in Greek units or in all-Jewish groups. Those of Spanish descent were also saved by Spanish intervention after much haggling between the Germans and Franco. They were sent to Bergen-Belsen. Some Jews were able to flee to Turkey and some of the Jewish youths who escaped this way enrolled in the Palestine Jewish Brigade and Free Hellenic Forces. The crowning act of Greek-Jewish resistance was the blowing up of two crematoria in Auschwitz. Led by Jose Levy and Maurice Aron, they managed to collect stores of dynamite and weapons from German warehouses. On September 6, 1944, with the help of French and Hungarian Jews, they blew up the crematoria and killed several German officers and soldiers, but they, too, were killed. The question: why did the Allies not bomb the whole death-complex at Auschwitz will be discussed in the last chapter. The total death count in all of Greece was over 60,000 Jews, almost total annihilation.

CHAPTER NINE

DEPORTATIONS FROM SOUTHEASTERN EUROPE

Bulgaria. Bulgaria, like Hungary and Romania, joined the Nazi camp mainly to gain and regain territory, but unlike Slovakia and Croatia, Bulgaria did not owe her existence to Hitler. She remained an independent, sovereign state. By history and cultural inclination, she felt much closer to Russia than to Germany, and hoped for a western alliance, but the Munich Pact seriously undermined Bulgaria's confidence in the western democracies, and the Nazi-Soviet Pact left her no room for exploring political choices. These developments combined with the desire to regain territory lost in the Second Balkan War and World War I led her to join the Axis in March 1941. It was in the same month that Hitler needed passage through Bulgaria on his way to Greece to rescue Mussolini, and the same month in which Bulgaria acquired Macedonia from Yugoslavia and Thrace from Greece. It was in these latter territories that about 14,000 Jews perished.

There were approximately 50,000 Jews in Old Bulgaria, over half of whom lived in the capital Sophia. They enjoyed complete civic and political equality and Jewish communal and religious life were respected. Jews were also well integrated economically and there was little anti-Semitism until the 1930s when Bulgarian students returned from German universities and joined a movement corresponding to the Nazis. However, there was little popular ideological support for National Socialism. The government, nevertheless, in its growing movement toward Germany, passed several anti-Jewish measures that affected the Jews in Old Bulgaria. In 1939, several thousand foreign Jews were expelled and in January 1941, severe restrictions were imposed: Jews had to register; they were excluded from certain types of employment and cultural activity, could not intermarry, suffered expropriations, and were restricted as to movement. Anti-Jewish propaganda intensified and after March 1941, over 10,000 Jewish men were conscripted for work in labor squads. In August, they were forced to wear a Jewish star, but not enough were made and many Jews refused to wear them.

The Germans, however, becoming impatient, stepped up their pressure. In the summer of 1942, a Commissariat for Jewish Affairs under

Alexander Belev was created to collaborate with the Germans in carrying out deportations. The first transports of 20,000 Jews were scheduled to leave in March 1943, but unexpected problems developed.

In September 1942, the Bulgarian government mildly reproached Germany about the harsh treatment of Bulgarian Jews in France. It was claimed that Jewish labor was needed to build roadways and railroad beds in Bulgaria. Members of the court of King Boris, the king himself, the cabinet, and other officials had intervened in behalf of individual Jews. Theodor Dannecker, the deportation specialist in France, was sent to Sophia and worked with Belev to plan for the deportations. They completed their work in February 1943. The whole operation was to be carried out in secret; Jews were to be told that they were being relocated to another part of Bulgaria.

Belev had made elaborate precautions to conceal the deportations, but some Jews and Bulgarians learned of the plans and began to protest. Bishop Kiril, who later became the patriarch of Bulgaria, sent a telegram to the king threatening civil disobedience. Noted writers and prominent citizens also saw the king and prime minister on behalf of the Jews. The most effective protests came from the Jews themselves. Several eminent Jews in Sophia learned of the proposed deportations through Belev's secretary who had close ties with a number of Jews in the capital. It became known that the Bulgarian cabinet authorized only the deportation of Jews from the annexed territories, but Belev and Dannecker fully intended to pull all Bulgarian Jews into their net. Altogether, the total number to be deported was 20,000. Belev's first list of Jews from the pre-1941 boundaries came to almost 2,500 more than his proposed 6,000. However, because of gathering resistance, he and Dannecker made their first assault against the over 4,000 Jews in Thrace.

These were Greek Jews now under Bulgarian control. Police blockaded the cities and towns at midnight March 4, 1943, and received lists of families to be assembled. Jews were abruptly awakened early in the morning and told that the government was sending them into the interior of Bulgaria for a short time. They were then marched through the main streets and assembled at tobacco warehouses. A few were able to escape to areas controlled by the Italians; some were granted Italian citizenship; some fled to Greece. Foreign Jews were rounded up and then later released. There were numerous reports of individual kindnesses, protests, and interventions, but the bulk of Thracian Jews experienced appalling conditions on the six-day journey to Treblinka:

absence of toilet facilities; women in childbirth without care; dysentery; death from hunger and exposure, and harsh treatment by guards. After many stops at camp sites, the deportees were taken to the port of Lom, and from there by barge to Vienna and then Treblinka. Over 4,000 of them perished.

In Macedonia, which Bulgaria had acquired from Yugoslavia, the morning of March 11, 1943, were the last hours for Jews. (*See Reading No. 85.*) At 2 A.M., several hundred men in various cities were mobilized as police and were instructed to collect Jews from their houses according to lists prepared in advance. They were told to try to convince the Jews that they were being temporarily moved to other parts of Bulgaria and that they would return to their homes as soon as the war was over. They were also told to take along all their cash and jewelry. Outside the police buildings, several hundred carts waited to transport sick Jews and their luggage. Along the streets were armed soldiers preventing escape. A survivor has described the scene: ''We were shivering, partly with cold, partly with terror. Everyone kept looking at his mother, sister, or brother as if he would not see them again. In the courtyard, a few tables were arranged, flanked by policemen and detectives. On the tables were spread out jewelry, gold articles and watches, and the pockets of the detectives were bulging. 'Take out all your money,' an agent kept shouting, 'for if I search you and find anything on you, I will shoot you like dogs.' '' As in Thrace, there were reports of humane individuals who tried to alleviate the suffering, of those who stood on railway wagons and threw bread over a wall into the temporary camps. These were momentary gestures. The three March transports that left for Poland carried 7,132 Jews to Treblinka, crossing Italian, Albanian, Serbian, Croatian, Hungarian, and German territory on the way.

In Old Bulgaria, meanwhile, the obstruction of the deportations reached a decisive stage. Early in March, the provincial governor of Kiustendil told a Jewish pharmacist, Samuel Baruh, about the deportation plans. Baruh sent word to his brother in Sophia, who then contacted the vice-president of the Bulgarian Parliament, Dimitri Peshev, who vigorously opposed the plans. Peshev then pressed the Minister of the Interior, Peter Gabrovski, to stop the action and threatened a public scandal. The plans were, at first, only postponed, for Peshev was not sustained in Parliament and was removed. However, by spring 1943, Bulgarian Jews became the subject of discussion abroad and the time, a time of crisis for Bulgaria as well as for Germany.

The Soviet victory at Stalingrad and the Allied threat against the Balkans, including Bulgaria, created great tension in the country. There were also numerous political assassinations and a great deal of partisan activity, including that of the police chief and a notorious German agent. The Bulgarian Orthodox Church under its head, Metropolitan Stephan, intensified its protests against anti-Jewish policies. Pro-Allied sympathy among Bulgarians began to surface. The Jews of Sophia were resettled in provincial towns, but they were not deported. The King met von Ribbentrop in Berlin in April and told him that he would deport only ''Communist elements'' among the Jews in prewar Bulgaria. Public and private protests intensified, including public demonstrations and further protests by the Bulgarian Orthodox Church. Russian victories and Soviet demands on Bulgaria as well as threatened Allied air attacks turned Bulgarian foreign policy around. By January 1944, there was some bombing. Deportation plans were shelved and some Jews were allowed to go to Palestine. Later in the year, a new government declared war on Germany. The Jews of Old Bulgaria survived.

Romania. In the interwar period, Romania had gained territory at the Paris Peace Conference in 1919, chiefly at the expense of Hungary, but suffered massive territorial losses in 1940 to Hungary, Russia, and Bulgaria. The fall of Poland and France led Romania to cut her pro-western ties and become Germany's ally. German troops were massed inside the country and Romania helped Germany in the invasion of Russia in June 1941. As a reward, Romania recovered Bessarabia and Bukovina which Russia had taken earlier. Romania was part of the Axis until the tide of war changed, when these territories were again lost. Romania then declared war on the Germans and recovered Transylvania. The opportunism of this switch and the vehemence of Romanian actions, first against the Russians, then against the Germans, were also evident in Romania's handling of the ''Jewish problem.'' The fate of Romania's Jews oscillated between Romanian opportunism and destructiveness. Each political change and each territorial loss or gain was a pretext for massacres of Jews.

Romania was considered one of the most virulently anti-Semitic countries in Europe, consistently denying its Jews minority rights that had been guaranteed at the Peace Conference and subjecting them to economic, political, and religious persecution. Most were denied or stripped of their citizenship; every political party had an anti-Jewish plank of one intensity or another. The pre-war Jewish population was approximately 800,000: 350,000 in Old Romania (Wallachia and Moldavia), 300,000 in Bukovina and Bessarabia, and 150,000 in Transylvania. Economically, because of the underdeveloped economy, corruption, and political instability, Jews were conspicuous in trade and commerce, constituting virtually the whole of middle-class activity, and arousing the envy of peasants and gentry.

King Carol was forced to abdicate in 1940 after the heavy territorial losses and a new government was formed in September. This was a military dictatorship under General Ion Antonescu, and immediately under him, Horia Sima, leader of the Fascist, vehemently anti-Semitic Iron Guard. Throughout the winter of 1940–41, the outrages and massacres of Jews continued, reaching a climax in January, with a butchery of Jews in Bucharest. The Guardists also struck against the Antonescu government, but their coup was crushed. Antonescu held power for the next four years, as long as the Romanian-German alliance lasted. The fate of the Jews hung partly on the state of this alliance, partly on the changing tide of war, and partly on the susceptibility of Romanians to bribes. The Jews in Old Romania, for the most part, survived; those in Bessarabia and Bukovina bore the brunt of Romanian killing frenzy and the *Einsatzgruppen;* in Transylvania, they were engulfed in the Hungarian deportations.

From the first contacts with Jewish leaders in September 1940, Antonescu showed a hypocritical courtesy that masked his own anti-Semitism and opportunism. He assured the most influential Jewish leader, Dr. Wilhelm Filderman, that no harm would come to the Jews as long as they did not boycott his government or damage Romanian trade and industry, in which Jews played a crucial role. Yet, these proved to be empty promises. On October 5, 1940, the state expropriated land owned by Jews, and in the following month, Jews began to be dismissed from jobs in commerce and industry and were liable to work in forced labor projects. Radios were surrendered. A General Commissar for the Jewish Question, Radu Lecca, was appointed to organize and then speed up ghettoization and deportation.

The anti-Jewish policies of Old Romania were outlined in a manual called *Richtlinien für die Behandlung der Judenfrage* (Instructions for the Treatment of the Jewish Question), personally handed to Antonescu by Hitler before the German invasion of the Soviet Union. Moreover, Gustav Richter was sent to Bucharest in April, 1941, to bring Romanian anti-Jewish legislation to the German level and to remain in

Romania until the ''Final Solution'' had been achieved. In the 89 anti-Jewish laws and decrees passed by the Romanian government between 1938 and May 1, 1942, the Romanians sometimes outdid their German model, but the effect of these measures was not uniform, mainly because of the Romanian propensity for bribery. At times, it was more profitable to extract money from live Jews, so long as they could keep paying, than to kill them.

Filderman learned of the ghettoization threat and in April 1941, sent a memorandum to the government exposing the potential economic harm it would cause the country. He also negotiated to free $100,000 that had been frozen in the United States, an agreement that was to be followed by a population exchange, enabling Romanian Jews to leave and Romanians in the United States to return to Romania. However, the German invasion of June 22 stopped the negotiations. Ghettoization was suspended, too, but a reign of terror descended upon Jews, now identified as ''suspicious persons,'' saboteurs, and spies. A massacre of Jews took place in Jassy on June 29 (*See Reading No. 86*), and the next day, 4,000 or more were packed in sealed railway cars, one destined for Poduloea, the other, for Calarasi. After several days, according to Romanian police reports, 2,530 had died of suffocation and thirst. In the weeks that followed, random shootings, beatings, thirst, and starvation claimed several thousand more. Romanian officials began to put the yellow badge decree into effect, but Filderman tirelessly argued against it, again warning of dire economic consequences if it were implemented. There were other pressures and Antonescu cancelled the order. Romanian destructive frenzy now fell upon the Jews of Bessarabia and Bukovina.

These ''lost'' provinces were recaptured from Russia by Romania and became not only a massive killing ground but a field of struggle between German and Romanian forces over the pace and methods of killing. In August 1941, the Romanians, on their own, drove 15,000 Bessarabian Jews across the Dniester River into a German military area in order to utilize the killing services of *Einsatzgruppe D*. But the German killers objected to the Romanian ''lack of discipline.'' They were ''disorderly'' in not burying the corpses. Elsewhere in Bessarabia, Germans also complained of excessive Romanian zeal which prevented systematic killing. In Odessa alone, the Romanians slaughtered 60,000 Jews, while locally instigated massacres claimed thousands more. Thousands more had to be disposed of. The so-called Tighina Agreement of August 30, 1941, was finally worked out between the German and Romanian military staffs, creating a huge dumping ground for Jews called Transnistria, between the Bug and Dniester rivers.

Transnistria was a vast penal colony in a barren stretch of the Ukraine laid waste by the retreating Russians. It was administered by Romanian Army officers who looted, murdered, tortured, took bribes, and then killed. In one of the camps called Bogdanovka, bread was sold for five gold rubles. When the gold gave out, the camp commander ordered mass shootings. In December, Jews were driven into stables and shot, and when the stables were filled with corpses, they were destroyed by fire. Those who could not be squeezed into stables were marched to a precipice above the Bug River. They were stripped, gold teeth were forcibly extracted, and if rings could not be removed easily, fingers were chopped off. Forced to stand naked in temperatures 40 degrees below zero, they were shot and the corpses dropped into the river. Within a week, 48,000 Jews were massacred in the camp. Further shootings in two other camps brought the total to 70,000. By May 1942, over 100,000 Jews from Bessarabia and Bukovina had been killed or died in Transnistria, two-thirds of those who had been deported. Filderman's petitions to stop these atrocities were unavailing. Antonescu was waging a war against Russia to avenge a national humiliation and Jews in Transnistria were considered "accomplices of Stalin."

By the summer of 1942, Eichmann had every reason to feel confident of Antonescu's cooperation in the planned deportations from Old Romania. The transports were scheduled to leave on September 10 for Lublin. But Antonescu was playing a double game. He gave his consent to the deportations but was actually turning away from them. By the fall, Germany's demand for more Romanian military aid met growing opposition; the tide of war was moving against Germany and the war effort was proving too costly and too bloody. Moreover, Romania's Commissar for Jewish Affairs was snubbed in Berlin. Certain Romanian religious and political leaders began to urge negotiations with the West, especially after the German defeat at Stalingrad, which caused staggering Romanian losses. Romanian political leaders were giving audiences to the papal nuncio, Swiss and Swedish ministers, and the International Red Cross and were listening to protests regarding the continued deportations to Transnistria. There was an appeal to allow Jewish orphans to go to Palestine. Antonescu maintained a vehemently anti-Jewish position, considering Jews "enemies of the state,'' but withheld permission for the deportations. In mid-1942, he had also become interested in profiting from Jewish emigration to Palestine—freeing 70,000 Jews still in Transnistria in exchange for $1,330 per Jew. Negotiations were begun, but the British Foreign Office and American State Department dismissed the proposal. However, early in October, deportations stopped. A doctor in Bucharest recorded the moment: ''The news spread like wildfire throughout the neighborhood. A huge crowd gathered to help free the poor wretches locked up for days in the filthy buildings from where they were to leave for Transnistria. Those present . . . witnessed scenes of almost unbearable delirium.''[1]

The Jews in Old Romania were still suffering, however, from forced labor, confiscation of property, even clothing, heavy taxes, and the rationing of bread. The Romanian regime continued its persecution, but by January 1943, the Germans were ready to give up Romania as a co-partner in the Final Solution. Himmler decided that nothing more could be done, and the SS left. The papal nuncio, Andreia Cassulo, was finally allowed to visit Transnistria (*See Reading No. 87*), and despite Antonescu's virulent self-confessed anti-Semitism, he permitted widows, the aged and disabled to move southward away from the front and obtain food and clothing that had been collected by other Jews. In August, the Allies bombed the Ploesti oil fields and Bucharest and the Romanians ordered all of the Germans to leave. A few months later there were American efforts to prod Romania to get out of the war and make peace with the Allies, but the rapid advance of the Red Army foreclosed this possibility. Ira Hirschmann, a representative of the newly-formed American War Refugee Board, met with the Romanian Minister to Turkey early in 1944 and urged him to have the prisoners in Transnistria released and 5,000 Jewish children in Romania permitted to go to Palestine. Antonescu apparently was willing, but the Allies could not find a refuge and Britain refused to open up Palestine for the children. By August, the Soviet army had broken through the Romanian-German lines in Bessarabia and Moldavia, and a new government was formed. Both Antonescus were arrested, an armistice was declared, and the German army was ordered to leave. Romania then declared war on Germany and within a few weeks Soviet forces and their new Romanian allies destroyed 26 German divisions. King

[1] Emil Dorian, *The Quality of Witness: A Romanian Diary, 1937–1944.* Philadelphia, Jewish Publication Society of America, 1982, p. 235.

Michael made contact with the previously outlawed Communist Party in Romania and a new and essentially Communist government was formed. The Soviet Union regained Bessarabia and Bukovina, and a curtain of silence was lowered over Transnistria. Estimates of the number of survivors vary from 48,000 to 60,000. In 1945, the Jewish population of postwar Romania was 430,000, indicating the destruction of approximately 370,000 Jews.

Hungary. In 1944, only one country in Europe, Hungary, stood intact against the destructive process that had swept the rest of the continent. The 750,000 Jews under Hungarian control lived in an enclave of time and space, only dimly aware of what was happening elsewhere, protected by a fragile political boundary. Once that boundary disappeared and the German army crossed the frontier, disaster overtook the Jews of Hungary. In 1944, in clear sight of the whole world, at a time when the war was obviously lost for Germany, Hungarian Jews suffered the most concentrated and methodical deportation and mass destruction of any in Europe. For 46 straight days, the Nazi machine of death worked ceaselessly and annihilated over 400,000 Jews.

Like Bulgaria and Romania, Hungary had joined the Axis to gain territory. With Germany's help she regained territory lost in 1919 to Romania, Yugoslavia, and Czechoslovakia (southern Slovakia, Bačka, Carpatho-Ukraine, and northern Transylvania). There were over 300,000 Jews in these newly annexed territories and they were subject to the first persecutions and deportations. The decisive moment for Hungary was April 1941, when the Germans insisted on the passage of their troops through the country for the attack on Yugoslavia.

Hungary had neither the conviction nor the force of arms to oppose German demands, but neither did she always yield to them. From 1938 to 1944, Hungarian prime ministers ranged from men who served Germany first to those who resisted pressures and tried to pull Hungary out of the German entanglement and the quicksand of a losing war. As prime ministers changed, the fate of Hungarian Jews changed also. The moderates slowed down the destructive process; the extremists hastened it. As a consequence, Hungarian Jews experienced sharply defined cycles off hope and despair. Periods of calm alternated with outbursts of deadly persecution. Undoubtedly, these sudden changes robbed Hungarian Jews and their leaders of realistically evaluating their predicament and depleted their psychological and physical energies.

There were about a half million Jews in prewar Hungary, half of them in Budapest, and most in middle-class occupations: self-employed businessmen, professionals, and white collar workers, all of them important in Hungary's economy, which had an anti-capitalist landed aristocracy and large peasantry. There was pervasive anti-Semitism and even pogroms, especially after the loss of territories after World War I and the short-lived communist regime under Béla Kun, a Jew. A counterrevolution soon swept Kun out of power and Admiral Miklos Horthy came to power as Regent. Conditions gradually settled down but below the surface of seeming stability lay the misery of landless peasants and the dangerous irredentism of many Hungarians.

In the early 30s, there was a noticeable German infiltration into Hungary and the growth of pro-Nazi groups, strengthened by the half-million Germans already in the country. On Easter Sunday in 1933, a number of German students wearing brown shirts attended a performance of the Passion Play near Budapest and brought with them a wreath containing a huge black swastika. Nazi newspaper correspondents and Nazi racial specialists came to Hungary in large numbers and German officials began to lecture Hungary on the need to deal decisively with the Jewish Question in order to regain the lost territory. In March 1938, the German absorption of Austria brought Nazi Germany to the very doors of Hungary, and very quickly the first anti-Jewish laws were passed, restricting Jewish economic activity and defining as Jews a number who had converted.

Between 1939 and March 1941, there was a lull. A moderate prime minister, Count Paul Telecki, tried to stave off German pressures and refused to be dragged into Germany's attack on Poland. When he could no longer prevail he committed suicide. The Hungarians were then enticed into declaring war against Russia in the summer of 1941 by the promise of territory from Romania, Under the new prime minister, Laszlo Bardossy, the first mass killings of Jews also took place in Nove Sad and Kamenets-Podolsk. Moreover, 130,000 Jewish men up to the age of 60 were drafted into labor gangs and often worked under conditions as inhumane as those in German concentration camps. Hangings, shootings, beatings, death by starvation, and disease were commonplace.

In March 1942 a new prime minister was appointed, Count Nicholas

Kallay, a political moderate who disliked the Germans. He yielded to German pressures somewhat by enlarging the labor units and confiscating more Jewish wealth, but he refused to introduce the yellow badge or to deport a single Jew. Some Jews from Poland, Austria, and Slovakia even found refuge in Hungary. In early 1943, Hungary appeared in Hitler's eyes to be acting more like a neutral than a German ally. Pressures intensified, but Kallay did not yield. He was, in fact, looking for a way out of the war, and he wanted to surrender to the Allies, not to Russia, but the Western powers refused to make a separate peace. Horthy met with Hitler and von Ribbentrop in April 1943 and was told that Hungarian Jews either had to be annihilated or sent to concentration camps. In Poland, Hitler said, they were "treated like tuberculosis bacilli. . . . Nations that did not rid themselves of Jews perished." (*See Reading No. 88.*) But the Kallay government stood firm and German mistrust grew. SS agents reported that the Hungarians would not consent to the liquidation of the Jews during the war. The Kallay regime was being viewed as the great stumbling block to closer German-Hungarian collaboration.

Kallay, in the meantime, was under great pressure from Döme Sztojay, the Hungarian Minister to Germany, to dissolve the Jewish obstacle and avoid German intervention. Right-wing movements also continued their agitation. The most extreme and violent was the Arrow-Cross movement which connived with the Germans to bring down the Kallay government.

In March, 1944, the German army invaded Hungary. Horthy now had to succumb to German control and Sztójay became prime minister. Eichmann then came in with a special unit of killing specialists. (*See Reading No. 89.*) He called together leaders of Budapest Jewry who were henceforth forced to operate under the authority of the SS and the Jewish Section of the Ministry of the Interior, dominated by László Baky and László Endre, primarily responsible for the deportations and murder of Hungarian Jews. Unlike Jewish leaders elsewhere, Hungarian Jewish leaders were aware of deportations of Jews elsewhere, but did not or could not keep Hungarian Jews or political leaders informed. At the same time, they did not know that Jews were being gassed at Auschwitz; most did not even identify the word "Auschwitz." Having had no experience in political struggles for exclusively Jewish causes, and considering themselves patriotic and loyal Hungarians, they took no initiatives that such extraordinary times required and continued being decent, honorable men used to traditional legal methods. They were, therefore, quite easily deceived by the calming words of Eichmann as to German intentions and lulled other Jews into a false sense of security. In part, they also justified their reliance on law and order by the reassurance that Horthy was still Regent, that they had sympathetic contacts among political leaders and that the Red Army was advancing toward the Carpathians. The imminence of a German defeat nourished these illusions.

The Jewish star decree was introduced on March 29, 1944, followed by movement restrictions and extreme economic and social measures. In April 2,500 Jewish apartments were ordered evacuated; 8,000 Jew were arrested for moving without permission. Hungary was then divided into six zones, and deportations were to start in the annexed provinces. While the Jews from the Carpatho-Ukraine and Transylvania were being removed, Jews in Old Hungary would be told that drastic measures affected only non-Hungarian Jews.

The first transport left on April 28, made up of 1,500 Jews suitable for labor. They were taken from an internment camp at Kistarcsa and then sent to Auschwitz. There, as had happened with other victims, they were compelled to write encouraging notes to their relatives, datelined "Waldsee." Early in May, 200,000 Jews in Zone I were concentrated in ten ghettos and camps, and on May 15, the massive deportations began.

The members of the Jewish Council in Hungary could not grasp the truth that the Germans were bent on annihilation of Hungarian Jews until it was too late. The Nazi machinery of deception, ghettoization, and deportation had been perfected and was now to work with unparalleled speed, this time with the full support of German military authorities as well as Sztójay's government, and the Hungarian police. There was no escape, no effective appeal for outside help, no Allied bombing of Auschwitz. By July 7, 437,000 Hungarian Jews had been deported to Auschwitz.

Meanwhile, Horthy, long inert and half-captive, under increasing foreign pressure to stop the deportations, told Edmund Veesenmayer, the German minister to Hungary, that he was being bombarded daily with telegrams from all sides, from the Vatican, the King of Sweden, the International Red Cross, the U.S. Government. He ordered the deportations stopped, but on July 14, von Ribbentrop threatened a total military occupation of Hungary if the deportations were not resumed. The warning was not heeded. Russian troops were already pouring into nearby Galicia. In August came the Romanian armistice with the Russians. Horthy appointed a new prime minister to conclude an armistice with the Allies and the Eichmann Special Operation Unit (*Sonderein-satzkommando*) withdrew. A Hungarian armistice mission left for Moscow. The Germans, however, were far from ready to quit Hungary and began concentrating troops for a new seizure of power by the Arrow Cross leader, Ferenc Szalasy. A power struggle in Hungary seesawed until the middle of October, when a German Panzer Division entered Budapest with orders to depose Horthy and Geza Lakatos, the prime minister. On October 16, both men surrendered and were imprisoned in Germany. Szalasy and the fanatically anti-Semitic Arrow Cross now resumed the hounding and killing of Jews in Zone No. 6, Budapest. Eichmann returned to the city on October 17 to accelerate the pace of the killing and resorted to forced marches to the Austrian border because railway lines had been bombed. Thousands walked through snow, rain, and sleet, without food for seven days, sleeping in stables, pigsties, or on the open roads. Those who collapsed were shot or died from exposure.

In Budapest, there remained about 100,000 Jews who were shoved into a huge ghetto. Arrow Cross atrocities rose to new excesses. (*See Reading No. 90.*) The murder gangs roamed the streets shooting at will, dragging Jews to the Danube and drowning them. Massacres continued until February 13, 1945, when the Russians finally took the city. The savageries of the last winter of the war in Budapest, when the Germans were in retreat on all fronts, have very few moments of humane intervention. The most shining were those in which Raoul Wallenberg, a young secretary to the Swedish Legation, acted to save as many Jews as possible. His work and other rescue efforts will be noted in the next chapter.

CHAPTER TEN

RESCUE EFFORTS AND FAILURES

Despite resistance to accepting the fact that the Nazis were systematically murdering Jews and planning to eliminate them physically from Europe, incontrovertible evidence, portions of which had been streaming in throughout 1942 and earlier (See *Reading No. 91*), in the reports of the *Einsatzgruppen* massacres, forced the United States, Great Britain, and the Soviet Union to make a solemn protest on December 17, 1942, against the German government's intention to exterminate the Jewish people in Europe, ''and condemned in the strongest possible terms this bestial policy of cold-blooded extermination.'' The British House of Commons even stood in silence for two minutes after the declaration was read by Anthony Eden. This was the first public, official acknowledgment of Nazi genocidal plans by the Allies. They pledged retribution and punishment of the perpetrators, but there was no rescue effort to save those still alive.

Fundamentally, any effective strategy of rescue had to come from the Allies, singly or collectively, but they never considered the rescue of Jews to be a major or incidental wartime objective. There were, however, numerous rescue schemes, but the results were meager, or, more often, non-existent. Jews, themselves, tried to organize rescue operations throughout the Nazi period, but lacking a state, arms, and political power, they accomplished very little. Moreover, the specific character of Hitler's war against the Jews was seldom acknowledged. The Allies often concealed the Jewish tragedy within the general European tragedy. For example, in January 1942, the American Jewish Congress asked nine Allied governments in conference in London to condemn the specific German crimes against Jews. The reply was that such a ''reference might be equivalent to an implicit recognition of the racial theories that we all reject.'' The president of the conference, Wladyslaw Sikorski, President of the Polish Government-in-Exile, further said that any reference to anti-Jewish crimes was purposely omitted because Jews were considered nationals of their respective states.

Throughout the crucial years 1942–43, there was deliberate obstruction, evasion, and indifference on the part of British and American bureaucrats and policy makers. The Soviet Union was not at all concerned with specifically saving Jewish lives. The American Secretary of the Treasury Henry Morgenthau Jr. experienced at first hand the diplomatic inertia that blocked rescue. "We knew in Washington," he wrote, "from August 1942 on, that the Nazis were planning to exterminate all the Jews of Europe. Yet for nearly 18 months, the State Department did practically nothing. Officials dodged their grim responsibility, procrastinated when concrete rescue schemes were placed before them, and even suppressed information in order to prevent an outraged public opinion from forcing their hand." Negotiations with the Romanians were hesitant and unfruitful, and the State Department doomed a Swedish offer to negotiate with the Germans for the release of 20,000 Jewish children from the continent. Breckenridge Long, Assistant Secretary of State, and his associates in the European Division postponed consideration of the proposal for six months, arguing that while Jewish philanthropists were prepared to underwrite the full cost of the operation, it was wrong to limit the plan to Jewish children alone. Norwegian children were than added by December 1943, but by that time, neither the Swedes nor the Germans were interested in the scheme. Morgenthau also knew that, despite State Department objections to direct talks with the Germans, Allies exchanged civilian internees, disabled prisoners of war and merchant seamen with the Axis. Moreover, the State Department refused to challenge Britain's power over the issuance of licenses to finance relief operations. This power rested with the Ministry of Economic Warfare and was used to veto a number of rescue efforts. Typical of the British position was the statement of December 17, 1943: "The Foreign Office is concerned with the difficulty of disposing of any considerable number of Jews should they be released from enemy territory. For this reason, they are reluctant even now to approve of the preliminary financial arrangements."

Thoroughly frustrated, Morgenthau, on January 16, 1944, accompanied by Randolph Paul, General Counsel in the Treasury Department, and John Pehle, Chief of the Foreign Funds Division, went to the White House to protest the suppression of information and inaction. (*See Reading No. 92.*) Finally, in January 1944, a fully independent agency funded largely by American Jewish funds, the United States War Refugee Board, was created with the power to negotiate and spend money without being hampered by the State Department or the British Foreign Office. By then, millions of Jews had perished, and within a few months, almost two million in Auschwitz alone. (*See Reading No. 93.*)

The British had not only blocked emigration and flight to Palestine but, after 1940, classified Jews in Nazi-occupied countries as enemy aliens. If any were able to flee Europe and go to Britain, they were interned as such. Yet, this stigma was not applied to the thousands of Dutch and Belgian immigrants who planned to emigrate to England in 1940.

In May 1943, Anthony Eden, British Foreign Secretary, discussed the possible rescue of 60,000 to 70,000 Bulgarian Jews with Cordell Hull, American Secretary of State. Eden declared that "the whole problem of the Jews of Europe is very difficult and that we should move very cautiously about offering to take all Jews out of a country like Bulgaria. If we do that, then the Jews of the world will be wanting us to make similar offers in Poland and Germany." He then added that "Hitler might take us up on any such offer" and there simply were not enough ships.[1] Yet ten days after this meeting, the British announced plans to take 21,000 non-Jewish refugees to East Africa, among the 100,000 non-Jewish refugees moved to the Middle East and Africa during the war. Over a million Italian and German prisoners of war were also put on ships to the United States.

The British were also involved in the fate of Hungarian Jewry in 1944. There was a strong pro-British element in Hungarian political life and in 1943 and 1944 England was viewed as the prime partner for peace negotiations with the Allies. Moreover, the main rescue operation of the Jewish underground, the Council for Assistance and Rescue in Hungary, was torpedoed by the British. This was the so-called "Blood for Goods" deal that Eichmann proposed in the midst of the massive Hungarian deportations—a ransom scheme that would have exchanged 10,000 trucks for 100,000 Jews. (*See Reading No. 94.*) Himmler was obviously putting out a peace feeler to the West. Emanuel Brand, a Hungarian Jewish leader, was sent to Istanbul, contacted the Jewish Agency and told them of Eichmann's fantastic offer, but the Jewish Agency lacked funds and political leverage. The offer was then taken to the British, but they said, "there must be no negotiations with the enemy," that the offer was simple blackmail. The Soviet govern-

[1] David S. Wyman, *The Abandonment of the Jews: America and the Holocaust, 1941–1945*. New York, Pantheon Books, 1985, pp. 97, 98.

ment was adamantly opposed to negotiations, but the Americans wanted to keep them open in order to gain time. Ultimately, the British arrested Brand in Cairo, and when he told the resident minister, Lord Moyne, that a million Jews were involved, Moyne protested: "What shall I do with these million Jews? Where shall I put them?"

The British refused to probe any variation of the ransom deal and exposed it as blackmail on July 20, 1944, in the British press. The British Foreign Office also bungled intelligence about the planned deportation of Hungarian Jews. Reports were often deficient and subject to poor evaluation; news would also arrive long after certain events had happened. For example, on May 19, 1944, when the Hungarian minister in Bern alerted the British of the planned deportations and suggested that the BBC warn the Hungarians not to assist the Germans, his cable lay unanswered at the Foreign office for many weeks. Even by the autumn of 1944, when many sources confirmed the murder of over 400,000 Jews, the British expressed doubts and reservations. They even accepted the Nazi fiction that Jews were being deported to the imaginary Waldsee. Much vital information was supplied by the Jewish Agency and the World Jewish Congress but was discounted or looked upon suspiciously because of anti-Jewish and anti-Zionist attitudes among many British officials.

The American government likewise had no intention of rescuing large numbers of Jews. Resistance against admitting refugees, even *within* quota limitations, has already been noted. The many resettlement schemes projected had only intellectual significance. The fear, shared by the British, was that Germany would unload masses of refugees upon a society with strong anti-Semitic and anti-immigration attitudes. The depression of the middle thirties and American involvement in the war after December 7, 1941, were additional elements in, as well as reasons for, the policy. Congress supported and helped shape this policy. Moreover, the mass media failed to publicize information about the planned killing of Jews, which was readily available.

The refusal of the Allies to bomb Auschwitz, the worst killing center, stands as one of the more serious indictments of their passivity and indifference. Pleas to bomb Auschwitz began to be numerous in the spring and summer of 1944. Two young Jews, Rudolf Vrba and Alfred Wetzler, managed to escape from Auschwitz on April 10, 1944, reached the underground in Slovakia, and dictated a 30-page report, containing details of the camp. This information was sent through many channels to Allied centers and insistent appeals to act urgently came from many quarters. By June, the Swiss, British, and American press carried reports of the purpose, location and layout of Auschwitz. Even earlier, from April 1944 on, there were aerial photographs of Auschwitz taken by American and British reconnaissance planes. (*See Reading No. 95.*)

On June 24, 1944, requests to bomb were received by the Operations Division of the War Department, but two days later the proposal was ruled "impracticable" because "it could be executed only by diversion of considerable air support essential to the success of our forces now engaged in decisive operations." Yet, by May 1944, the U.S. Fifteenth Air Force (which had not been consulted) clearly had the capacity to strike Auschwitz. The I. G. Farben plant producing synthetic fuels less than five miles from the gas chambers was repeatedly bombed in the last year of the war. On August 20, 127 flying fortresses dropped over a thousand 500-pound high explosive bombs on the factory areas of Auschwitz, and all groups reported success in striking the target area. The excuse of "diversion" was thus based not on any serious analysis of operational capacity, but on policy.

The British, too, rejected appeals. On July 7, after a meeting with the Jewish leader Chaim Weizmann, Eden wrote to the British Air Minister, asking for his opinion regarding the bombing. A month later the British Air Command wrote that it did not possess accurate information on the location of the camp and that the operation would require reconnaissance flights that would result in casualties. No, said the British, there were "technical difficulties". They would not bomb the camp or the railway lines leading to it, but perhaps the Americans could be persuaded.

For the Germans, gassing was a very efficient means of killing Jews. Two thousand could be killed in less than a half hour, requiring only a few SS men. If these killing installations had been destroyed at this late stage in the war, in 1944, it would have been virtually impossible for the Germans to rebuild them. Those who could have been saved included: 437,000 Hungarian Jews murdered up to July 8, 1944, and another 100,000 gassed up to November when Himmler ordered the crematoria to be dismantled. Two were dismantled and the buildings blown up. But Auschwitz still existed with its 64,000 imnates, 6,000 of whom were too ill to move; the other 58,000, starving and emaciated, were sent in freezing weather on their death march. Some of these prisoners also could have been rescued had the camp or railway lines been bombed.

Jews in the ghettos and camps clung to the hope for salvation from the Allies. There is ample testimony of these hopes. Jews also hoped for and expected help from institutions of moral stature and humanity such as the Vatican and International Red Cross, but those hopes, too, were bitterly thwarted.

Nearly 80 percent of German-invaded Europe owed religious allegiance to the Vatican, but this great institution remained silent through the Holocaust. Except in the case of Slovakia, which we have mentioned earlier, the Vatican did not condemn the mass murder of Jews nor the murderers. Not even the chief architects of mass murder: Hitler, Himmler, and Heydrich—all Catholics—were excommunicated, nor were they threatened with excommunication. Nor was the myth of resettlement ever publicly exposed, although the Vatican knew what deportation meant.

The question of Vatican silence is still being argued. Defenders of Pope Pius XII claim that protests would have made the situation facing the Jews worse than it already was, that practical aid could be rendered quietly where it was needed, as in the case of hiding the Jews of Rome. They also argue that as spiritual ruler of all Christendom, the Pope could not specify atrocities, but had to condemn broadly all acts of inhumanity committed on both sides. Pius XII undoubtedly suffered much personal anguish in having taken the path of caution and reserve, but very few gained strength or comfort from his generalities condemning *all* inhumane actions. The Poles, indeed, were the first to protest his cautious Christmas message of 1942, by which time Nazi savagery against them was intense. But he withheld identification of the persecutor.

Politically and ideologically, Vatican policy regarding the Jews of Europe resulted from centuries of Christian religious anti-Semitism, from the Pope's abhorrence of bolshevism, his own deep love for Germany and German culture, and his preference for a German as against a Soviet victory. The Vatican also split hairs in trying to distinguish between religious anti-Semitism, which was, after all, religiously permissible, and racial anti-Semitism, which was not. It is also clear that Vatican relations with German Catholics in Germany were critical. German churchmen as a whole were sympathetic to the Nazi regime.

A forceful stand aginst Nazi persecution of Jews might well have led to wide-scale desertions of Germans from the Church. Moreover, the spiritual, economic, and political power of the Vatican was declining, and Pius XII was unwilling to lose even more ground by possible desertions. Local conditions were significant. We should recall the indifference of the Slovakian officials, who were Catholic priests, when the Vatican tried to stop deportations. Elsewhere, the influence of the Vatican was less important than the vigor or lack of it of the local clergy, and many Catholic priests and nuns struggled heroically to save Jews.

In sharp contrast to the Pope, the Orthodox Patriarch of Constantinople wrote all of his bishops in the Balkans and in central Europe urging them to help Jews and to announce in their churches that concealing Jews was a sacred duty. This explains the strange fact that in Slovakia, more Jews temporarily escaped deportation by being converted to the Orthodox Church than to Roman Catholicism.

Another great institution from which Jews hoped for aid also failed them. This was the International Committee of the Red Cross, which was the prisoner of old international conventions when these were meaningless and destructive. Its function has been to preserve some elements of civilized conduct in wartime and to relieve the suffering of prisoners and other victims of war. When the victims were Jews, the Red Cross was shackled or shackled itself with outmoded terms. It admitted that Nazism had condemned Jews to persecution and systematic extermination, but being neither prisoners of war nor civilian internees, they formed a separate category, without the benefit of any convention. They were classed as detainees, which gave them a penal status. Yet, they were not considered prisoners-of-war. Thus, the Red Cross did not figure out how to provide services for such a category, or change their rules until October 1944, and until that time they could not or would not intervene. (*See Reading No. 96.*) The argument was a familiar one: unwillingness to make a special case of the Jews. One of their reports after the war reads: ''Perhaps we should have resorted to pounding tables and making a scandal. Maybe so? But if assistance to the Jews would have been our only task, one could possibly have envisaged such an attitude. But this was not our only mission. To make a rumpus on account of the Jewish question would have meant to put in jeopardy everything without saving a single Jew.''

There were, however, some non-Jews who protested the persecution, even risking or sacrificing their lives, "to make a rumpus," to save Jews. They have been identified by Yad Vashem[2] as the "Righteous Among the Nations," and about 3,000 men and women from all of the countries of Nazi-occupied countries have been so honored, but there are undoubtedly more who remain obscure or are too modest to reveal themselves. These were individuals, not governments, and occasionally groups or agencies who hid Jews, took their children to convents or adopted them, provided false papers, supplied food for Jews in attics or bunkers, and helped smuggle Jews over borders. Many were simple folk who felt the pull of conscience, Christian charity, or basic humanity. In France, farmers and teachers were conspicuous. The whole village of Le Chambon devoted itself to saving Jews. In Poland, a group called Żegota, which spanned all class lines, formed solely to save Jews. (*See Reading No. 97.*) In Hungary, in the summer of 1944, Raoul Wallenberg printed thousands of certificates of Swedish protection and brought protective houses for Jews in Budapest, saving them from deportation. (*See Reading No. 98.*) A German businessman, Oscar Schindler, operated an armaments factory in the Sudetanland, where he employed a thousand Jews and saved them, providing them with food, medicine, and clothing and outwitting Nazi police. He forwarded letters to Poland where Jewish children were hidden and was even able to extricate 300 women from Auschwitz, the wives, mothers, and daughters of the men in his factory. The great, compassionate Monsignor Angelo Roncalli, who later became Pope John XXIII, served as apostolic delegate to Turkey and distributed many baptismal certificates to Jews in the Balkans. Many of the people of Denmark, Italy, Belgium, Bulgaria, and Holland showed the world that human goodness had not vanished during an inhumane time.

In the United States, Jewish organizations worked to inform political leaders of the urgent need to acknowledge the unique Nazi victimization and annihilation of Jews and to act to save those still alive. The World Jewish Congress and Zionist organizations also gathered intelligence and shared it and tried to energize governments to act. There was, as yet, no Jewish state to serve as political and military arm of the Jews of Europe, to act for them as other national states had been doing.

In the last months of the war, Nazis still in power were pulling in opposite directions, some fully aware that Germany had lost the war, like Wisliceny, Walter Schellenberg, and Kurt Becher; others, like

[2] The Holocaust documentation center in Jerusalem, Israel.

Eichmann, an unwilling agent in the Brand talks, were hounding and killing Jews to the very end. Himmler, the mastermind, ordered the gassings to stop in November 1944 and, aiming to disrupt the unity of the Allies and create alibis for the murderous criminals, initiated contacts with the Western Allies. (*See Reading No. 99.*) These had only very limited results. Some of the most ghastly experiences of the victims were the death marches from Hungary to Germany, planned by Eichmann in the last weeks of the war. (*See Reading No. 100.*)

After the death camps and concentration camps were liberated, some survivors were guided to Italian ports and found boats bound for Palestine; many others died as they were being liberated; most were taken or themselves stumbled into Displaced Persons camps or hospitals, waiting to gain enough strength to start the long search for lost families. Two-thirds of Europe's Jews had perished (*See Reading No. 101.*), and with them, centuries old cultures which can never be recovered. Survivors have, in general, made remarkable adjustments to life and have taken their place in many communities. They will bear emotional and often physical scars forever. Their children suffer as well from dilemmas and guilt in trying to assimilate the experiences of their parents and the human void left by the loss of their past, the destruction of relatives, photos, letters and other memorabilia that connect generations. There is great disappointment and bafflement over the deliberate delays and sabotage of American prosecution of Nazi war criminals and the protection and prosperity many of the murderers enjoy in the West. Perhaps most painful for the survivors to endure is the rise of a revisionist movement that claims that the Holocaust never happened, that it is a Jewish hoax. There has also been an ominous rise in anti-Semitism throughout the world and repetitions of the old lies and libels about Jews which the Nazis spread. In Germany itself, myths and legends idealizing Hitler and Nazism abound. One hopes and trusts that a sober and thoughtful consideration of the readings that follow will reveal sufficient facts to refute the revisionists and offer glimmers of humanity found even in this dark history, expressions of human compassion and solidarity that help sustain civilization.

PART 2

READINGS

READING NO. 1

THE PROTOCOLS OF THE ELDERS OF ZION[1]

The Protocols *were based on a satire on the ambitions of Napoleon III,* Dialogue aux Enfers entre Montesquieu et Machiavel, *written by a French radical lawyer Maurice Joly. The authors of the* Protocols *substituted "Elders of Zion" for Napoleon and remade some of the material. Many passages were changed, but almost half were taken literally. The book as a whole was exposed as a forgery in 1921. The idea of "Elders of Zion" meeting secretly came from a German novelist, Herman Goedsche, who wrote in the 1860s under the pseudonym of Sir John Retcliffe. The Russian version of the* Protocols *was extensively spread throughout Europe by White armies after the Bolshevik Revolution. The German translation was published in 1919.*

γ   γ   γ

Protocol No. 3 In order to incite seekers after power to a misuse of power we have set all forces in opposition one to another, breaking up their liberal tendencies towards independence. To this end we have stirred up every form of enterprise, we have armed all parties, we have set up authority as a target for every ambition. Of States we have made gladiatorial arenas where a host of confused issues contended. . . . A little more, and disorders and bankruptcy will be universal. . . . Abuses of power will put the final touch in preparing all institutions for their overthrow and everything will fly skyward under the blows of the maddened mob.

Protocol No. 5 The second secret requisite for the success of our government is comprised in the following: To multiply to such an extent national failings, habits, passions, conditions of civil life, that it will be impossible for anyone to know where he is in the resulting chaos, so that the people in consequence will fail to understand one another. This measure will also serve us in another way, namely, to sow discord in all parties, to dislocate all collective forces which are still unwilling to submit to us, and to discourage any kind of personal initiative which

[1] Herman Bernstein, *The Truth About the "Protocols of Zion."* New York, 1935, pp. 303, 311–12.

might in any degree hinder our affair. . . . From this collision arise grave moral shocks, disenchantments, failures. *By all these means we shall so wear down the goyim that they will be compelled to offer us international power of a nature that by its position will enable us without any violence gradually to absorb all the State forces of the world and to form a Super-Government.* In place of the rulers of to-day we shall set up a bogey which will be called the Super-Government Administration. Its hands will reach out in all directions like nippers and its organisation will be of such colossal dimensions that it cannot fail to subdue all the nations of the world.

Protocol No. 6 We shall soon begin to establish huge monopolies, reservoirs of colossal riches, upon which even large fortunes of the *goyim* will depend to such an extent that they will go to the bottom together with the credit of the States on the day after the political smash.

READING NO. 2

ARYAN RACE-SOUL[2]

Chamberlain was an Englishman, drawn to German philosophy and militarism, who settled in Bayreuth and married Richard Wagner's daughter. He became a German citizen while still a young man and became the prophet of the Nazi Party because of his glorification of the German people who, he believed, were the master race of the world. The Jews, by contrast, were a "negative" race, a "bastardy," fully justifying the Aryan rejection of them:

γ   γ   γ

For Chamberlain the Germans were held together by their shared blood, but he also believed in a Germanic Christianity quite similar to that of Wagner. To begin with, Chamberlain founded his theory on Kant, who, according to his interpretation, postulated an essence of things beyond reason and pragmatism. This essence was the "German religion," which bestowed infinite vistas upon the soul and served to keep science within narrowly defined bounds. And for Chamberlain, this religion was a monopoly of the Aryan "race-soul." Such a soul made Germans honest, loyal, and industrious; thus middle-class morality became once more a quality of the German race. Moreover, Chamberlain believed in the Aryan stereotype, and here he accepted anthropological and cranial measurements. But as not all Germans possessed the outward appearance proper to Aryans, it seemed best to retreat to the race-soul which they did share.

In the light of the Aryan ideal-type and its racial soul, Chamberlain transformed Christ into an Aryan prophet. Christ's disposition revealed an Aryan soul, for he exemplified love, compassion, and honor, and his soul was devoid of all materialism. . . . A supposedly factual argument was also adduced, namely, that the Jews had never settled in Galilee and that actually an Aryan people lived in the place where Christ was born. This was however of secondary importance compared with Christ's "Aryan race-soul."

According to Chamberlain, the Germanic race entered history as the

[2] George L. Mosse, *Toward the Final Solution: A History of European Racism.* New York, 1978, pp. 105, 106–107.

saviours of mankind and as the heirs of the Greeks and Romans. German Aryans had to wage a bitter struggle against their enemies in order to fulfill their civilizing mission; for Chamberlain, Catholic Christianity was one such enemy, which sought to enslave the race-soul under foreign laws first invented by St. Paul, the Jew. The Protestant Reformation put an end to that and liberated the racial soul. German racism was always to think of Luther as the great liberator from foreign oppression. The real enemy of the Aryan, however, was the Jew. Chamberlain saw in the Jews an Asian people who had entered European history at the same time as the Germans, and like the Germans had managed to preserve their racial purity. He held that the Jewish soul was materialistic, legalistic, and devoid of tolerance and morality, drawing upon the Old Testament for his proof.

In Chamberlain's view, the Jews were the devil and the Germans the chosen people; between them existed a chaotic mixture of peoples—passive spectators at the crucial battle of history. The outcome of the battle between Aryans and Jews would decide whether the base Jewish spirit would triumph over the Aryan soul and drag the world down with it. Chamberlain wrote that the Germans had never strayed far from their original stock, while the Jews, though they had kept themselves apart from Gentiles for centuries originally, were a mixture of the most diverse peoples imaginable (Syrians, Amorites, Hittites) and therefore a bastard people. The Aryans must struggle against this bastard race, which was the very epitome of all evil.

The defeat of the Jews would lead not to social or economic change, but to a spiritual revolution, as a result of which the Aryan race-soul would dominate the world. . . .

READING NO. 3

RACIST ANTI-SEMITISM[3]

Under traditional Christian views of Jews, it was possible for them to achieve salvation by converting to Christianity. The Enlightenment further held that any individual, including Jews, could rise to a higher cultural level through general good-will and education. Racial anti-Semitism, however, eliminated this possibility:

γ　　　　　　γ　　　　　　γ

By ascribing the character of man to his hereditary qualities and by accepting the neo-Darwinist view that acquired characteristics cannot be inherited, this theory ruled out any prospect of improvement by God or man. If everything stems from nature, there is no room for the optimistic belief that man can change his character at will. Race is an eternal law. This theory, under the mantle of which pseudo-scientific principles were generalized and deified, left no room for man's ability to change his nature; neither did it leave room for divine grace: good and evil are ingrained in the blood—from the dawn of creation until the end of all time.

As to the Jewish question, the conclusion to be drawn from this approach was obvious. The curse which, according to popular belief, was brought upon the Jewish people with the victory of Christianity, was now thought to be manifested in the Jews' evil racial characteristics. The "Judaeus perversus" of earlier Christian doctrine now became that perverse racial type of Jew who formed the subject of modern caricatures. The Jew ceased to be a mere dogmatic concept and a synonym for all that is bad and contemptible in the world: he became a physical entity, a definite human type whose characteristics could be defined and even measured. His characteristic appearance, his build, features, crooked nose and gestures could be visually described and pictured in a general manner easily recognized by all. The Jewish stereotype, created in the course of many generations as a result of the interaction of dogma and reality, was proved with a scientific basis by racial anti-Semitism. . . . This development also removed the basic

[3] A. Bein, "Modern Anti-Semitism and its Effect on the Jewish Question," *Yad Vashem Studies*, III, 1959, pp. 13–14.

principle from the Christian theory about the Jews. From now on, the Jew was considered accursed from the dawn of the ages until the end of the world. No amount of education could overcome the eternal barrier of race. Assimilation would only poison the healthy body of the nations by the penetration of parasitic elements. The obvious conclusion, drawn without shame or inhibitions from these pseudo-scientific premises, was that there really was no longer any room for the Jews within the nations. The only solution was the removal of the Jews by concentrating them in their own country or, even better and more logically, by annihilating them.

These alternative possibilities are suggested more or less explicity by most anti-Semitic theorists of the day. Repeatedly the Jews are compared with germs and bacilli which, according to Paul de Lagarde "one does not educate—one destroys them as thoroughly and speedily as possible." I should like to draw attention to the semantics of the Jewish question which have not yet been adequately investigated. For many years Jews were called such names as "germs," "parasites" or "vermin" which must be exterminated, just as they had earlier been called the children of Satan who must be fought.

READING NO. 4

HITLER IN VIENNA[4]

Besides consuming the abundant anti-Semitic literature in Vienna, Hitler saw Eastern European Jews for the first time, and was filled with hatred and disgust:

γ   γ   γ

While walking through the Inner City of Vienna [he wrote], I suddenly encountered an apparition in a black caftan and black sidelocks. Is this a Jew? was my first thought. For, to be sure, they had not looked like that in Linz. I observed the man furtively and cautiously, but the longer I stared at this foreign face, scrutinizing feature for feature, the more my first question assumed a new form: Is this a German? . . . Wherever I went, I began to see Jews and the more I saw, the more sharply they became distinguished in my eyes from the rest of humanity. . . . Was there any form of filth or profligacy, particularly in cultural life, without at least one Jew involved in it? If you cut even cautiously into such an abscess, you found, like a maggot in a rotting body, often dazzled by the sudden light—a kike! [There follow lurid allusions to uncouth Jews seducing innocent Christian girls and adulterating their blood, a theme frequently found in later Nazi literature.] Gradually [he continues], I began to hate them. . . . For me, this was the time of the greatest spiritual upheaval I have ever had to go through. I had ceased to be a weak-kneed cosmopolitan and became an anti-semite.

The cosmopolitan atmosphere of Vienna, which once captivated so many, also sickened him.

My inner revulsion toward the Hapsburg State steadily grew. . . . I was repelled by the conglomeration of races which the capital showed me, repelled by this whole mixture of Czechs, Poles, Hungarians, Ruthenians, Serbs and Croats, and everywhere the eternal mushroom of humanity—Jews and more Jews. To me, the giant city seemed the embodiment of racial desecration.

---

[4] Adolf Hitler, *Mein Kampf.* Tr. by Ralph Manheim. Boston, 1943, pp. 56–59, 123–124.

READING NO. 5

THE DESTRUCTION OF DEMOCRACY IN PRUSSIA[5]

Prussia, the dominant state in Germany and the last bastion of republican democracy, blocked von Papen's plan to transform the country into an authoritarian state. To achieve this, he had to dissolve Prussia as a political entity and incorporate it into the Reich, a process which anticipated Hitler's own policy of coordination (Gleichshaltung.) This action was unconstitutional and might possibly have been challenged by the Reichsbanner, *the armed units of the Social Democratic Party, but the party leaders wanted to avoid civil war at all costs, appealing instead to a court. The court declared the action unconstitutional but would not rescind Article 48, which had been invoked:*

γ   γ   γ

On 19 May 1932 the Braun–Severing minority coalition of Socialists and Centrists in Prussia resigned, finally worn down by the continuous harassment of their opponents, the Nazis and Communists. As the two extremist parties were clearly unable to provide an alternative coalition, Braun and Severing agreed to continue as a caretaker government, placing themselves in an even more vulnerable position. Papen prepared for his attack on Prussia: he obtained Hindenburg's signature to an emergency decree under the powers granted by article 48 of the Constitution, which would replace the Prussian parliament by a Reich Commissioner in order to 'defend Prussia against the threat of a Communist takeover which the Land government ignored'. There was, of course, no real threat nor any danger that, as Papen hinted, the Socialists would form a coalition with the KPD, and the application of article 48 was therefore illegal.

A suitable pretext for the *coup d'état* presented itself on 17 July. As part of their rabble-rousing election campaign, the Nazis organized a deliberately provocative street demonstration in Altona, a Prussian town contiguous with Hamburg, whose population was almost exclu-

---

[5] John R. P. McKenzie, *Weimar Germany, 1918–1933*. Totowa, N.J., 1971, p. 232.

sively working-class. Communist snipers fired on the Nazis, killing fifteen of the demonstrators. On 20 July Severing and Braun were informed in the Reich Chancellery that, as their government was clearly no longer maintaining law and order within Prussia, a state of emergency had been declared; they were to be removed form office and replaced by Papen as Reich Commissioner.

READING NO. 6
AN ELECTORAL SET-BACK FOR THE NAZIS, NOVEMBER 1932[6]

Election Results of July 31 and November 6, 1932

		Votes cast (to nearest thousand)		Number of seats		Percentage of total vote	
		July	Nov.	July	Nov.	July	Nov.
KPD	Communist	5,370,000	5,980,000	89	100	14·3	16·9
SPD	Social Democratic	7,960,000	7,251,000	133	121	21·6	20·4
DDP (DStP State)	Democratic	373,000	339,000	4	2	1·0	1·0
Z	Centre	4,589,000	4,230,000	75	70	12·4	11·9
BVP	Bavarian People's	1,203,000	1,097,000	22	20	3·2	3·1
DVP	People's	436,000	661,000	7	11	1·2	1·9
DNVP	Nationalist	2,187,000	3,131,000	40	51	5·9	8·8
NSDAP	National Socialist	13,779,000	11,737,000	230	196	37·3	33·1
Others		985,000	1,003,000	11	12	2·6	2·9
Total (to nearest hundred thousand)		37,200,000	35,700,000	608	584		

80·6 per cent of the electorate voted compared with 84·0 per cent in July 1932

[6] McKenzie, *op. cit.*, p. 239

138

READING NO. 7

DACHAU, THE FIRST
CONCENTRATION CAMP[7]

On March 20, 1933, just eleven days after becoming chief of police in Munich, Himmler announced the establishment of Dachau concentration camp at a press conference:

γ   γ   γ

The first group of Dachau prisoners taken into "protective custody" were originally guarded by the Bavarian police. None of them could have conceived that this place, an abandoned First World War munitions factory, would one day become a powerful reservoir of slave labourers comprised of prisoners from all over Europe, that it would be, for the SS, the ideal training ground for murder.

When the SS took control of the camp on April 11, 1933, the prisoners lost the last traces of their civil rights and were left defenseless to the despotism of their guards.

On becoming commmander of the Dachau camp in June 1933, Theodor Eicke set up a scheme of organization with detailed regulations for camp life. This came to be used, with local variations, for all concentration camps. Even the basic lay-out of the concentration camps came from Eicke. Each camp had its prisoners' quarter surrounded by a high tension fence and guard towers and, separate from these, a command area with administrative buildings and barracks.

In 1934 Eicke was appointed Inspector General for all concentration camps. With Daachau as his model, he developed an institution which was intended, by its very existence, to spread fear among the populace, an effective tool to silence every opponent of the regime. Dachau became, in effect, a training ground for the SS. Here its members first learned to see those with different convictions as inferior and to deal with them accordingly, not hesitating to murder when the occasion arose. In later years the SS was able, without a thought, to annihilate millions of innocent people in the gas chambers. The transformation

---

[7] Barbara Distel, *Dachau Concentration Camp*. Brussells, Comité International de Dachau, 1972, pp. 1, 2, 3.

of the theories of National-Socialism into a bloody reality began in the concentration camp at Dachau.

The Prisoners of the Dachau Concentration Camp

When the camp opened, only known political opponents of the National-Socialists were interned. Social Democrats, Communists, and Monarchists who had passionately opposed each other before 1933 found themselves together behind barbed wire. Having prohibited political organizations, parties, and trade unions, the Nazis extended this ban later in 1933 to include membership in the Jehovah's Witnesses. The latter were subjected to the ugliest forms of derision and maltreatment in the camp.

By the beginning of the war in 1939, the concentration camps, a continually expanding network, were gradually being filled. The inmates included political opponents of all shades, Jews, and gypsies, who were classified as racially inferior, clergyman who resisted the political coercion of the churches, and many who had been denounced for making critical remarks of various kinds.

Dachau's first Jewish inmates had been arrested because of their political opposition to National-Socialism. Not until the sytematization of the persecution of the Jews did their numbers increase. After the "Crystal Night" of November 1938 over 10,000 Jews from all over Bavaria were brought to Dachau. Many of them were later released, and whoever could, left Germany.

At Dachau, as elsewhere, Jewish prisoners received even worse treatment than other prisoners. During the war, when the systematic extermination of the Jews began, they were dispatched from the concentration camps in Germany to their death in the extermination camps which the Germans had built in the occupied areas in the East. . . . . When the camp was liberated, prisoners from over thirty countries were found there, the German prisoners forming only a small minority.

READING NO. 8

STREICHER AND THE
APRIL 1, 1933 BOYCOTT[8]

The first official act of the Nazi government directed against Jews was the boycott of Jewish shops and offices on April 1, 1933. Julius Striecher, editor of Der Stürmer, *organizer of the action, called on the German people to "strike the world enemy":*

γ γ γ

The same Jew who plunged the German people into the blood-letting of the World War, and who committed on it the crime of the November Revolution [Weimar] is now engaged in stabbing Germany, recovering from its shame and misery, in the back . . . The Jew is again engaged in poisoning public opinion. World Jewry is engaged again in slandering the German people. . . . Millions of Germans longed to see the day on which the German people would be shaken up in its entirety to recognize at last the world enemy in the Jew. . . . At 10 A.M. Sat., 1 April, the defensive action of the German people against the Jewish world criminal will begin. A defensive fight begins, such as never has been dared before throughout the centuries. . . . National Socialists! Strike the world enemy!

---

[8] *Völkischer Beobachter,* March 31, 1933, PS 2410.

READING NO. 9

GERMAN ANTI-NAZI RESISTANCE IN THE 1930s [9,10]

Because of the imprisonment, flight, or murder of most anti-Nazi forces in Germany, any expression of resistance to Nazism was not only rare and life-threatening, but had to be expressed in subtly coded forms. German children in anti-Nazi families were particularly vulnerable:

γ   γ   γ

My dad was a civil servant in municipal administration. He also belonged to the Socialist Party, the SPD in Germany, and he lost his position in 1933.

I had one younger brother and we sustained ourselves throughout these years because we had a big garden and a very good family and everybody chipped in. That's how we survived until my dad retrained himself and worked in the economy. He became an accountant. You were taught from early on in Germany that the way to greet people was to use the ''Heil Hitler'' salute and if you refused to do that as an adult, you could occasionally run a risk of being turned in. My father told us not to use that. We could use it in school—that was beyond his control—but, privately, when we went for walks and met people we would always say, ''Gutentag'' and never ''Heil Hitler.'' As the Nazi time progressed and we entered the war, that became actually an act of opposition and it was quite risky. My father listened, even before the war, to the BBC in the middle of the night. That was a dangerous thing because if they ever caught you or anybody denounced you, you would end up in the penitentiary or in a concentration camp. Since the papers were censored very heavily and subject to Nazi propaganda, this was really his only source of genuine information. I remember that we had an elderly couple next door, in that same house, and they were Jehovah's Witnesses and the husband was taken and he did not survive. They made him abjure in prison. If he promised to sign that he would

[9] Testimony of Anne Dore Weidemann-Russell, April 17, 1984. Gratz College Holocaust Archive.

[10] Testimony of Herta Besse, October 12, 1983. Gratz College Holocaust Archive.

never follow his faith, they said they would let him go, and he didn't, and I think he was beaten to death. I remember that.[9]

* * * *

Then I myself was drawn into the resistance work through a Jewish family and also the "Red Help." I always took my children along in a baby carriage—though they were actually too old for that—and we met in garden plots of friends. I had a friend who is today 96 years old, Gustav Betlow. He came always with a butterfly net pretending to look for butterflies. This is how we were able to hold out. But the owners of the garden plots who had harbored us—most of them were arrested and perished. One woman returned after more than ten years after she had been arrested in 1934. After 1933 all our friends worked together in order to build up some form of resistance. Some foolish errors were made by some friends. For example, some honest people kept a list of their donations with all full names and how much they had given. It was not much because we all did not have much to give. Some of these lists fell into the hands of the Gestapo who found cause for another search of our homes. When they asked me what I had to do with these lists I answered, "Sorry, I did not even know what the money was collected for. I was sure it was for one of *your* organizations." So we could not do this any more. From then on we worked only on a "friendship" basis.

As an example, we would tell one friend that he has to renovate his kitchen now. So four of us went to paint his kitchen. Another one "needed" his garden worked over, so four or five went there to work. Then we went to the Jewish neighborhood or what was left of it—Alexander Platz—and bought old bicycles. Then we met on bikes, first four, then six and eight or more. We had discovered an island in the middle of a lake that belonged to a farmer. It could be reached only by boat and the boat was always on the island when we were there. The farmer built huts out of straw for us and we could sleep in them, on the floor. We met there on weekends and we were safe. At night we crossed the lake with the boat and went home on our bikes. So we always looked for and found means of evasion. In the Nazi years 1933–1945 I did not experience a single betrayal.

Even as a little girl I was exposed to the political activities of my parents and experienced everything with them. I must have been ready to absorb all this. All visitors who came to our house were functionaries of the SPD like August Bebel, Marie Juchacz, Louise Schroeder (who after 1945 became Mayor of Berlin). I admired all of them.

Then we had an apartment on the ground floor that belonged to a Jewish family. They had to give up their apartment. The woman who was Jewish had married an Italian who was also Jewish. The Nazis found out and started to harass them. They left Berlin and left us their apartment as still *their* residence. We used it as a "hotel," as a hide-out. We closed the shutters permanently and we put up once a couple, once a single, once several people at the time.[10]

READING (CHART) NO. 10

ABSORPTION OF STATE POLICE AND SECURITY FUNCTIONS BY RSHA[11]

The engulfment of the state by the SS advanced rapidly after Himmler became Reichsführer SS in 1937. By 1938, all members of the Gestapo *and Criminal Police* Kriminalpolizei, *or (*Kripo*) were required to join the SS, and in 1939, the* Gestapo *and* Kripo *were joined to form the Main Office Security Police, technically an agency of the state. Parallel with this structure was the Nazi Party Security Service, the SD. In September 1939, after the war started, state and party systems were merged into the massive* Reichssicherheitshauptamt—*RSHA. Section IV B 4, headed by Eichmann, in the years 1941–44, was to become the center of the Nazi machinery of deportation and death for the Jews of Europe:*

γ   γ   γ

[11] Nora Levin, *The Holocaust: The Destruction of European Jewry, 1933–45*. New York, 1973 p. 57.

Absorption of State Police by RSHA

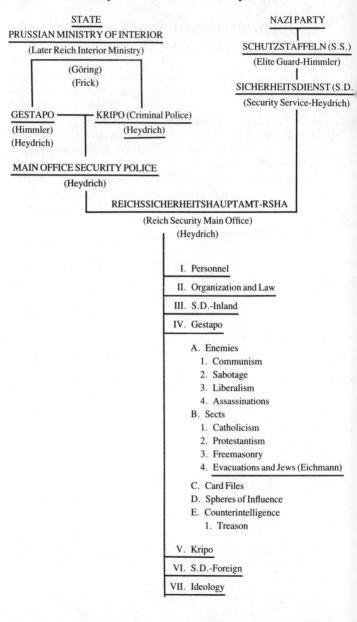

STATE
PRUSSIAN MINISTRY OF INTERIOR
(Later Reich Interior Ministry)
(Göring)
(Frick)

NAZI PARTY
SCHUTZSTAFFELN (S.S.)
(Elite Guard-Himmler)
SICHERHEITSDIENST (S.D.)
(Security Service-Heydrich)

GESTAPO — KRIPO (Criminal Police)
(Himmler)   (Heydrich)
(Heydrich)

MAIN OFFICE SECURITY POLICE
(Heydrich)

REICHSSICHERHEITSHAUPTAMT-RSHA
(Reich Security Main Office)
(Heydrich)

I. Personnel

II. Organization and Law

III. S.D.-Inland

IV. Gestapo

   A. Enemies
     1. Communism
     2. Sabotage
     3. Liberalism
     4. Assassinations
   B. Sects
     1. Catholicism
     2. Protestantism
     3. Freemasonry
     4. Evacuations and Jews (Eichmann)
   C. Card Files
   D. Spheres of Influence
   E. Counterintelligence
     1. Treason

V. Kripo

VI. S.D.-Foreign

VII. Ideology

READING NO. 11

PROFOUND DILEMMAS FOR
GERMAN JEWRY[12, 13]

Nourished on the liberal values of the Enlightenment and the first among all European Jews to experience Emancipation, German Jews had enthusiastically pursued acculturation and assimilation into secular German culture and society. Thus, when the Nazi storm broke, they were much less prepared for the tasks of survival than were the Jews of Eastern Europe. The shock, bewilderment, and complete disorientation caused some to commit suicide; others clung to their loyalty and attachment to the "other Germany" and their faith in the traditional appeal to law and to a state based on law:

γ   γ   γ

New distress has overtaken us. Jewish people are torn away from their work; the sense and basis of their lives has been destroyed . . .

We are faced with new tasks of unknown magnitude. It is not enough to give bread to those who do not know how they are to survive the next few days. Of course it is our first task to make sure that none of our people goes hungry or lacks a roof over his head. Of course we must make sure that the institutions remain that we have built for our children, for our old and our sick. . . . German Jews, show that you are able to rise to the magnitude of your task! Do not imagine that the problems of German Jewry can be solved without the greatest of sacrifices, by means of undirected emigration. There is no honor in leaving Germany in order to live untroubled on your income abroad, free of the fate of your brothers in Germany. It will not help anybody to go abroad aimlessly, with no prospect of making a living, but only increase the numbers there who are without work and means. Every prospect will be examined, every possibility exploited to help those who no longer have a prospect of earning a living in their German Fatherland to find some means of settling abroad! But don't leave Germany senselessly! Do your duty *here!* Don't push people off blindly to an uncertain fate.[12]

[12] *C. V. Zeitung,* April 27, 1933, quoted in Yehuda Bauer, *A History of the Holocaust.* New York, 1982, pp. 115–116.

* * * *

. . . the great majority of German Jews remains firmly rooted in the soil of its German homeland, despite everything. There may be some who have been shaken in their feeling for the German Fatherland by the weight of recent events. They will overcome the shock, and if they do not overcome it then the roots which bound them to the German mother earth were never sufficiently strong. But according to the ruling of the laws and regulations directed against us only the ''Aryans'' now belong to the German people. What are we, then? Before the Law we are non-Germans without equal rights; to ourselves we are Germans with full rights. We reject it, to be a folk or national minority, perhaps like the Germans in Poland or the Poles in Germany, because we cannot deceive our own innermost (feelings). We wish to be subject as Germans with equal rights to the new Government and not to some other creation, whether it is called League of Nations or anything else . . .

Thus we are suspended between heaven and earth. We will have to fight with courage and strength in order to get back to earth, in the eyes of State and Law too . . . [13]

[13] *C. V. Zeitung*, June 1, 1933, quoted in Bauer, *ibid.*, pp. 116–117.

READING NO. 12

EMIGRATION HELP FROM GERMAN OFFICIALS BEFORE 1939[14]

Until January 1939, when the Gestapo *took control of Jewish emigration (i.e., expulsion), certain officials in the* Reichswanderungs-samt *(Reich Office of Emigration) in the Reich Ministry of the Interior handled Jewish emigration. Many had been members of the Center Party or other non-Socialist parties and had served in the ministry for a long time. They worked conscientiously to plan an orderly emigration until they found themselves quite helpless toward the end of 1938. They were firmly convinced that:*

γ   γ   γ

Jewish emigration had to take place only after the most careful preparation for which an adequate period of time had to be allowed. Sufficient preparation of emigrants concerned one of the points in which we were most interested: vocational preparation, i.e. mainly vocational re-training by means of courses and institutions established by the *Reichsvertretung der Juden in Deutschland* (National Representation of the Jews in Germany). Another aspect of emigrants' preparation was teaching them foreign languages. For this purpose the *Hilfsverein* had set up entire institutes and organised courses of study, accompanied by widespread publicity. Last but not least, there was preparation by the dissemination of factual information on the conditions for emigration into the various countries and individual channelling of emigrants according to their personal abilities. For the promotion of this individual channelling, the *Hilfsverein* used to publish copious material of which the periodical *"Jüdische Auswanderung"* (Jewish Emigration) in particular used to be sold in tens of thousands of copies. In addition, the *Hilfsverein* maintained a network of numerous advisory offices throughout the Reich which were continually kept informed by circulars of every change in immigration conditions. All this was done in the closest coordination with the Reich Office of Migration. After the first issue of our periodical had appeared, the officials of that office

---

[14] Arthur Prinz, ''The Role of the Gestapo in Obstructing and Promoting Jewish Emigration,'' *Yad Vashem Studies*, II, Jerusalem, 1958, pp. 206, 207–208.

even told us that such a publication should actually have been issued by them but that they had never found the time for it. . . .

Apart from the need for the individual channelling of emigrants, the *Reichswanderungsamt* and its branch offices showed, above all, full understanding for the fact that Jewish emigration must take place *on a strictly legal basis*, i.e. that all the documents of the emigrant had to be in order and to conform to the legal requirements of his country of destination. This led, among other things, to the realization that there were also people who were unfit for emigration. These included not only persons whose age, physical ailments, etc. made them undesirable immigrants to any country, but also, in particular, the so-called antisocial elements. When we negotiated with the Reich Office of Migration we were dealing with *experts* who fully appreciated this attitude and were well aware of the fact that the emigration of ten unsuitable persons might eventually wreck the emigration prospects of a hundred suitable people. The *Reichswanderungsamt* had thought this problem through to its logical end and had drawn the necessary conclusions as far as it was in its power.

In 1936 and 1937 the officials of the *Reichswanderungsamt* still felt themselves safe, within their own sphere of activity. They fearlessly declared that, in their view, if emigration had to be forced on the Jews at all, it should be carried out ''in a manner befitting a civilized nation''. This produced an extremely benevolent attitude in all questions of transfer of Jewish property. The *Reichswanderungsamt* by no means wanted to chase the Jews penniless across the frontier.

These circumstances made it possible to pursue a productive and efficient directed Jewish emigration policy in the period between the adoption of the Nuremberg Laws in 1935, and the so-called ''Juniaktion'' (June Operation) of June 1938. It is mainly due to this policy that a great part of the Jewish emigrants reached countries in which they were able to take root, build a new life and often find a new homeland.

But even in this period a constant shift of the political centre of gravity in Germany was noticeable, a shift which also affected Jewish efforts at emigration in an ever-increasing degree. It has been stated above that in 1936–1937 the officials of the *Reichswanderungsamt* as well as a large part of the older officials of other ministries still considered themselves masters in their own homes who dared to take decisions. But this situation radically changed in the course of 1938. When in December 1938 officers of the *Hilfsverein* and of the *Reichsvertretung* called at the *Reichswanderungsamt* in order to secure alleviation of the terms for the release of 30,000 Jews who had been detained in concentration camps—namely emigration within a few weeks—the situation was as follows: the entire pogrom and the mass arrest of nearly 30,000 Jews had been staged absolutely without the knowledge of the *Reichswanderungsamt* whose officials openly showed their consternation at the news we reported.

READING NO. 13

UNIFICATION OF GERMAN JEWRY IN 1933[15]

Under the Nazi assaults, the 525,000 Jews of Germany needed a central voice to speak on their behalf and to try to negotiate with government and party officials. A normally long process of coordination had to be telescoped into several months because of the sudden crisis facing Jews in 1933. Ideological and organizational divisions were fairly serious and ran deep. The Reichsvertretung *was able to attain its authority largely because of the universal regard for Rabbi Leo Baeck and because the organization became the center for relief, vocational training, and emigration of youth, goals upon which German Jewish leaders could agree. Among the numerous reminiscences of this early period is one by Georg Lubinsky who stressed the importance of financial aid from Jews in the United States and England and the solidarity of the leaders, yet who regretted their failure to dissolve the organized community sooner:*

γ   γ   γ

I believe that without the stream of money sent from outside Germany by the American Joint Distribution Committee (AJDC) and the ''British Council for German Jewry'', the *Reichsvertretung* would not have so rapidly reached its dominant position in Jewish life in Germany. . . .

For a start it was important to establish contact with the AJDC and the Jews of England, a task which was entrusted to Tietz and Senator. I still remember Tietz's reports on his meeting with Weizmann in London in 1933. This was the first meeting between these two men. The foresight of Weizmann and the men of the AJDC was very helpful when we drew up a plan for the rescue of the Jews of Germany. They decided in particular to treat vocational training and emigration as the most urgent problems.

In one respect we do, however, see our achievements of the past in a bright light. I hold that in those days we were able to establish one important positive fact: the feeling of brotherhood born in distress.

[15] K. Y. Ball-Kaduri, ''The National Representation of Jews in Germany—Obstacles and Accomplishments at its Establishment,'' *Yad Vashem Studies II*, Jerusalem, 1958, pp. 173, 174.

This brotherhood did indeed give a great deal to all those who took part in this work. But I must repeat that we were all guilty of lack of foresight and imagination. I dare say that the successful organization of the *Reichsvertretung* which had its cultural peaks, such as the Conference on Adult Education at Herrlingen, often induced us excessively to slow down the process of disbandment of German Jewry. We still believed at that time that in Hitlerite Germany it would be possible to work for a renaissance of Jewish culture and to achieve orderly organization of Jewish life. A joint historic guilt here lies upon the shoulders of all those who were responsible for this form of our communal life in Germany. We believed that we had very, very much time. I remember the discussion we had where we expressed the opinion that the existence of the *Kehillot* should be maintained. By so doing we held up for too long the programme for the dissolution of enterprises both of individuals and of the community; in one form or another we all bear part of the blame for this.

READING NO. 14

THE TRAUMAS OF JEWISH CHILDREN IN SCHOOL[16]

The school law of April 25, 1933 was a humiliating and degrading experience for Jewish children and a foretaste of subsequent persecutions. Cities rushed to set up "Jews' benches" in their schools while "racial science" became a permanent part of daily school studies. The plight of Jewish children was described by Martin Buber:

γ   γ   γ

The children are experiencing what is happening and are silent. But at night they awaken from their nightmares and stare into the darkness. The world has become so uncertain and untrustworthy.

One had a friend; the friend was taken for granted like the sunlight. But suddenly he has become a total stranger and mocks at you.

One had a teacher. One felt that in his presence all was in order; but suddenly he lost his voice, refusing to answer questions.

In the field where one played with his schoolmates, one has become unwelcome.

What happened? No one seems completely competent to answer the child. The child becomes angry, but no one seems to be able to calm him. Parents, educators—how can we help our children? Parents—you cannot dismiss the child with a mere verbal explanation. It may sound pathetic and sympathetic—but no more. However, you can conduct yourself in a way that may help your child. You can translate Jewish values into Jewish living. You can study our language, rich lore, Hebrew, and our heroic history. Nay, study is not enough; it must become part of our daily living; it must enter our bloodstream. We must live, yes, live as Jews, as a people, as a community! Teach your children Jewish values! Make your lives Jewish! Begin with yourselves—and your children will follow.

---

[16] Martin Buber, "Die Kinder," *Jüdische Rundschau*, May 30, 1933, p. 227. Quoted in Solomon Colodner, "Jewish Education under National Socialism," *Yad Vashem Studies* III Jerusalem, 1959, pp. 165–166.

READING NO. 15

NAZIFIED SCHOOLING[17]

Non-Jewish German youth, meanwhile, were being thoroughly organized and conditioned to hate Jews in Hitler youth groups and in schools. There teachers as well as students mocked and denounced Jewish children, and Hitler's vehement views on education were applied. The aim would be achieved, he said, " . . . by burning into the heart and brain of the youth . . . an instinctive and comprehended sense of race":

γ   γ   γ

. . . in the winter of 1933, all teachers of "non-Aryan" or Jewish descent were relieved of their posts. An edict was issued on July 11, 1933, that included teachers with all other State officials, ordering them to subordinate their wishes, interests, and demands to the common cause, to devote themselves to the study of National Socialist ideology, and "suggesting" that they familiarize themselves with *Mein Kampf.* Three days later, a "suggestion" was sent to all those who still maintained contact with the Social Democratic Party, that they inform the Nazi Party of the severance of these connections. Committees were formed to see that it was carried out, and whoever hesitated was instantly dismissed. The purge was on.

It was decided, in Prussia first (November, 1933), and later in all German schools, that public school teachers must belong to a Nazi fighting organization; they were to come to school in uniform, wherever possible, and live in camps; and, during the final examinations, they were to be tested in *Geländesport*—military sports

This was all deadly serious, and the teachers knew it. Hitler had cried in Weimar, "If there are still people in Germany today who say, we will not join your community, we will remain as we are, then I reply, 'You will pass on, but after you will come a generation that knows nothing else!' "

Rhineland Children, a primer written by Richard Seewald and Ewald Tiesburger, is the most effective introduction to the military life. Children learned to read, in the past, through words more peaceful than:

---

[17] Erika Mann, *School for Barbarians.* New York, Modern Age Books, 1938, pp. 5, 7, 9, 10.

Hört, wir trommeln, bum, bumbum—
Hört, wir blasen, tä terä tä tä!
Nun, das Lager räumen!

Listen to the drums, boom, boom, boom—
Listen to the trumpets, tateratata!
Come on, clear the camp!

The supplement to this primer was published by the *Stürmer Verlag*, is highly recommended officially, and, although it is an expensive book, has already reached a sale of more than seventy thousand copies. By Elvira Bauer, it has a title astonishing both in length and content: *Trau keinem Fuchs auf grüner Heid! Und keinem Jud bei seinem Eid!* (Trust no fox on green heath! And no Jew on his oath!) On the bright red cover are two pictures with the title. One is of the fox, peering around a corner maliciously eager for his prey; and the other, a typical Nazi caricature of the Jew, beneath a star of David—huge nose, thick lips and bleary eyes, swearing his false oath with fat fingers raised. The book is printed in a luxurious edition, with many colored illustrations, and with two-color text. That is, those words which the authors wish to impress upon their readers are printed in red—"Devil," "Jews," "thick-lips," "gangster." It is impossible to describe the level of sadistic cruelty, the dishonesty and barbarism of this book, the core of all future training.

And the *N.S. Educator* publishes a history curriculum which finds it by no means "sufficient merely to relate events."

Weeks	Subject	Relations to the Jews	Reading Material
1–4	Pre-war Germany The Class War Profits, Strikes	The Jew at large!	Hauptmann: *The Weavers*
5–8	From Agrarian to Industrial State Colonies	The peasant in the claws of the Jews!	Descriptions of the colonies from Hermann Löns
9–12	Conspiracy against Germany, Encirclement, Barrage around Germany	The Jew reigns! War plots	Beumelburg: *Barrage Life of Hindenburg, Wartime Letters*

Weeks	Subject	Relations to the Jews	Reading Material
13–16	German Struggle German Want Blockade! Starvation	The Jew becomes prosperous! Profit from German want	Manke: *Espionage at the Front* *War Reports*
17–20	The Stab in the Back Collapse	Jews as leaders of the November insurrection	(?) On Secret Service in Enemy Country Bruno Brehm: *That Was the End*
21–24	Germany's Golgotha Erzberger's Crimes! Versailles	Jews enter Germany from the East Judah's triumph	Volkmann: *Revolution over Germany* Feder: *The Jews* *The Stürmer* newspaper
25–28	Adolf Hitler National Socialism	Judah's foe!	*Mein Kampf* Dietrich Eckart
29–32	The Bleeding Frontiers Enslavement of Germany The Volunteer Corps Schlageter	The Jew profits by Germany's misfortunes Loans (Dawes, Young)	Beumelberg: *Germany in Chains* Wehner: *Pilgrimage to Paris* Schlageter—a German Hero
33–36	National Socialism at Grips with Crime and the Underworld	Jewish instigators of murder The Jewish press	Horst Wessel
37–40	Germany's Youth at the Helm! The Victory of Faith	The last fight against Judah	Herbert Norkus The Reich Party Congress

READING NO. 16

THE NUREMBERG LAWS OF SEPTEMBER 1935[18]

The problem of defining a Jew, of prime importance in subsequent Nazi persecutions and ultimate annihilation, had created problems for earlier generations of racist anti-Semites and was to prove a stumbling block for Nazis as well. "Semitic" is not a racial category, nor is "Jew." Moreover, "non-Aryan" and "Aryan" likewise are not designations for race. Nazi bureaucrats struggled for a long time over these difficulties, and finally had to resort to the religious descent of one's ancestors. Even so, persons of "mixed Jewish blood, or Mischlinge,*created dilemmas for racial anthropologists under Himmler during the war, when they had to decide whether* Mischlinge *had any "Germanizable" traits that could be salvaged for the Fatherland:*

γ   γ   γ

TRANSLATION OF DOCUMENT 1416-PS

1935 REICHSGESETZBLATT, PART 1, PAGE 1146

The Reich Citizenship Law of 15 Sept 1935

The Reichstag has adopted unanimously, the following law, which is herewith promulgated.

Article 1

1. A subject of the State is a person, who belongs to the protective union of the German Reich, and who, therefore, has particular obligations towards the Reich.

2. The status of the subject is acquired in accordance with the provisions of the Reich- and State Law of Citizenship.

Article 2

1. A citizen of the Reich is only that subject, who is of German- or kindred blood and who, through his conduct, shows that he is both desirous and fit to serve faithfully the German people and Reich.

[18] 1416-PS, 1417-PS. *Nazi Conspiracy and Aggression*, vol. IV, 1946.

2. The right to citizenship is acquired by the granting of Reich citizenship papers.

3. Only the citizen of the Reich enjoys full political rights in accordance with the provision of the laws.

Article 3

The Reich Minister of the Interior in conjunction with the Deputy of the Fuehrer will issue the necessary legal and administrative decrees for the carrying out and supplementing of this law.

Nurnberg, 15 Sept 1935 at the Reichsparteitag of Liberty

> The Fuehrer and Reichs Chancellor
> Adolf Hitler
> The Reichs Minister of the Interior
> Frick

On the basis of Article 3, Reichs Citizenship Law, of 15 Sept. 1935 (RGBI I, page 146) the following is ordered:

Article 1

1. Until further issue of regulations regarding citizenship papers, all subjects of German or kindred blood, who possessed the right to vote in the Reichstag elections, at the time the Citizenship Law came into effect, shall, for the time being, possess the rights of Reich citizens. . . .

Article 2

1. The regulations in Article 1 are also valid for Reichs subjects of mixed, Jewish blood.

2. An individual of mixed Jewish blood, is one who descended from one or two grandparents who were racially full Jews, insofar as does not count as a Jew according to Article 5, paragraph 2. One grandparent shall be considered as full-blooded if he or she belonged to the Jewish religious community.

Article 3

Only the Reich citizen, as bearer of full political rights, exercises the right to vote in political affairs, and can hold a public office. . . .

Article 4

1. A Jew cannot be a citizen of the Reich. He has no right to vote in political affairs, he cannot occupy a public office.

2. Jewish officials will retire as of 31 December 1935. If these officials served at the front in the World War, either for Germany or her allies, they will receive in full, until they reach the age limit, the pension to which they were entitled according to last received wages; they will, however, not advance in seniority. After reaching the age limit, their pension will be calculated anew, according to the last received salary, on the basis of which their pension was computed.

3. The affairs of religious organizations will not be touched upon.

4. The conditions of service of teachers in Jewish public schools remain unchanged, until new regulations of the Jewish school systems are issued.

Article 5

1. A Jew is anyone who descended from at least three grandparents who were racially full Jews. Article 2, par. 2, second sentence will apply.

2. A Jew is also one who descended from two full Jewish parents, if: (a) he belonged to the Jewish religious community at the time this law was issued, or who joined the community later; (b) he was married to a Jewish person, at the time the law was issued, or married one subsequently; (c) he is the offspring from a marriage with a Jew, in the sense of Section 1, which was contracted after the Law for the protection of German blood and German honor became effective (RGBl.I, page 1146 of 15 Sept 1935); (d) he is the offspring of an extramarital relationship, with a Jew, according to Section 1, and will be born out of wedlock after July 31, 1936.

Article 6

1. As far as demands are concerned for the pureness of blood as laid down in Reichs law or in orders of the NSDAP and its echelons—not covered in Article 5—they will not be touched upon.

2. Any other demands on pureness of blood, not covered in Article 5, can only be made with permission form the Reich Minister of the Interior and the Deputy of the Fuehrer. . . .

READING NO. 17

THE "JUNE ACTIONS" OF 1938[19]

Although the pogroms of November 9–10, 1938, are generally considered to have marked a decisive turn in Nazi policy, there were a number of incidents in June that foreshadowed the radical changes later:

γ   γ   γ

The same outrages which are usually believed to be peculiar to the November riots had already occurred earlier in 1938.

1) *The destruction of synagogues.* On 9 June, the Great Synagogue of Munich was destroyed on the personal order of Hitler, after notice had been given one day before. Upon this, Streicher made haste to carry out the destruction of the Great Synagogue of Nuremberg with pomp and ceremony. The synagogue of Dortmund, too, was destroyed and the 100,000 Mark compensation which the community was promised was fictitious, for before it was paid out, the community was fined for exactly this amount.

2) *Mass arrests and enforced emigration.* On 31 May the American *chargé d'affaires* in Vienna sent the Secretary of State the following cable: "Since morning of 27th wholesale arrests of Jews. Many reported sent to Dachau. Action reliably attributed to direct orders of Himmler and presumably intended further to demoralize Jews, facilitate spoilation and expedite exodus." On 15 June, about 1,500 Jews were arrested all over Germany, 'asocial' elements in the language of the Nazis i.e. not only persons who had at some previous time transgressed the law and been convicted; but also violations of traffic regulations and the like were included in the list of "crimes". These convicts were the first to get the full taste of the concentration camps. The tendency to "break" the prisoners, even if this meant to kill them, was only too clear. These men were set free only if they undertook to emigrate at once.

3) *Destruction and looting of shops.* "The entire *Kurfuerstendamm* was plastered with scrawls and cartoons. 'Jew' was smeared all

[19] Shaul Esh, "Between Discrimination and Extermination," *Yad Vashem Studies,* II, 1958, pp. 80–83.

over the doors, windows, and walls in waterproof colors. It grew worse as we came to the part of the town where poor little Jewish retail shops were to be found. The S.A. had created havoc. Everywhere were revolting and bloodthirsty pictures of Jews beheaded, hanged, tortured, and maimed, accompanied by obscene inscriptions. Windows were smashed, and loot from the miserable little shops was strewn over the sidewalk . . . '' All this was put down in Berlin, not in November but on the 28 June, 1938, in the diary of the journalist Bella Fromm, and it all was nothing but a means in the all-out fight for:

4) *Ousting the Jews from German economy.* All through 1938 laws were enacted with this aim. . . . During the summer the process of "Aryanization" was markedly intensified. It follows that in Germany there was method even in rioting and violence; everything was tried out till in November, after careful preparation and organization, and in possession of a pretext which they regarded as excellent, they organized riots which were in no way different from the preceding ones except in their scale.

READING NO. 18

INTENSIFICATION OF
ANTI-JEWISH MEASURES, 1938[20]

Hitler's plan to physically exclude Jews from German life through economic, political, and social measures up to 1938 had not succeeded. Nor had the pressures to emigrate. Only about 20 percent of Jews in Germany had left. A series of new measures in 1938 was intended to speed the process.

γ　　　　γ　　　　γ

. . . In the beginning of the year (5 January), a law about change of names was decreed which must have been prepared as early as the end of 1937. The Jews do not seem to have understood what this law meant for them. Paragraph 12 of the law provided that the Minister of the Interior was authorized to decree regulations about the bearing of names, and to order the change of names which did not conform to these regulations. After only eight months the hidden intention was revealed. So-called "Jewish names" and the addition of "Israel" and "Sarah" became compulsory. The intention was clearly to put a stain on the Jews in the eyes of the people and to make pariahs of them. In March, the law concerning "Jewish Communities" was enacted. According to this decree the recognition of Jewish communities by public law was abolished, which meant that membership was no more compulsory and the communities had lost the legal right of imposing taxes. This was a severe shock, the first official stroke against the Jewish community as a religious congregation. This law clearly intended to strike at the roots of the organic and financial existence of German Jewry, but by the outside pressure against the status of every Jew the Nazis helped to preserve these organic forms to a high degree. About one month later the Jews were ordered to register their property with the authorities. . . . The confiscation of Jewish property now seemed absolutely necessary to the rulers and in particular to Göring who knew very well how great were the needs of the German economy with its continually

---

[20] Shaul Esh, "Between Discrimination and Extermination," *Yad Vashem Studies*, II, 1958, pp. 87, 88–89.

rising expenditure and its continually dwindling exports. Whoever had any doubts left about these intentions could dispel them when in the middle of June, 1938 the "third regulation concerning the law of citizens of the Reich" was published. Here the term "Jewish enterprises" was defined and registration made compulsory. The provisions for the execution of the law, which the Minister of the Interior published one month later, stressed that the registration of Jewish enterprises had to be carried out "with the utmost possible speed", that is to say that still in summer an imposition was decided upon such as was announced in November as a fine, amounting to one milliard Mark. In a speech made by Funk, the Minister of Economy, on 15 November, 1938, this was quite openly admitted. The riots happened, he said, at a moment when "we had nearly completed the economic measures for expelling the Jews from economic life in Germany". He revealed that the compulsory registration had established that Jewish property in Germany amounted to about 7 milliards of Mark. He prided himself that of this amount 2 milliards had already been seized and said that he saw in his mind's eye the desired aim, the complete pauperisation of German Jewry.—But let us return to the chronological succession of facts, to the month of July. On 22 July identity cards were made compulsory for persons of 15 years of age and above. On the following day a special regulation for Jews was added. Jews of any age had to have identity cards, even infants. . . Still in the same month Jewish physicians were removed from their professional activity, two months later followed the removal of Jewish lawyers. Both physicians and lawyers were branded as pariahs, the few who were still allowed to continue working in their profession were forbidden to use their professional titles: the physician (*Arzt*) became a "sick-attendant" (*Krankenbehandler*) and the lawyer was called "consultant" (*Konsulent*). In the autumn the passports of German Jews were confiscated. Again, there was nothing new in this decree; it was only the official condensation and final stage of a development which had started long before. In particular, the secret provision of the Minister of the Interior must be kept in mind, namely that Jews must not be allowed to travel abroad except for the following reasons: emigration, travels in the interest of German economy (i.e. travels the necessity of which is approved by the Chamber of Commerce), serious illness or death of near relatives, illness of the applicant, visit of children at educational institutes. This strict control was made possible by the practice of seizing the passports of Jews on their return from abroad. And now, on the 5th of October 1938, the validity of all Jewish passports was annulled. Those who needed a passport for emigrating from Germany were given passports with a distinctive mark, the notorious 'J,' following the initiative of a Swiss official who was worried about the refugees fleeing into his country.

READING NO. 19

NAZI FOREIGN POLICY GOALS AND WESTERN EMIGRATION FAILURES[21]

By 1938 Hitler's power was unquestioned and his control over domestic and foreign policy matters, absolute. This consolidation paralleled drastic social, economic, and political measures against Austrian and German Jews, the failure of the West to provide refuge for them, and influenced the passage of anti-Jewish measures in Poland, Italy, and Hungary. It also cast a deep shadow all over Europe, with its threat of further conquest and nazification:

γ   γ   γ

3358-PS

Ministry for Foreign Affairs.   Berlin, 25th January 1939.
83–26 19/1

Contents:

The Jewish Question as a factor in German Foreign Policy in the year 1938.

1. The German Jewish Policy as basis and consequence of the decisions for the foreign policy of the year 1938.
2. Aim of German Jewish Policy: Emigration.
3. Means, ways and aim of the Jewish Emigration.
4. The emigrated Jew as the best propaganda for the German Jewish Policy.

It is certainly no co-incidence that the fateful year 1938 has brought nearer the solution of the Jewish question simultaneously with the realization of the "idea of Greater Germany", since the Jewish policy was both the basis and consequence of the events of the year 1938 . . .

To All diplomatic and qualified consular representatives abroad:

The necessity for a radical solution of the Jewish question arose however also as a consequence of the foreign political development, which resulted in a further 200,000 Jews in Austria in addition to the 500,000 of the Jewish Faith living in the Old Reich. . . .

---

[21] 3358-PS, *Nazi Aggression and Conspiracy*, vol. VI, 1946.

The final goal of German Jewish Policy is the emigration of all the Jews living in Reich territory. It is foreseen that already the thorough measures in the economic sphere, which have prevented the Jew from earning and made him live on his dividends, will further the desire to emigrate. Looking back on the last 5 years since the assumption of power, it is, however, obvious that neither the Law for the Reestablishing of the Professional Character of the Civil Service nor the Nurnberg Jewish laws with their executive regulations, which prevented any tendency of Jewry being assimilated, contributed to any extent to the emigration of German Jews. On the contrary every period of domestic political tranquility has resulted in such a stream of Jewish immigrants returning, that the Gestapo has been obliged to put Jewish immigrants with German passports into a training camp for political supervision.

The Jew was excluded from politics and culture. But until 1938 his powerful economic position in Germany was unbroken, and thereby his obstinate resolve to hold out until "better times" came. . . .

But the Jew has underestimated the consequences and the strength of the National Socialist purpose. . . . Italy stood at Germany's side, with her racial laws in the fight against Jewry . . . Jewry in Hungary and Poland was subjected to special laws. Everywhere the success of German foreign policy now begins to shake Jewish strongholds which have been established for hundreds of years from Munich and in far off States, like the tremours of an earthquake.

It is also understandable that World Jewry, "which has selected America as its Headquarters" regards as its own downfall the Munich Agreement, which in American opinion signifies the collapse of the democratic front in Europe. . . .

The emigration movement of only about 100,000 Jews has already sufficed to awaken the interest if not the understanding of many countries in the Jewish danger. We can estimate that here the Jewish question will extend to a problem of international politics when large numbers of Jews from Germany, Poland, Hungary and Rumania are put on the move as a result of increasing pressure from the people of the countries where they are living. Even for Germany the Jewish problem will not be solved when the last Jew has left German soil. . . .

READING NO. 20

GREAT BRITAIN AND THE EVIAN CONFERENCE OF JULY 1938[22]

From 1933 to the time of the Evian Conference, about 11,000 Jews had been admitted to Great Britain; after the pogroms of November 9–10, 1938, thousands more found refuge there, although after war was declared September 3, 1939, many were interned as enemy aliens. The restrictive British attitude regarding immigration generally and regarding Palestine as a possible refuge, however, was made abundantly clear at the Evian conference:

γ   γ   γ

On 5 July, the day before the opening of the Evian conference final instructions to the British delegation were prepared. They emphasized again why the discussion should not include potential refugees from Rumania, Poland, Hungary and possibly Czechoslovakia. All these countries might be watching these deliberations and 'it was important to avoid giving the impression that the meeting was going to create such facilities for emigrants that other countries would with impunity force sections of their population to leave. The United Kingdom delegates should constantly bear in mind the relation of the discussion to this wider problem.' This attitude forced the British into an unenviable position. They sincerely wanted Evian to succeed but on a limited scale only. If resettlement could be easily achieved, masses of newly-expelled refugees would further exacerbate the problem both for the potential host countries and for the individuals concerned.

As to Britain herself, the instructions were explicit: 'His Majesty's government are bound to have regard to their domestic situation and to the fact that the United Kingdom is not a country of immigration and to recognise that for demographic and economic reasons', the traditional haven for the oppressed and persecuted had become very restrictive. Persons who had no resources and would be seeking employment could only be admitted in very limited numbers. (If, however, the newly-formed co-ordinating committee of private societies interested in refugee work could find methods of livelihood in non-competitive

---

[22] Joshua B. Stein, ''Great Britain and the Evian Conference of 1938,'' *Weiner Library Bulletin*, (London), 1976, XXIX New Series, Nos. 37/38, pp. 48, 49.

fields for a certain number, the government would be willing to admit some of this class.) Students were allowed to enter more freely, the presumption being that they were to remain in Britain only temporarily. The government was prepared to admit such academically qualified people as could be placed by the Society for the Protection of Science and Learning. The entry of doctors and dentists would have to be limited in response to the opposition of the British medical and dental societies. Lastly, the government would accept transient refugees—people not intending to settle permanently in Britain but anxious to learn a new skill before going elsewhere.

Attention was then drawn to Palestine. Delegates were instructed that 'reference to the possibilities of immigration into Palestine should be avoided if possible'. Governments pursuing the issue should be informed 'that His Majesty's government, as a mandatory power, has a special obligation to facilitate Jewish immigration into Palestine under suitable conditions and has discharged and will continue to discharge that responsibility in the light of circumstances prevailing in the territory'. Palestine was not to be discussed and with Lord Winterton as her chief delegate, Britain could rest assured that these instructions would be inflexibly followed. The guidelines were supplemented by a 15-page documentation showing why the colonies could accept only a few if any refugees apart from the odd farmer, dentist or vet. . . .

Of the many meetings the British delegation held, perhaps the one with the *Reichsvertretung der Juden in Deutschland* (Jewish Council of Germany) may be singled out as typical of the rest. The group's leader, Dr Otto Hirsch, destined to die in a Nazi prison camp in 1941, had a proposal for the evacuation of 300,000 German and Austrian Jews. He was informed by Winterton that perhaps a few hundred selected families might be settled in parts of Africa, but his Lordship refused even to discuss a specific scheme Hirsch had prepared allowing for the settlement of substantial numbers in Palestine. Having achieved nothing, the supplicants left empty handed, as did all the others who spoke to the British delegation.

READING NO. 21

KRISTALLNACHT—THE POGROMS OF NOVEMBER 9–10, 1938[23, 24, 25, 26]

The German press referred to the violence of these pogroms as the "spontaneous demonstration of the German people," who were reacting to the death of vom Rath, but oral instructions by Goebbels to party leaders ordered them to "organize and execute" the actions. Further, Goebbels insisted that only party courts investigate any cases of "excesses." No blame was ever incurred by the arsonists or murderers, nor punishment meted out:

γ   γ   γ

SECRET
National Socialist German Labor Party
Supreme Party Court [Oberstes Parteigericht]
The Chief of the Central Office   Munich 33

Report about the events and judicial proceedings in connection with
the anti-semitic demonstrations of 9 November 1938

On the evening of 9 November 1938, Reich propaganda director Party Member Dr. Goebbels told the party leaders assembled at a social evening in the old town hall in Munich, that in the districts [Gauen] of Kurhessen and Magdeburg-Anhalt it had come to the hostile Jewish demonstrations, during which Jewish shops were demolished and synagogues were set on fire. The Fuehrer at Goebbels's suggestion had decided, that such demonstrations were not to be prepared or organized by the Party, but so far as they originated spontaneously, they were not to be discouraged either. In other respects, Party Member Dr. Goebbels carried out the purport of what was prescribed in the teletype

---

[23] 3063-PS, *Nazi Conspiracy and Aggression,* vol. V, 1946.

[24] Testimony of Fred Stamm, Jan. 25, 1981, Gratz College Holocaust Archives.

[25] Testimony of Susan Neulaender Faulkner, November, 1983, Gratz College Holocaust Archives.

[26] Jeanette Wolff, *Mit Bibel und Bebel.* Bonn, 1980. Tr. by Hanna Silver. Gratz College Holocaust Archives.

of the Reich propaganda administration of 10 Nov. 1938 (12:30 to 1 o'clock).

(Enclosure 2)

It was probably understood by all the Party leaders present, from the oral instructions of the Reich propaganda director, that the Party should not appear outwardly as the originator of the demonstrations but in reality should organize and execute them. Instructions in this sense were telephoned immediately (thus a considerable time before transmission of the first teletype) to the bureaus of their district [Gaue] by a large part of the Party members present. . . .

The deputy of the Fuehrer agreed with the interpretation of the chief Party Court, that known transgression in any case should be investigated under the jurisdiction of the party. . . . Dr. Goebbels' instruction that the Party was not to organize this demonstration was most likely interpreted by each Party leader present in the town-hall to mean that the Party should not appear as the organizer. Party Member Dr. Goebbels probably meant it in that way for politically interested and active circles who might participate in such demonstrations are members of the Party and its branches. Naturally they could be mobilized only through offices of the Party and its branches. Thus a series of subordinate leaders understood some unfortunately phrased orders which reached them orally or by phone, to mean that Jewish blood would now have to flow for the blood of Party Member von [*sic*] Rath, that at any rate the leadership did not attach importance to the life of a Jew, for example, not the Jew Gruenspan but all Jewry was guilty of the death of Party Member von [*sic*] Rath, the German people were therefore taking revenge on all Jewry, the synagogues were burning in the entire Reich, Jewish residences and businesses were to be laid waste, life and property of Aryans had to be protected, foreign Jews were not to be molested, the drive was being carried out by order of the Fuehrer, the police were withdrawn, pistols were to be brought, at the least resistance the weapon was to be used without consideration, as an SA man each one would certainly know what he had to do, etc. . . . The public, down to the last man, realizes that political drives like those of 9 November were organized and directed by the Party, whether this is admitted or not.

When all the synagogues burn down in one night, it must have been organized in some way and can only have been organized by the Party. But the soldiers should never be put in a position of having any doubts in regard to the intention of the commander—whether the order really means what it says; for there is a possibility that such doubts may lead to the wrong results in important matters, or there might be doubts in a case when the commander wants to be certain that his order is understood and carried out literally. In any case, soldierly discipline and with it the National Socialist concept of discipline is undermined thereby . . .

Also in such cases as when Jews were killed without an order (enclosures 13, 14 and 15) or contrary to orders (enclosures 8 and 9), ignoble motives could not be determined. At heart the men were convinced that they had done a service to their Fuehrer and to the Party. Therefore, exclusion from the Party did not take place. The final aim of the proceedings executed and also the yardsticks for critical examination must be according to the policy of the Supreme Party Court. . . . At that time most of the killings could still have been prevented by a supplementary decree. Since this did not happen it must be deduced from this fact as well as from the remark itself that the final success was intended, or at least considered as possible and desirable. The individual active agent carried out not only the assumed, but also the vaguely expressed and correctly understood will of the leaders. For that he cannot be punished.

[signature] Schneider
Schneider

[Seal]
Nat.Soc.Ger.Worker Party
Supreme Party Court.[23]

* * * *

The following are accounts of individual Jews who were witness to the events of November 9–10, 1938:

One day one of my father's friends came . . . He told my father that he should stay home and that he should send his sons away. The best thing to do is to give them some money and tell them to ride the railroad wherever they wish to ride, not to stop anywhere, just ride the railroad. He said, ''But they must leave immediately.'' So my father borrowed some money somewhere . . . And my brother and I started a journey of three days. We rode on the railroad to Frankfurt, Kassel, Paderborn. We rode anywhere, wherever a train would take us. After two days we called a Gentile neighbor who had a grocery store, whose son was my closest friend, and I asked him what was happening, whether we could come home. He said, ''Don't come home yet. But also, I want you to know, don't ever call me again. I will not report you but don't ever you call me again.'' My father was not taken . . . I do remember though that we were the only three males in town who were not taken to a concentration camp . . . The synagogue was completely destroyed. The community house was not destroyed because it was occupied by the Brownshirts . . . I found our house . . . the doors were destroyed. Some of the windows were destroyed, which I repaired properly. And I found a mood of desperation among the members of my family because we had a large house and people from the villages who had suffered even more than we had, they had come to us and my parents took them in.[24]

* * * *

It was a dark, sort of a greyish day, hazy and slighty warm for November and somehow there was some kind of electricity in the air that we sort of had a feeling to stay at home, be cautious. . . . Then after dark, my aunt with her husband [came] and they told us that there was already destruction going on outside. . . . I was walking over the sidewalks with glass crunching under my feet, and on the next street— Fasanenstrasse. . . . the oldest synagogue in Berlin . . . was in flames. The firetrucks were there training their hoses on the neighboring houses, but letting the synagogue burn. . . . And the entire sidewalk across from the synagogue was filled with hundreds of people . . . as if it was like a carnival to them . . . applauding and laughing . . . flames lighting up in the sky . . . and the people standing in the reflected light, in the glow of the flames . . . laughing. . . . [I] tried to walk past them in such a way that they wouldn't see that I was crying. . . . Then . . . there were some brown shirts and they were beating up an old Jewish man with a long beard . . . and there were people standing around laughing and applauding . . . like a Roman circus. . . . I came home and I was promptly sick all over the kitchen floor.[25]

* * * *

. . . armed SA hordes broke into our house on Munster Street, [Dortmund], where I had a 7 room apartment with my pension—mistreated my guests, broke up all the furniture and threw it into the street from the third floor. Before intruding into our place, the SA and SS men had raged through the apartment below ours where two Jewish families lived. The man of one family was in bed and very sick. The hordes tore the chandelier from the ceiling and beat the sick man with it until he was unconscious. A few weeks later the forty year old man died of the consequences of this mistreatment. (Our two girls Edith and Kathe were hidden by the janitor in his place in the attic when the raging pack came to us.)

The intruders did not only mistreat the guests in our pension but broke up all the furniture, the book shelves, ruined the books and threw chairs and small tables into the street, until the curious people standing there howled because some of them were hit. Then they cut open all the upholstered furniture and after that they wanted to throw my 80-year old mother-in-law who challenged the horde, into the street from the third floor. They would have done that if not at that moment SS Obersturmführer Wissmann, who knew me (he had an uncle in my hometown), entered and called the men to order.

My oldest daughter Juliane worked at that time in the Jewish hospital in Frankfurt. Later she went with us to the Riga Ghetto and KZ where she perished.

Our apartment was one big pile of rubble. We received a summons from the police to remove the debris by noon next day. Also, we had to replace the broken windows the same day at our own expense. They arrested all my dinner guests; they were loaded onto a wagon and driven away. The next evening they came for my husband. Since the day when I was declared "enemy of the State" and taken into "protective custody," he was not permitted to enter his own shop. So he started to work as a bill collector for the Victoria Insurance. . . . After the "Kristallnacht" my husband was deported to the concentration camp Sachsenhausen and put into the hardest kommando, the Klinker Werke. He returned in February 1939, a wreck in body and soul. I never learned what had happened to him at the camp. His silence can be explained thru the special Nazi method: he had to sign never to mention a word about the camp—otherwise he would be returned immediately to the camp. This method worked so well with all former terrified KZ inmates so that everybody kept silent and thus the world never knew about the happenings in the camp.[26]

READING NO. 22

FURTHER ECONOMIC PUNISHMENT—A BILLION RM FINE[27]

On the night of November 10, Göring spoke to the German people on the radio. "Everything is quite official," he said. "The Jews have to pay a collective fine of one billion marks, twenty percent of their property." This fine was referred to a Sühneleistung, *an "atonement payment" to be paid by Jews for their "abominable crimes" in causing the death of vom Rath. Two billion Reichsmarks of Jewish wealth had already been confiscated. The additional one billion was collected in four installments ending August 15, 1939. Another five percent was added, payable November 15, 1939. Jewish insurance claims were paid for by insurance companies, but these monies, too, were confiscated by the government (Finance Ministry). Jewish property owners were also ordered to repair all property damage and Jewish communities ordered to clear the rubble from the streets:*

γ γ γ

TRANSLATION OF DOCUMENT 1412-PS

1938 REICHSGESETZBLATT, PART I, PAGE 1579

Decree relating to the payment of a fine by the Jews of German nationality of 12 Nov. 1938.

The hostile attitude of the Jewry towards the German people and Reich, which does not even shrink back from committing cowardly murder, makes a decisive defense and a harsh punishment (expiation) necessary. I order, therefore, by virtue of the decree concerning the execution of the 4-year Plan of 18 Oct. 1936 (RGBl. I, page 887) as follows:

Section 1

On the Jews of German nationality as a whole has been imposed the payment of a contribution of 1,000,000,000 Reichsmark to the German Reich.

[27] 1412-PS, *Nazi Conspiracy and Aggression*, vol. IV, 1946.

Section 2

Provisions for the implementation are issued by the Reich-Minister of Finance in agreement with the Reich-Ministers concerned.
Berlin, 12 November 1938.

The Commissioner for the Four Year Plan
Goering
General Field-Marshal.

READING NO. 23

ANTI-JEWISH TERROR IN VIENNA, MARCH 1938[28, 29]

The acquisition of Austria was one of Hitler's cherished ambitions and the country fell under increased Nazi pressure to admit members of the Austrian Nazi Party into the government after 1934. Franz von Papen became the German Minister to Vienna with the explicit purpose of organizing the overthrow of the existing Schuschnigg regime. In 1936 and 1937 various concessions were extracted, the Austrian police were infiltrated, and ultimately Schuschnigg was worn down and capitulated after Hitler threatened an invasion. On March 15, 1938, the day after Hitler's entry into Vienna, Austria was declared a province of the German Reich. Huge crowds cheered the Nazi advance. The American journalist William L. Shirer wrote in his diary:

γ   γ   γ

VIENNA, *March* 22

Tess's condition still critical. And the atmosphere in the hospital has not helped. First, Tess says, there was a Jewish lady whose brother-in-law committed suicide the day Hitler entered town. She screamed all the first night. Today she left in black mourning clothes and veil, clutching her baby. There was a second Jewish lady. No one in her family was murdered, but the S.A., after taking over her husband's business, proceeded to their home and looted it. She fears her husband will be killed or arrested, and weeps all night long.

On the streets today gangs of Jews, with jeering storm troopers standing over them and taunting crowds around them, on their hands and knees scrubbing the Schuschnigg signs off the sidewalks. Many Jews killing themselves. All sorts of reports of Nazi sadism, and from the Austrians it surprises me. Jewish men *and* women made to clean latrines. Hundreds of them just picked at random off the streets to clean the toilets of the Nazi boys. The lucky ones get off with merely cleaning cars—the thousands of automobiles which have been stolen from the Jews and "enemies" of the regime. The wife of a diplomat, a

[28] William L. Shirer, *Berlin Diary: The Journal of a Foreign Correspondent, 1934–1941.* New York, 1941, pp. 110–111.
[29] Testimony of L. T. February 24, 1981, Gratz College Holocaust Archives.

Jewess, told me today she dared not leave her home for fear of being picked up and put to "scrubbing things."[28]

VIENNA, *March* 25

Went with Gillie to see the synagogue in the Seitenstättengasse, which was also the headquarters of the Jewish *Kultusgemeinde*. We had been told that the Jews had been made to scrub out toilets with the sacred praying-bands, the *Tefillin*. But the S.S. guards wouldn't let us in. Inside we could see the guards lolling about smoking pipes.

* * * *

A nine-year old Jewish child in Vienna had the following memory:

I remember walking to the trolley one day after school with Gerda, and we came by a crowd of people, and the police standing around, and the crowd of people had just obviously looted a man's clothing store and the people were just streaming out, loaded with men's clothes, and there was the big *Jude* on the plateglass window and there was the poor man, obviously a Jew who was being beaten up and there was a soldier . . . I mean, the policeman, just standing by. And another episode that I remember right next door to us, was a friend of my father's and his wife, an elderly couple. . . . One night, I have no idea how late it was, but it was during the night sometime. I woke up, looked out the window, and saw this woman being pushed down her front steps. She was wearing a red coat and I watched to see what was happening. I couldn't quite figure it out, there were two Gestapo men behind her. I went back to bed, and the next morning I discovered that what had happened, they had rounded a number of middle-aged Jewish woman, and they were wearing nothing but red coats. They were driven by Gestapo to a central square where there were statues of heroes riding on a horse, and they had to take off their coats and, totally in the nude, were given pails, were given scrubbing brushes, and had to scrub the statue of this hero. Again, people standing around, people cheering, you know, nobody really saying anything. That was the problem . . . The one incident really that I think really got to my father took place the day after the *Anchluss*. Viennese always go to coffee houses and they have their own coffee house and they have a table and they have a waiter, and my father also had this coffee house that he had been going to for 20–30 years, and he had been sitting at this one table and he had been waited on by this one waiter, and the day after the *Anchluss* when my father went to his coffee house, as usual, the waiter looked at him and pretended not to know him. My father said, ''Hello, Franz,'' whatever his name was, and the waiter just looked at him, and said . . . looked at him up and down, turned over the lapel of his coat and showed a long-time Nazi membership button and said, ''I don't wait on dirty Jews.'' Now, how he even knew that my father was Jewish, I think is an interesting question. My maiden name was Glaser, which is not necessarily Jewish.[29]

READING NO. 24

GERMAN-JEWISH IMMIGRATION TO THE UNITED STATES, 1933–1938[30, 31]

For the period from 1933 to 1938, although the German quota was 26,000 per year, it was never filled. In 1930, President Hoover had urged American consuls abroad to demand stringent proofs from visa applicants that they would be self-supporting. He made it clear that if the consul believed that the applicant might become a public charge at any time, the visa could be refused. The Immigration Act of 1924 further required the applicant to furnish a police certificate of good character. Jewish organizations frequently protested the incongruity of this rule, but it was repeatedly invoked:

γ   γ   γ

In August 1933 the State Department's legal adviser, Green H. Hackworth, commented on these complaints: " . . . it is believed that the mere fact that a Jew has been driven out of Germany into another country, or has found it desirable to flee from Germany to escape persecution, does not in and of itself excuse him from producing the documents required by Section 7(c) if it is reasonably possible for him to obtain such documents upon applying therefor to the appropriate German authorities." Such pronouncements, divorced from the reality of life in Nazi Germany, were issued regularly by the legal adviser. . . .

In a report dealing with immigration from January to August 1934 . . . the vice-consul in Berlin noted that German police departments habitually expunged records of minor crimes five or ten years after their occurrence. This prompted C. Paul Fletcher of the Visa Division in Washington to note: "The statement relative to the unavailability in Germany of complete police records strengthens the contention that the United States is being made the dumping ground for criminals."

Stringent quotas, the "public charge" provision and the necessity

---

[30] Arthur D. Morse, *While Six Million Died: A Chronicle of American Apathy.* New York, 1968, pp. 137, 139, 140.

[31] Werner Rosenstock, "Exodus 1933–1939, A Survey of Jewish Emigration from Germany," *Leo Baeck Institute Year Book* I. London, 1956, p. 376.

to provide police certificates ''if available'' were not the only barriers facing the potential immigrant. There was also the ''contract labor'' provision which made it impossible for workers to enter under employment contracts. Thus the prospective immigrant, attempting to meet the ''public charge'' provision, might assure himself of a job and then be barred because of his foresight. . . .

A further restriction in the Immigration Act of 1917 called for the ''exclusion of persons whose ticket or passage is paid for by any corporation, association or society, municipality or foreign government either directly or indirectly.'' The originators of this provision could not have foreseen the plight of the German Jews, who were stripped of all their possessions before being cast adrift on endless seas. They were expected to be self-sufficient though penniless, capable of supporting themselves though unemployed, and prepared to pay their passage without accepting help from friends. In October 1934 the Third Reich issued its most dramatic currency restriction, limiting each emigrant to a total of 10 reichsmarks (about $4). The Jews were thus trapped by both German and American regulations.

The harshness of American immigration policy was not lost on Hitler, who turned each aspect of the world's apathy into a weapon for himself. A month after he had assumed power he issued a statement that American citizens had no right to protest his anti-Semitism in view of the United States' own racial discrimination in its immigration policies. ''Through its immigration law,'' said Hitler, ''America has inhibited the unwelcome influx of such races as it has been unable to tolerate in its midst. Nor is America now ready to open its doors to Jews fleeing from Germany.''[30]

* * * *

Jewish Immigration from Germany to the United
States of America, January 1933 to June 1938[31]

January 1933 to December 1933	535
January 1934 to December 1934	2,310
January 1935 to June 1935	658
July 1935 to June 1936	6,750 (estimated)
July 1936 to June 1937	6,750
July 1937 to June 1938	10,000
Total (approx.)	27,000

READING NO. 25

HITLER REJECTS SCHACHT EMIGRATION PLAN[32]

Schacht was deeply, and properly, concerned with Germany's precarious financial situation in 1938, but his reasonable economic analyses were no match for the Nazi extremists, not only Heydrich and Hitler, but Göring as well. As head of the Four-Year Plan, Göring geared his program to German self-sufficiency, which included production of synthetics and substitutes and increased public borrowing. Purchases of foreign exchange were also made for rearmament expenditures and drove up Germany's debt. In December 1938, Schacht went to London to discuss his emigration plan with George Rublee, director of the intergovernmental committee created after Evian, but was dismissed the following month by Hitler, who refused to "give up" Jewish assets:

γ   γ   γ

Ministry for Foreign Affairs   Berlin, 25th January, 1939
83–26 19/1

The Jewish Question as a Factor in German Foreign Policy in the year 1938

. . . The American President Roosevelt "who it is well known is surrounded by a whole row of exponents of Jewry among his closest confidants" called a State Conference as early as the middle of 1938 to discuss the refugee questions, which was held in Evian without any particular results. Both of the questions, the answering of which is the first essential for organized Jewish emigration remained unanswered: firstly the question of *how* this emigration should be organized and financed and secondly the question: emigrate *to where?*

In answer to the first question, International Jewry in particular did not appear willing to contribute. On the contrary the Conference—and later the Committee formed by it in London under the direction of Rublee, an American—regarded its main task as that of forcing Germany by international pressure to release Jewish property to the greatest possible extent. In other words Germany was to pay for the emigration of

[32] 3358-PS *Nazi Conspiracy and Aggression,* vol. VI, 1946.

her 700,000 Jews with German national property. It is at the same time to be doubted whether International Jewry ever seriously desired the mass emigration of their fellow Jews from Germany and other states at all, unless there was an equivalent of a Jewish State. The tactics hitherto employed in Jewish proposals, were in every case aimed less at mass emigration of Jews than at the transfer of Jewish property.

It goes without saying, that the transfer of even a fraction of Jewish property, would be impossible from the point of view of foreign exchange. The financing of a mass emigration of German Jews is therefore still obscure. . . .

Schaumburg

READING NO. 26

NAZI PROMOTION OF ANTI-SEMITISM IN BLOCKING EMIGRATION OUTLETS[33]

Germany not only wanted all of its Jews to leave, but had no interest in an orderly process. Quite the reverse—the radical Nazis helped to incite anti-Semitism in those countries where they established their influence or had surrogates and relished reports of anti-Semitism elsewhere:

γ   γ   γ

. . . After over 100,000 Jews even in 1933/34 had succeeded either legally or illegally in escaping abroad and establishing themselves in someone else's country either with the help of their Jewish relatives living abroad or circles sympathetically disposed from a humanitarian point of view, almost every State in the World has in the meantime hermetically sealed its borders against these parasitical Jewish intruders. The problem of Jewish emigration is therefore for all practical purposes at a standstill. Many States have already become so cautious, that they demand a permit made out by German authorities from Jews travelling in the ordinary way with German passports, saying that there is nothing against them returning. . . . Germany is very interested in maintaining the dispersal of Jewry. The calculation, that as a consequence boycott groups and anti-German centres would be formed all over the world, disregards the following fact which is already apparent, the influx of Jews in all parts of the world invokes the opposition of the native population and thereby forms the best propaganda for the German Jewish policy.

In North America, in South America, in France, in Holland, Scandinavia and Greece, everywhere, wherever the flood of Jewish immigrants reaches, there is today already a visible increase in anti-semitism. A task of the German foreign policy must be to further this wave of anti-semitism. This will be achieved less by German propaganda abroad, than by the propaganda which the Jew is forced to circulate in his defense. In the end, its effects will recoil on themselves. The reports from German authorities abroad, emphasize the correctness of this interpretation:

[33] 3358-PS, *Nazi Conspiracy and Aggression,* vol. VI, 1946.

The press and official correspondents continually report anti-semitic demonstrations by the population of North America. It is perhaps indicative of the domestic political development in USA, that the listening-audience of the "Radio Priest" Coughlin, who is well known to be Anti-Jewish, has grown to over 20 millions. The Embassy in Montevideo reported on 12 December last year "that the Jewish influx continues for months, week by week. It goes without saying, that anti-semitism is growing"—Salonica reported on 30 November 1938: "that forces are at work to stir up the hate against the Jews" and that at the same time Greek Freemasonry is endeavoring to stem the anti-semitic movement. In France, the Paris Town Council (Stadtversammlung) was in April of this year to discuss a proposal, by which the naturalization of Jews was in future to be refused. . . . These examples from reports from authorities abroad, can, if desired be amplified. They confirm the correctness of the expectation, that criticism of the measures for excluding Jews from German Lebensraum. . . . would only be temporary and would swing in the other direction the moment the population saw with its own eyes and thus learned, what the Jewish danger was to them. The poorer and therefore the more burdensome the immigrant Jew is to the country absorbing him, the stronger this country will react and the more desirable is this effect in the interests of German propaganda. The object of this German action is to be the future international solution of the Jewish question, dictated not by false compassion for the "United Religious Jewish minority" but by the full consciousness of all peoples of the danger which it represents to the racial composition of the nations.

By Order

Schaumburg

READING NO. 27

HEYDRICH'S ORDER OF
SEPTEMBER 21, 1939[34, 35]

*Heydrich's ominous letter contained the results of a conference held
in Berlin on September 21 and was sent to* Einsatzgruppen *chiefs, the
High Command of the Army, officials of several Reich ministries, and
the chief of the civil administration of the occupied territories. It is very
likely that Heydrich was already thinking about and planning for the
physical destruction of Jews:*

γ γ γ

Berlin, 21 September 1939

The Chief of the Security Police
PP (II)—288/39 secret
Special Delivery Letter
To *The Chiefs of all detail groups [Einsatzgruppen] of the Security Po-
lice.*
Concerning: The Jewish problem in the occupied zone.

I refer to the conference held in Berlin today, and again point out that
the *planned joint measures* (i.e. the ultimate goal) are to be kept *strictly
secret.*

Distinction must be made between

(1) The ultimate goal (which requires a prolonged period of time)
and

(2) the sectors leading to fulfillment of the ultimate goal. (each of
which will be carried out in a short term).

The planned measures require thorough preparation both in tech-
nique and in the economic aspect.

Obviously the tasks at hand cannot be laid down in detail from here.
The following instructions and directives serve at the same time for the
purpose of urging chiefs of the detail groups to practice consideration
of problems.

[34] 3363-PS, *Nazi Conspiracy and Aggression*, vol. VI, 1946.
[35] Ibid.

I

*The first prerequisite for the ultimate goal is first of all, the
concentration of the Jews from the country
to the larger cities.*

This is to be carried out speedily. In doing so distinction must
be made:

(1) between the zones of Danzig and West Prussia, Poznan, Eastern Upper Silesia;
and

(2) the other occupied zone.

If possible, the zone mentioned under item 1 shall be cleared completely of Jews, or at least the aim should be to form as few concentration centers as possible.

In the zones mentioned under item 2, there shall be established as
few concentration points as possible so that future measures may be
accomplished more easily. One must keep in mind that only such cities
are chosen as concentration points which are located either at railroad
junctions or at least along a railroad.

On principle, all Jewish communities *under 500* heads are to be dissolved and to be transferred to the nearest concentration center. . . . . [34]

II

Councils of Jewish Elders

(1) In each Jewish community, a Council of Jewish Elders is to be
set up which, as far as possible, is to be composed of the remaining
influential personalities and rabbis. The Council is to be composed of
24 male Jews (depending on the size of the Jewish community).

It is to be made *fully responsible* (in the literal sense of the word) for
the exact execution according to terms of all instructions released or
yet to be released.

(2) In case of sabotage of such instructions, the Councils are to be
warned of severest measures. [35]

(3) The Jewish Councils are to take an improvised census of the
Jews of their area, possibly divided into generations (according to age)

a. up to 16 years of age,

b. from 16 to 20 years of age,

c. and those above and also according to the principal voca-
tions—

and they are to report the results in the shortest possible time.

(4) The Councils of Elders are to be made acquainted with the time and date of the evacuation, the evacuation possibilities and finally the evacuation routes. They are, then, to be made personally responsible for the evacuation of the Jews from the country.

The reason to be given for the concentration of the Jews to the cities is that Jews have most decisively participated in sniper attacks and plundering.

(5) The Councils of Elders of the concentration centers are to be made responsible for the proper housing of the Jews to be brought in from the country. The concentration of Jews in the cities for general reasons of security will probably bring about orders to forbid Jews to enter certain wards of that city altogether, and that in consideration of economic necessity they cannot for instance leave the ghetto, they cannot go out after a designated evening hour, etc.

(6) The Council of Elders is also to be made responsible for the adequate maintenance of the Jews on the transport to the cities. . . .

III

All necessary measures, on principle, are always to be taken up in closest agreement and collaboration with the German civil administration and the competent local authorities.

In the execution of this plan, care must be taken that economic security suffer no harm in the occupied zones.

(1) The needs of the army, should particularly be kept in mind e.g. it will not be possible to avoid leaving behind here and there some Jews engaged in trade who absolutely must be left behind for the maintenance of the troops, for lack of any other way out. In such cases, the immediate aryanization of these plants is to be planned for and the emigration of the Jews is to be completed later in agreement with the competent local German administrative authorities.

(2) For the preservation of German economic interests in the occupied territories it is self understood that Jewish war and ordinary industries and factories and those important to the 4-Year Plan must be kept going for the time being.

In these cases also, immediate Aryanization must be planned for and the emigration of the Jews must be completed later.

(3) Finally, the food situation in the occupied territories must be

taken into consideration. For instance, as far as possible, real estate of Jewish settlers should be provisionally entrusted to the care of neighboring German or even Polish peasants to be worked by them in order to insure harvesting of the crops still in the fields, or cultivation.

In regard to this important question contact should be made with the agricultural experts of the (C.d.Z.).

(4) In all cases in which a conformity of interests of the Security Police [Sicherheitspolizei] on the one hand, and the German civil administration on the other hand, can be reached.

I am to be informed of the individual measures in question as quickly as possible before their execution and my decision is to be awaited.

IV

The Chiefs of the detail groups [Einsatzgruppen] are to report to me continuously on the following matters:

(1) Numerical survey on the Jews present in their territories (if possible according to the above mentioned classification).

The number of Jews who are evacuated from the country and those who are already in cities are to be listed separately.

(2) Names of cities which have been designated as concentration points.

(3) The time set for the Jews to be evacuated to the cities.

(4) Survey of all Jewish war and ordinary industries and factories or those important to the 4-Year Plan in their territory.

If possible the following should be specified:

> *a.* Kind of factory (also statement on possible reconversion of factory to really vital or war-important factories or those important to the 4-Year Plan);
>
> *b.* which factories should be most urgently Aryanized (in order to avoid loss); what kind of Aryanization is suggested? Germans or Poles, (the decision depends on the importance of the factory);
>
> *c.* number of Jews working in these factories (include leading positions).

Will it be possible to keep the factory going after the Jews have been removed or will German or Polish workers respectively have to be assigned for that purpose? To what extent?

If Polish workers have to be used, care should be taken that they are mainly taken from the former German provinces in order to somewhat ease the problem there. These questions can only be solved by incorporation and participation of the labor offices [Arbeitsaemter] which have been set up.

V

For the fulfillment of the goal set, I expect the full
cooperation of all forces of the Security Police
[Sicherheitspolizei] and the Security Service
[Sicherheitsdienst].
The Chiefs of the neighboring detail groups shall immediately establish contact with each other in order to be able to cover completely the territories in question.

VI

The High Command of the Army [OKH]; the commissioner for the 4-Year Plan, (c/o State Secretary Neumann) (Staatssekretaer); the Reich Minister of the interior (c/o State Secretary Stuckart); the Reich Ministry for Food and Economy [fuer Ernaehrung und Wirtschaft] (c/o State Secretary Landfrie(d)); as well as the Chief of the civil administration of the occupied territories have received copies of this decree.

Signed: Heydrich
Certified:
signed: Schmidt
Office employe.

Responsible for
correct copy
signed: signature
    Major on the General Staff (Major i.G.)

READING NO. 28

GHETTOIZATION—PREPARATION FOR ANNIHILATION[36]

The period from 1939 to 1941 marked the transition stage from the forced emigration (i.e. expulsion) of Jews to physical annihilation. Heydrich had sketched the blueprint in his September 21, 1939 Order. Registration and segregation through the process of ghettoization were the preliminary, prerequisite steps:

γ   γ   γ

A. *Registration.*

The first step in accomplishing the purpose of the Nazi Party and the Nazi-dominated state, to eliminate the Jew, was to require a complete registration of all Jews. Inasmuch as the anti-Jewish policy was linked with the program of German aggression, such registration was required not only within the Reich, but successively within the conquered territories. For example, registration was required, by decree, within Germany (*Reichsgesetzblatt* Part I, 1938, page 922, 23 July, signed by Frick); within Austria (*Reichsgesetzblatt*, Volume 1, 1940, page 694, 29 April); within Poland (*Kurjer Krakowski*, 24 October, 1939); in France (*Journal Official* No. 9, page 92, 30 September, 1940); in Holland (*Verordnungsblatt*, No. 16, 10 January, 1941, signed by Seyss-Inquart).

B. *Segregation into Ghettos.*

The second step was to segregate and concentrate the Jews within restricted areas, called ghettos. This policy was carefully worked out, as is illustrated by the confidential statement taken from the files of Rosenberg (*212-PS*). This memorandum of Rosenberg's, entitled "Directions for Handling of the Jewish Question", states:

"The first main goal of the German measures must be strict segregation of Jewry from the rest of the population. In the execution of this, first of all, is the seizing of the Jewish population by the intro-

---

[36] *Nazi Conspiracy and Aggression*, vol. IV, 1946.

duction of a registration order and similar appropriate measures. . . .

* * * *

" . . . All rights of freedom for Jews are to be withdrawn. They are to be placed in ghettos and at the same time are to be separated according to sexes. The presence of many more or less closed Jewish settlements in White Ruthenia and in the Ukraine makes this mission easier. Moreover, places are to be chosen which make possible the full use of the Jewish manpower in case labor needs are present. These ghettos can be placed under the supervision of a Jewish self-government with Jewish officials. The guarding of the boundaries between the ghettos and the outer world, is, however, the duty of the Police.

"Also, in the cases in which a ghetto could not yet be established, care is to be taken through strict prohibitions and similar suitable measures that a further intermingling of blood of the Jews and the rest of the populace does not continue." (*212-PS*)

READING NO. 29

JEWS IN FORCED LABOR[37]

Jews were concentrated in forced labor columns by a decree of October 26, 1939, but the unplanned evacuations and uprooting of vast numbers precluded any rational or systematic use of Jewish labor. A half million Jews of the 1,500,000 (at the end of 1940) in the Government-General were technically eligible for labor, but the Germans made little productive use of them. Hans Frank, the administrator of the Government-General, wanted to make short shrift of this mass of Jews, squeezing food and property from them, and taking "measures which will lead, somehow, to their annihilation." His diary entries reveal his hatred and intent:

γ   γ   γ

FRANK DIARY, 1939,
from 25 October to 15 December
2233-G-PS

[Page 44].
. . . By spring 1,000,000 Poles and Jews from East and West Posen, Danzig, Poland and Upper Silesia must be received by the general government. The resettlement of the ethnic Germans and the taking on of Poles and Jews (10,000 daily) must be accomplished according to plan. Especially urgent is the instituting of *forced labor for the Jews*. The Jewish population if possible must be extracted from the Jewish cities and be put to *work on roads*. The critical question of housing and feeding are still to be cleared up. . . .

FRANK DIARY, 1940
Vol. IV, October-December
2233-C-PS

10/7/40
The Governor-General then addresses the assembly with the following words:
My dear Comrades!

[37] 2233-PS *Nazi Conspiracy and Aggression*, vol. IV, 1946.

. . . It would not be a bad idea then to send our dear ones back home a picture, and tell them: well now, there are not so many lice and Jews any more, and conditions here in the Government General have changed and improved somewhat already. Of course, I could not eliminate all lice and Jews in only one year's time. (public amused) But in the course of time, and above all, if you help me, this end will be attained. After all, it is not necessary for us to accomplish everything within a year and right away, for what would otherwise be left for those who follow us to do?

FRANK DIARY, 1951 Oct-Dec.
2233-D-PS

CABINET SESSION
Tuesday 16 December 1941 in the Government
Building at Krakow
Speech of the Governor General
Closing the Session

As far as the Jews are concerned, I want to tell you quite frankly, that they must be done away with in one way or another. The Fuenrer said once: should united Jewry again succeed in provoking a world-war, the blood of not only the nations, which have been forced into the war by them, will be shed, but the Jew will have found his end in Europe. . . . As an old National-Socialist, I must say: This war would only be a partial success, if the whole lot of Jewry would survive it, while we would have shed our best blood in order to save Europe. My attitude towards the Jews will, therefore, be based only on the expectation that they must disappear. They must be done away with.

READING NO. 30

DESTRUCTION OF JEWISH LABOR[38]

There was a continuous struggle between army and civilian officials on the one hand, and the German SS police, on the other, over the utilization of Jewish labor. Not only Jews, but the Wehrmacht *and civilian leaders, found the waste and destruction of this great reservoir of skilled labor incomprehensible:*

γ   γ   γ

These different ordinances . . . have destroyed the economic bases of Jewish life . . . The creation of a Jewish quarter right in the center of the city Warsaw ruthlessly split up important economic units. Prohibiting the crossing of this quarter caused losses in time and material. Two thousand Aryan businesses were moved out and 4,000 Jewish concerns were moved in. . . . Despite such complications and difficulties . . . the policy of the total expulsion of the Jews from economic life has been continued. . . . This, despite the fact that the civil administration could not deny that the Jew was practically irreplaceable in certain areas of economic life.''

---

[38] ''The War Economy in Poland, 1939–40,'' quoted in Leon Poliakov, *Harvest of Hate: The Nazi Program for the Destruction of the Jews of Europe.* Syracuse, New York, 1973, pp. 39–40.

READING NO. 31

THE LUBLIN RESERVATION[39, 40, 41]

From the beginning of their occupation of Poland, the Nazis used the district of Lublin in the southeastern part of the Government-General as an area in which to experiment with population shifts and upheavals. In the midst of numerous projects involving Germans and non-Jewish Poles, the deportation of Jews to Lublin could easily pass as another population transfer. There was, therefore, no suspicion at first that behind the mask of "resettlement" a very different plan was being prepared. The German propaganda machine publicized the idea of Lublin as a Jewish reservation, and in October 1939, thousands of Jews from Germany, Austria, and Poland began to arrive. Nothing, however, had been prepared for them. They found shelter in old dilapidated schools, barracks, warehouses and stables and when these gave out they suffered in the open fields:

γ   γ   γ

The haste with which the reservation has been established out of nothing is leading to desperate situations. Sometimes trains drive on for 40 kilometers beyond Lublin and halt in the open country, where the Jews alight and have to find themselves primitive accommodations in the surrounding villages. Up to November 10, about 45,000 Jewish men, women and children from Cieszyn, Bogumin, Moravska, Ostrava, Prague, Pilzno, other towns of the Protectorate and from Vienna and the new Reich provinces, Danzig-Westpreussen and Posen-Warthegau, have been sent to the reservation. Under the supervision of the men of the SS-Death's-head Corps, the Jews are compelled to work at road-building, draining marshes and rebuilding the damaged villages. There is compulsory labor service for men up to 70 years and for women up to 55.[39]

[39] Jacob Apenszlak, ed., *The Black Book of Polish Jewry*. New York, 1943, p. 236.
[40] Comer Clarke, *Eichmann: The Man and His Crimes*. New York, 1960, pp. 46–47.
[41] S. Moldawer, "The Road to Lublin," *Contemporary Jewish Record,* Vol. 3, March–April, 1940, p. 130.

* * * *

The following report was made by a Dutch national who saw two trainloads of Eichmann's captives pass through Breslau on their way East:

The sick, the aged and babies in arms were crushed into barred cattletrucks. From my train compartment I could see that the occupants were in a terrible state. The train was in a siding, and while we were held up by railway signals, I heard scores crying for help. One Jewish mother said she had been driven from her home in Vienna a week before and was kept with hundreds of others in a stockade outside the town until trucks took them to the railway yard for shipment. They had been aboard the train for two days and had only once received food. She said that some babies had suffocated in the crush and that the SS guards had even then forced in more people and then bolted the door. One or two children were still left over so they threw them in over the heads of those already there. The day was bitterly cold and what those poor people must have suffered at night is beyond comprehension. An old man told me the train stopped in open country once a day for twenty minutes and the doors opened for the captives to relieve themselves in the open fields. The stench was appalling and many of the occupants had been bilious. People were standing with their arms limply hanging through the slats of the wagons as if they were dead or half dead.[40]

* * * *

Among the firsthand accounts of Lublin was a report by a journalist from Leipzig who had the necessary papers for America and a ticket for a German liner, but was forbidden to sail in September 1939, put on a freight car and told that he was going "to the Jew-state Lublin." He survived in Lublin until November 15, when the American consul in Warsaw enabled him to leave:

Lublin is a vale of sorrow. No human beings are they who walk its streets; all are phantoms, shadows, haunting a world that is no longer in existence. Nobody speaks in Lublin; nobody exchanges greetings. They have even ceased to weep. . . . In normal times, Lublin has a population of 72,000 Gentiles and 40,000 Jews. Today [November 1939] the number of Jews cannot be computed, but it must run into at least 200,000, perhaps a quarter of a million. The congestion, the stench, the poverty, the disease and the chaos which reign in Lublin cannot be paralleled anywhere on earth. Men live in the streets, in cattle-stalls, in cellars, in carts and in the debris of devastated houses.[41]

READING NO. 32

THE SEALING UP OF THE WARSAW GHETTO, NOVEMBER 15, 1940[42, 43]

A ghetto for Warsaw Jews was proposed as early as November 4, 1939, but administrative conflicts beset German officials and ghettoization was deferred. However, Jews were registered, had to wear a Jewish star, could not visit certain streets, and could be arrested without warrant and carried off for any sort of work. Confiscation of Jewish property was swift and severe and earnings were limited to 500 zlotys per month—about $100. Newspapers and radios were confiscated. In December 1939 the Jewish Council was compelled to set up large wooden signs reading "Danger: Epidemic Zone," at 34 street corners. In the summer of 1940, before the ghetto was officially established, ten-foot walls were built separating the Jewish area from the rest of the city. This severance was justified as a quarantine measure, but it had a more sinister purpose. In September 1940, the 80,000 "Aryan" Poles still living within the "infected" area were ordered to move out, and on October 3, the ghetto was officially proclaimed. The wall measured eleven miles long, ten feet high and two bricks wide. It was covered with plaster and broken glass to prevent those inside from climbing out. The cost of building the wall was borne by the Jewish Council. And then came November 15, 1940:

γ   γ   γ

. . . the day that none of us will ever forget.

In the morning, as on every other, men and women set out on their way to work, storekeepers, employers, executives, most of whom worked in the non-Jewish section. As they came to the various points where thoroughfares and streets crossed from the Jewish section into the non-Jewish districts, they ran against barbed wire strung across and guarded by German police who were stopping all traffic out of the Jewish section. Hastily they tried other streets, avenues, alleys, only to find in every case barbed wire or a solid brick wall well guarded. There was no way out any more.

[42] Tosha Bialer, "Behind the Wall," *Collier's*, February 20, 1943, p. 17.
[43] Mark Edelman, *The Ghetto Fights*. New York, 1946, p. 4.

Quickly the news spread through the section. Other people came out of their houses and started to stare at the barricades, pathetically silent, stunned by the frightful suspicion that was creeping into their minds. Then, suddenly, the realization struck us. What had been, up till now, seemingly unrelated parts—a piece of wall here, a blocked-up house there, another piece of wall somewhere else—had overnight been joined to form an enclosure from which there was no escape.[42]

* * * *

. . . The walls and barbed wire surrounding the ghetto grew higher every day until, on November 15, they completely cut off the Jews from the outside world. Contacts with Jews living in other cities and towns were, naturally, also made impossible. For Jewish workers all possibilities of earning a living vanished. Not only all factory workers, but all those who had been working in "Aryan" enterprises, as well as government agencies, became unemployed. The typically wartime group of middlemen, tradesmen appeared. The great majority, however, left jobless, started selling everything that could possibly be sold, and slowly approached the depths of extreme poverty. The Germans, it is true, widely publicized their policy of "increasing the productive power of the ghetto," but actually they achieved the complete pauperization of the population. The ghetto population was increased by thousands of Jews evicted from neighboring towns. These people with practically nothing to their names, alone, in strange surroundings where others were preoccupied with their own difficulties, literally dying of malnutrition, tried to build their existence anew.[43]

READING NO. 33

JEWISH AUTONOMY—
A NAZI DECEPTION[44]

The Nazis used the term Jewish self-government to deceive Jews into thinking that, although isolated and ghettoized, they would be able to manage their lives, albeit under extremely adverse conditions, and thus survive. The reality was otherwise. Shmuel Zygelboim, a member of the Warsaw Jewish Council, escaped from the the ghetto, but left the following record of the first meeting of the council. (He later became a members of the Polish National Council in London and committed suicide in May 1943 after failing to obtain Allied help for the perishing Polish Jews.)

γ　　　　　γ　　　　　γ

The first meeting of the Judenrat took place in the middle of October. A Gestapo officer by the name of Mende came to the meeting and delivered a speech as if he were speaking to criminals. He ordered the Judenrat to stand while listening. He said that the fate of the Jews and of the Judenrat was in the hands of the Gestapo. The Judenrat is not to approach any other Nazi officer. No discussions. "The *Führer* law reigns here." What the Gestapo orders has to be executed promptly and meticulously, "not in the Jewish manner. . . ."

Three weeks after the appointment of the Judenrat in Warsaw, its members were suddenly called to an urgent meeting. It was on a Sabbath. At 12 o'clock Gestapo men came to the chairman and ordered him to call a meeting for 4 o'clock the same day. Out of the 24 members of the Judenrat only 16 could be located. With heavy hearts and grave thoughts we waited in the conference room of the Jewish community building. It was not the first time that the Gestapo had suddenly summoned us. Each time we had been faced with some new persecution order or with some obnoxious assignment which we refused to carry out. . . . At quarter past four the doors were abruptly forced open.

[44] From the *Zygelboim Book*, compiled by J. S. Herz, quoted in Nora Levin, *The Holocaust: The Destruction of European Jewry, 1933–45*. New York, 1973, pp. 213–214.

Gestapo men entered, rifles, pistols, and whips in their hands. They took up places in half-circle around us and looked at us with angry, evil eyes without saying a word. They appeared so unexpectedly, with such force and in such a terrifying manner that all sixteen people seated around the table jumped up. For a long time there was an agonizing, stifling stillness in the room. The Gestapo men, standing around, saying nothing, looked at each one of us, some artfully smiling, until one of them barked out in barracks-like tone: "All present?"

The chairman handed him the attendance list and the Gestapo man called out each member. . . . The roll call finished, the Gestapo men, taking along the chairman, went into the latter's office. After fifteen minutes, a Gestapo officer came out and said: "You listen and be careful! The Judenrat consists of 24 members and 24 alternates. Only 16 are present. I give you half an hour to fetch the others. Forty-eight Jews must be present. No discussion. . . . " After some deliberation it was decided that in order to produce the full contingent of the membership, we will enlist Jews from outside the Judenrat wherever we may find them. We called in all clerks of the Judenrat who were present in the building at the time, and a few Jews who happened to pass by the building and a few Jews from the Jewish funeral parlors which were located close by. A list of all those present, of whom more than half were included by sheer accident, was then submitted to the Gestapo officer. He then ordered that all assemble in the meeting hall and form two lines—one of the members of the Judenrat and the other of alternates.

Thus we stood for a long time, waiting until the door was thrust open once again and about 50 Gestapo men under the command of an officer entered the hall. All carried pistols or whips. . . .Finally, in a threatening, harsh voice the officer uttered: "Jews, you listen to me, and listen carefully! The commandant has ordered that all Jews of Warsaw must leave their present homes and move to the streets that have been designated for the ghetto, not later than Tuesday. To assure that the order is strictly carried out, all 24 alternates will be taken hostages. With their heads they are responsible for the exact execution of the order. You, the members of the Judenrat, are also responsible with your heads. We are not taking you away now simply because somebody must remain here to take care of the execution of the order." The 24 Jews, present only by accident, were then surrounded by the Gestapo men. Orders were shouted:

"About face, forward march" and they marched out. Outside, in the street, trucks were waiting and the Jews were carried away.

READING NO. 34

HUNGER AND DISEASE KILL JEWS IN THE GHETTOS[45, 46]

The Jewish Councils tried to alleviate hunger and disease, to provide shelter and work, and to organize a chaotic society, but they worked against impossible odds. The fear of German punitive measures was stark and the measures brutal. In April 1941, there was an official warning to the Warsaw Jewish Council threatening already diminished food supply, retaliatory raids and executions, if the council did not meet its labor quota. Over 43,000 Jews starved to death during the first year of the ghetto; 15,000 died of typhus in 1941. Famine conditions made smuggling a matter of life and death:

γ   γ   γ

In the beginning the penalty for smuggling food into the ghetto was six months in jail. Later it was increased to ten thousand zlotys and one year in jail. Then an order was issued making death the penalty for leaving the ghetto without authorization. Since most forms of smuggling required periodic visits to the ''Aryan'' side, this was a severe blow. Many were shot for smuggling food.

But hunger broke through all barriers. Smuggling was organized spontaneously on a large scale. It was carried on through various channels and by the most artful means. Along with the daring and cunning and the extraordinary improvisations operated one simple and powerful mechanism, bribery, which reached to the police of all varieties and the gendarmes of all ranks. So important were the operations of the smugglers that prices in the illegal ghetto market rose or fell depending on the results of the day's smuggling.

Children used to steal over to the ''Aryan'' side by digging holes under the walls or by hiding near the ghetto gates and sneaking through when the guard momentarily turned his back. Then they would make their way to an apartment, cautiously and timidly knock on the door, and with eloquent eyes beg for food. Occasionally they would get a crust of bread or a few potatoes. With their hard-earned treasure they

[45] Bernard Goldstein, *The Stars Bear Witness*. New York, 1949, pp. 75–77.
[46] Marek Edelman, *The Ghetto Fights*. New York, 1946, pp. 12–13.

would crawl back through breaks or chinks in the ghetto barrier. Parents would sit home all day nervously awaiting the return of their only breadwinner. In tears they would gulp the food brought at such great risk.[45]

* * * *

. . . In the meantime the terror within the ghetto kept increasing, while the ghetto's isolation from the outside world became more and more rigid. More and more people were being arrested for sneaking onto the "Aryan" side, and finally "special courts" were established. On February 12, 1941, seventeen people previously sentenced to death for illegal trespassing in the "Aryan section" lost their lives. The execution took place in the Jewish jail on Gęsia Street. At four A.M. shrill cries notified the neighborhood that "justice" was being meted out, that seventeen outcasts, including four children and three women, were being duly punished for leaving the ghetto in pursuit of a piece of bread or a few pennies. Cries from other jail cells could also be heard, the voices of future victims awaiting trial for the same offense, a total of seven hundred people.[46]

READING NO. 35

RESPONSIBILITIES OF JEWISH COUNCILS[47]

The cutting off of Jews in the ghettos from their former sources of living, homes, and familiar round of daily life, and their isolation from the outside world created wholly new tasks for the Jewish councils:

γ   γ   γ

It was necessary to organize trade and industry in the ghetto, set up a network for the rationing of food, which was available only in very limited supply, establish postal connections with the outside world in those ghettos in which postal services for the Jews had been cut off, obtain from the municipal census department the registration certificates of the ghetto inhabitants, handle domestic services (in some ghettos, such as the Lodz Ghetto, this included electricity and gas supplies), organize primary school education from which the Jews were barred, set up a medical service where necessary, provide social and medical assistance for the needy of the region and from outside it, etc.

There was no uniform number of departments in the administrative organization of the Jewish Councils in the various ghettos; the number varied according to the size of the community, the special requirements of the ghetto population, the economic structure of the ghetto and other local factors. It also depended on whether life in the ghetto was under the complete control of the administration staff, as it was at Lodz, where the individual was entirely dependent on the ghetto administration in everything determining his position and his conditions of living, or whether the individual was left with a slight possibility of exercising his own initiative and was not entirely subject to the Jewish Council. In any case, the uprooting of the Jews from their former municipal framework and the constantly increasing demands of the au-

---

[47] Isaiah Trunk, "The Organizational Structure of the Jewish Councils in Eastern Europe," *Yad Vashem Studies*, VII, 1968, pp. 151–152.

thorities were the objective reasons for the establishment of the large number of departments. The duties and importance of the various departments in the ghetto administration changed as changes occurred in the position of the ghetto and in the nature of the orders and demands of the authorities.

READING NO. 36

CULTURAL LIFE IN THE GHETTOS[48]

Despite the abnormal overcrowding, hunger, and disease in the ghettos, a very intense cultural life has been documented in many memoirs and diaries. Because educational and religious activity was forbidden in all of the ghettos at a certain time, it had to be carried on clandestinely, at risk of death. In June 1942, a month before the deportations, Dr. Emanuel Ringelblum, historian and founder of an important archive, wrote a long entry in his diary on the kinds of books people were reading. "We did not lose our human characteristics," he wrote; "our minds are as busy as they were before the war"—an exaggeration, undoubtedly, but an indication that some Jews at least were still able to read and distract themselves.

γ   γ   γ

Under the cloak of the children's kitchens and homes of CENTOS, a net of underground schools of various ideologies was spread . . .

The secular schools using Yiddish as the language of instruction were particularly active. They were organized by the unforgettable leaders Shakhne Zagan and Sonia Nowogrodzki, both of whom were led to their death in Treblinka . . .

Lively underground educational activities were conducted by almost all parties and ideological groups, particularly youth organizations. During almost the entire time in which the ghetto existed, an underground press issued newspapers, journals and miscellaneous volumes. . . .

Extensive educational activity among children and youth was conducted by the Central Organization for the Protection of Children and Orphans (CENTOS) under the leadership of . . . [Dr. Adolf Berman] and of the unforgettable Rosa Symchowitz (died of typhus contracted at her work with homeless children). With the aid of teachers, educators and artists, hundreds of children's programs were presented in dormitories, homes and clubs.

---

[48] Philip Friedman, *Martyrs and Fighters: The Epic of the Warsaw Ghetto*. New York, 1954, pp. 94, 95–96.

A central library for children was organized by . . . [Basia Temkin-Berman], a theatre under the direction of . . . [Bluma Fuswerk] with the cooperation of (four persons named) and others, courses in Yiddish language and literature. In connection with the activities of the "Children's Month" especially impressive programs were presented to which thousands of persons came to free themselves for a few hours from the pressure of reality and to pass the time with the children in a carefree way. Several hundred children from the CENTOS institutions and schools participated in these highly artistic productions. Today there are no more Jewish children left in Poland. Hitler's criminals murdered ninety-nine percent of the children.

A symphony orchestra under the able leadership of Szymon Pullman was active in the ghetto. Whenever an occasion was presented, concerts of beautiful orchestral and chamber music provided moments of rest and escape. Pullman and almost all the members of the orchestra including the violinist Ludwik Holcman were killed in Treblinka. The young concert master Marian Neuteich was murdered in the Trawniki camp. New talents appeared in the ghetto. The phenomenal young singer Marysia Ajzensztat, "the nightingale of the ghetto," daughter of the choir director of the Warsaw synagogue, shone like a meteor. She was murdered by the *S.S.* during the "liquidation campaign." Choirs were organized. Of especially high quality was the children's chorus under the direction of J. Fajwiszys. He was killed in the Poniatów camp. Other choir leaders like Gladstein, Zaks, and others were murdered in Treblinka. The Jewish artists and sculptors living in extreme poverty occasionally prepared exhibitions . . . All Jewish artists were put to death in Treblinka . . . This is all that we wanted to tell you, dear friends. Not many of us are still alive. . . .

Warsaw, March 1, 1944
Signed by Dr. E. Ringelblum and Adolf Berman

A week later, on March 7, 1944, Ringelblum, his wife, son, and thirty-five other persons hidden on the "Aryan" side were tortured and shot.

READING NO. 37

THE UNDERGROUND PRESS[49]

Except for a few secret radios and couriers who disguised themselves as "Aryans" and went from ghetto to ghetto bringing news, messages, and, occasionally arms, the ghettos were cut off from all outside sources of information. Rumors abounded and every scrap of hope and wishful thinking was fanned into fact. Under conditions in which it was impossible to validate reality, the Jewish underground press helped those readers who could obtain copies grasp their true situation. In the Warsaw ghetto, these crudely hectographed papers were published in Polish, Hebrew, and Yiddish:

γ   γ   γ

The function of the press derived mainly from its determination to strengthen Jewish resistance and the stamina of the masses in the face of the terrible repression to which the latter were subjected. Its object was also to give them faith that despite the persecution they were subjected to they could hold out and would yet see the overthrow of their enemies. Under the conditions obtaining in the Ghetto, when despair and apathy began to take root, the crumbs of consolation and encouragement which these clandestine broadsheets had to offer were important in raising the flagging spirits of the Jews.

The illegal youth publications fulfilled a special mission. These publications spoke to the hearts of its readers, strengthened them, and provided them with spiritual and intellectual guidance. Thus, to cite one example, the object of the "Yunge Gvardye" ('The Young Guard') was to encourage the youth that while it must continue its fight it must not neglect its education. The same can be said of the organ of Hashomer Hatzair, "Plomienie" ("Flames") and "El Al" (Upwards'), which fought depression and despair. With this object in view they called upon the young people to continue their studies and fostered the spirit of struggle and revolt. "Under the im-

[49] Joseph Kermish, "On the Underground Press in the Warsaw Ghetto," *Yad Vashem Studies* I, 1957, pp. 86, 96–97, 98–99. ("Instructions" from *Yugent Shtimme* No. 3, December 1940, p. 40.)

pact of our ideals the walls of apathy and servility will be breached,''
wrote ''Plomenie'' of 1st September, 1940. . . .

Practically all the periodicals published in the Warsaw Ghetto were
distributed among the Jewish masses and in the provincial towns, and
sometimes were surreptitiously introduced into the concentration
camps. In this variety of smuggling mostly Jewish couriers were engaged. A number of daring girls of the type of Tossia Altman, Frumke
Plotnitzka, Tema Shneiderman (Wanda Mayevska), Lea Kozibrod-
ska (Lonka), Chaika Grossman, Frania Beatus, Miriam Heinsdorf,
Chavka Follman and others, visited the closely-guarded ghettoes on
behalf of their organizations. Their journeys from Ghetto to Ghetto
with illegal material (mainly underground publications), sometimes to
distant places, despite the extreme personal risk involved and the necessity to smuggle across the borders of the various districts (such as
from Vilna to Bialystok, Bialystok to Warsaw, Warsaw to Kovel, etc.)
made possible communication and exchange of information between
the various Ghettoes . . .

*Even so, the danger of informers and untrustworthy readers required
special care in determining ''who is capable of being a reader,'' as
indicated in the following ''Instructions'':*

γ   γ   γ

1. Who is capable of being a reader? Not everyone is worthy of getting
   the ''Yugent Shtimme.'' Anyone receiving it must be well-known
   and reliable. He must not be unstable, confused or talkative. To distribute the paper indiscriminately would be an act of madness if not
   a crime.
2. Don't ask questions! Only you and the distributor of the paper know
   each other. No one else knows anything. You do not know from
   whom the distributor gets the paper. You must not know this and
   you must not ask.
3. Don't take notes! Do not write down any addresses. Always keep
   in mind that if you must note anything, you must do it in cypher.
   When you have done what is necessary, burn your notes.
4. Nobody else may take your place in receiving the paper and in passing it on. You must do it yourself, with your own hands. We have
   confidence in you.

5. Keep your house clean! Don't leave things to be done tomorrow. If you get the paper today, hand it on. Don't accumulate.

6. Don't talk! Talk as little as possible about the work of the organization. Many people are curious; some of them are paid for their curiosity. If by any chance you know the names of the active members, don't talk! Never mention a name, because by talking too much you may betray some one.

READING NO. 38

THE RINGELBLUM ARCHIVES
("*ONEG SHABBAT*")[50]

Ringelblum could have gone to Palestine from Geneva in August 1939, but decided to return to his home in Warsaw. After the fall of the city he devoted himself to relief activities and, as he wrote, "News came to me of every event affecting Jews in Warsaw and its suburbs . . . and the Polish provinces." At night he made notes of what he had seen and heard and in May 1940, he found a nucleus of workers to help him accumulate accounts of the unfolding experiences of Polish Jewry. Communal leaders among the refugees who had been expelled to Warsaw wrote histories of the towns and cities they had left. Monographs were written on religious life, relations with the Poles, labor camps, Jewish Councils, German atrocities, the diminishing economic life in the ghettoes. At first, the O.S. notes were written in an atmosphere of hope. Later, the work became a pure historical act, witness to the imminent annihilation. In the summer of 1942, during the massive deportations, preparations had been made to seal the materials in crates and bury them, and on August 3,

γ   γ   γ

they were buried at 68 Nowolipki and 34 Swietojerska. In the midst of the preparations, one of the workers, eighteen-year-old Naum Grzywacz wrote: "We have decided to describe the present time. Yesterday we sat up till late in the night, since we did not know whether we would survive till today. Now I am in the midst of writing, while in the streets the terrible shooting is going on. . . . Of one thing I am proud: that in these grave and fateful days, I was one of those who buried the treasure . . . in order that you should know of the tortures and murders of the Nazi tyranny."

His colleague, nineteen-year-old David Grober added:
"We must hurry, because we are not sure of the next hour. . . . I want the coming generations to remember our times. . . . With what ardor we dug the holes for the boxes . . . with what joy we received every

[50] Marek Edelman, *The Ghetto Fights*. New York, 1946, pp. 134–135.

bit of material. . . . How I would like to live to the moment when the treasure is dug out and the whole truth proclaimed. . . . But we certainly will not live to see it.''

Remarkably enough, one portion of the archives was found in rubber milk containers in the rubble of the ghetto in September 1946, and another portion in December 1950.

READING NO. 39

THE CHRONICLE OF LODZ GHETTO[51]

The Lodz Ghetto was the first ghetto in Poland to be enclosed and it became the one most hermetically sealed from the rest of the world. By May 1940, over 160,000 Jews were pushed into the slum quarter of the city, the Baluty area, and all Poles and ethnic Germans were forced to leave. The ghettoization process, outlined in Heydrich's Order of September 21, 1939, was followed remorselessly: the marking of Jews with a yellow star, confiscation of property, conscription into forced labor and the setting up of a Jewish Council. Periodically, Jews from other towns in Poland and Jews from Germany, Austria, and Czechoslovakia were brutally thrust into the Lodz Ghetto. The Chronicle *was composed in the Department of Archives, one of the sections in the large Ghetto Administration headed by the Eldest of the Jews, Mordecai Chaim Rumkowski. The Archives were known to the German authorities but the* Chronicle *was not, and entries were couched in language that was cautious and guarded. The authors had to be constrained by fear of discovery by the Germans who were in the Ghetto every day. They were also constrained in their references to and appraisal of the otherwise severely criticized, authoritarian Rumkowski.*

γ   γ   γ

The *Chronicle* was written by a group of men of different cultural and professional backgrounds and ages, but all were drawn together by the common experience of ghettoization and the desire to record that experience—the life of a Jewish community *in extremis . . .* Cukier, Hecht and Heilig died in the Ghetto; Kamieniecki, Rosenfeld, Singer, Zelkowicz and all but one of the archivist staff perished in the final liquidation of the Ghetto in August 1944.

The first entry in the *Chronicle* was written January 12, 1941 and continued almost every day until July 30, 1944, first in longhand, then typed. Altogether about 1000 entries or bulletins were produced, ranging from a half-page to ten or more pages. Until September 1, 1942, the *Chronicle* was written in Polish; after that time for a few months,

---

[51] N. Levin, Book Review, *Martyrdom and Resistance*, May–June, 1986.

it was written in Polish and German, and after December 1942, in German, by deportees from the West. Certain headings such as weather, births and deaths, shootings, suicides, food supplies and rations, public health and disease matters, news of the day, resettlements, inspections of the Ghetto, incidents of smuggling, and cultural events are frequently repeated, supplemented occasionally by more discursive articles and sketches. The tone of the entries is, in the main, straightforwardly factual, almost clinical. There is almost no interpretive analysis of the events recorded, but occasionally the dread, horror, and ghastliness of those events breaks out: "macabre lines of corpses awaiting burial"; "a horrendous rise in price of necessities"; resettlement actions causing "severe depressions in the ghetto"; "March [24, 1942] will long be remembered . . . From morning on, for twenty hours nonstop, processions of deportees headed on foot for Marysin"; " . . . now the eye has already grown accustomed to seeing spring-carriages pass loaded with people who are more dead than alive. Wrapped in rags, barely visible, they lie motionless on the wagons. Their blank gazes fixed on the sky, their faces bloodless and pale, hold a silent but terrible reproach to those who have remained behind"; "the despair of parents and other family members who had been parted from their brothers and sisters is beyond description."

Pervading the *Chronicle* are the urgent exhortations of Rumkowski to work, to work at all costs, and to be prepared for the consequences—resettlement—for not working.

As is well known, Rumkowski's sole solution to Nazi demands and the only salvation for Jews in the Lodz Ghetto was a highly productive work force, and although he succeeded in sustaining a remnant of Jews in the Lodz Ghetto longer than occurred in any other ghetto, he was a much hated man against whom vehement attacks have been leveled in many Holocaust sources—but not in the *Chronicle*. There he appears as an efficient, caring Chairman of the *Ältestenrat*, ruling a beseiged community along principles of law and order, who must obey the German overlords, and thus must himself be obeyed. . . .

Undoubtedly he enjoyed the power and honor, but, as Dr. Philip Friedman has noted, "he was also impelled by a profound feeling of historical mission, which only a chosen few merit and which he was obliged to fulfill." He was convinced, as were other Jews, that proper behavior, appropriate approaches, and, above all, work, would persuade the Nazis to come to a *modus operandi* with the Ghetto. The working remnant and Rumkowski himself exhausted themselves in struggling to live by his obsession, but the Nazis held to their plan for total annihilation. Rumkowski was, as a Lodz journalist put it, at the "wheel of a hell-ship." He was a vain man who wanted to be a surrogate father to orphans and deluded himself into thinking that he could be a Jewish savior.

READING NO. 40

THE COMPLICITY OF THE GERMAN ARMY IN MASS MURDER [52] [53]

On March 30, 1941, prior to the invasion of the Soviet Union, Hitler told 200 senior army officers that the coming campaign would be "more than a mere conflict; it is a collision between two different ideologies," necessitating the elimination of the "Bolshevist-Jewish intelligentsia" and Soviet officials, who, when captured, "were to be handed over to the Field Sections of the SD, or shot on the spot by the troops." In his dealing with the "hostile inhabitants," the German soldier need not be bound by the letter of the laws of war or military discipline. On the contrary, "any type of attack by the inhabitants against the Wehrmacht" *should be handled with the utmost severity, including summary execution. "German soldiers guilty of breaking international law . . . will be excused." Special operational units,* Einsatzgruppen, *were assigned "special Security Police tasks."*

The officers were shocked and some later admitted to having to "overcome scruples," but none protested. Hitler was determined to erase the boundary between military and ideological warfare. On June 6, the Commissar Order, signed by General Walter Warlimont, regarding the treatment of "political commissars," was followed by "operational orders" involving execution of "all important officials of the State and Party, "agitators and fanatical Communists," and "all Jews." Years of indoctrination of the Wehrmacht *regarding the "danger" of "Jewish Bolshevism" drew the army into collaboration with the* Einsatzgruppen. *At the beginning of October, von Reichenau, commander of the Sixth Army, who had already provided active support to the mass killings by Action Group C, issued the order concerning the "Conduct of Troops in the Eastern Territories," which was distributed to all army groups and armies:*

γ   γ   γ

---

[52] International Military Tribunal. *Trial of the Major War Criminals Before the International Military Tribunal,* XXXV, pp. 84–86.

[53] IMT XXXIV, pp. 129, 132.

In the Eastern Territories the soldier is not merely a combatant according to the rules of the art of warfare; he is also the harbinger of an unwavering racial concept and an avenger for all the bestialities inflicted upon the German and related nations. That is why the soldier must have total comprehension of the necessity of the harsh but just punishment meted out to Jewish sub-humanity. A further objective is to nip in the bud rebellions in the rear of the Wehrmacht which, as we know from experience, are invariably instigated by Jews . . . Far from all political considerations, the soldier is called upon to accomplish two goals: 1. The complete extermination of the Bolshevik heresy, the Soviet State and its armed forces. 2. The merciless annihilation of alien treachery and cruelty in order to safeguard the life of the German Wehrmacht in Russia. Only thus will we do justice to our historical task of freeing the German nation once and for all from the Asiatic-Jewish danger.

* * * *

General von Manstein, commander of the Eleventh Army, which operated in the Crimea, where Action Group D conducted mass executions, on November 20, 1941, called upon his soldiers to understand "the necessity of the harsh punishment of Jewry":

This struggle is not only being waged against the Soviet Armed Forces in the established manner laid down by European rules of warfare. Behind the front, too, the fighting continues . . . Jewry acts as the middle man between the enemy in rear and the still fighting remainder of the Red Army Forces and the Red leadership. More than in Europe, it holds all the key positions in the political leadership and administration, controls trades and guilds and, further, forms the nucleus for all unrest and uprising. The Jewish-Bolshevist system must be eradicated once and for all. Never again must it encroach upon our European *Lebensraum* . . .

READING NO. 41

MASS KILLINGS BY THE *EINSATZGRUPPEN*[54]

The Einsatzgruppen, *or special action units, were conceived by Heydrich as special strike forces for the political police (SS) and security intelligence (SD) in the invasion of Austria, Czechoslovakia, and Poland, to follow directly behind the advancing army. At first the army generals opposed their violation of army regulations and discipline, but by the time of the invasion of the Soviet Union, the army had succumbed to the primacy of the* Einsatzgruppen *in the annihilation program. Earlier, in Heydrich's September 21, 1939, order, the* Einsatzgruppen *chiefs were reminded that the "planned overall measures (i.e. the final aim) are to be kept strictly secret." Those measures were openly described and revealed as the* Einsatzgruppen *swept through the Soviet Union. The mass killing, as described by Ohlendorf, was repeated at countless sites:*

γ   γ   γ

In the implementation of this extermination program, the special commitment groups were subdivided into special commitment detachments, and the *Einsatzkommandos* into still smaller groups, the so-called Special Purpose Detachments [*Sonderkommandos*] and Unit Detachments [*Teilkommandos*]. Usually, the smaller units were led by a member of the S.D., the Gestapo or the criminal police. The unit selected for this task would enter a village or city and order the prominent Jewish citizens to call together all Jews for the purpose of resettlement. They were requested to hand over their valuables to the leaders of the unit, and shortly before the execution, to surrender their outer clothing. The men, women and children were led to a place of execution which in most cases was located next to a more deeply excavated anti-tank ditch. Then they were shot, kneeling or standing, and the corpses thrown into the ditch. I never permitted the shooting by individuals in the group D, but ordered that several of the men should shoot at the same time in order to avoid direct personal responsibility. The leaders

[54] Affidavit of Otto Ohlendorf, November 5, 1945, 2620-PS. *Nazi Conspiracy and Aggression*, vol. 5, 1946.

of the unit or specially designated persons, however, had to fire the last bullet against those victims that were not dead immediately. I learned from conversations with other group leaders that some of them demanded that the victims lie down flat on the ground to be shot through the nape of the neck. I did not approve of these methods.

READING NO. 42

LOSS OF JEWISH MANPOWER DEPLORED[55]

Economic considerations and armament needs were neglected or ignored in the single-minded obsession to destroy Jews. Prof. Seraphim wrote of his misgivings in a secret letter addressed to General Georg Thomas, Chief of the Industrial Armament Department, dated December 2, 1941:

γ   γ   γ

"For the personal information of the Chief of the Industrial Armament Department I am forwarding a total account of the present situation in the Reichskommissariat Ukraine in which the difficulties and tensions encountered so far and the problems which give rise to serious anxiety are stated with unmistakable clarity. . . .

"Jewish problem:

"Regulation of the Jewish question in the Ukraine was a difficult problem because the Jews constituted a large part of the urban population. . . . The majority of Jews remained under German administration. The latter found the problem more complicated through the fact that these Jews represented almost the entire trade and even a part of the manpower in small and medium industries besides the business which had in part become superfluous as a direct or indirect result of the war. The elimination therefore necessarily had far-reaching economic consequences and even direct consequences for the armament industry (production for supplying the troops)."

* * * *

"The attitude of the Jewish population was anxious—obliging from the beginning. They tried to avoid everything that might displease the German administration. That they hated the German administration and army inwardly goes without saying and cannot be surprising. However, there is no proof that Jewry as a whole or even to a greater part was implicated in acts of sabotage. Surely there were some terrorists or saboteurs among them just as among the Ukrainians. But it cannot be said that the Jews as such represented a danger to the

---

[55] 3257-PS, *Nazi Conspiracy and Aggression*, vol. V, 1946.

German armed forces. The output produced by Jews who, of course, were prompted by nothing but the feeling of fear, was satisfactory to the troops and the German administration.

"The Jewish population remained temporarily unmolested shortly after the fighting. Only weeks, sometimes months later, specially detached formations of the police executed a planned shooting of Jews. The action as a rule proceeded from east to west. It was done entirely in public with the use of the Ukrainian militia, and unfortunately in many instances also with members of the armed forces taking part voluntarily. The way these actions, which included men and old men, women, and children of all ages were carried out was horrible. The great masses executed make this action more gigantic than any similar measure taken so far in the Soviet Union. So far about 150,000 to 200,000 Jews may have been executed in the part of the Ukraine belonging to the Reichskommissariat; no consideration was given to the interests of economy.

"Summarizing, it can be said that the kind of solution of the Jewish problem applied in the Ukraine which obviously was based on the ideological theories as a matter of principle had the following results:

"(a) Elimination of a part of partly superfluous eaters in the cities.

"(b) Elimination of a part of the population which hated us undoubtedly.

"(c) Elimination of badly needed tradesmen who were in many instances indispensable even in the interests of the armed forces.

"(d) Consequences as to foreign policy—propaganda which are obvious.

"(e) Bad effects on the troops which in any case get indirect contact with the executions.

"(f) Brutalizing effect on the formations which carry out the execution—regular police."

READING NO. 43

THE DESTRUCTION OF
THE VILNA GHETTO[56]

*The 60,000 Jews of Vilna, known as the "Jerusalem of the East,"
were confined to a ghetto on September 6, 1941. Dina Abramovitz,
who worked in the ghetto library kept a diary:*

γ   γ   γ

1941

. . . We were segregated, set apart with yellow badges and with
barbaric regulations calculated to insure that everything human should
be forbidden to us. They began to exterminate us, individually, in
groups, en masse. We were thrown into the ghetto and the gates were
locked behind us. . . .

The Days of Awe arrived . . . We had premonitions . . . we
awaited something. . . .

With some other people of our house, we went up into the attic. A
great dark, cold attic with open windows. But this was ridiculous. It
was comic. They were already in the ghetto, the emissaries of death,
the Lithuanian troops with blue uniforms and red epaulettes; they went
everywhere and they would come here too. It is foolish, childish, to
hide from them in an open attic. . . . We climbed back down from the
attic. The house was deathly still. . . . But then there was some mur-
muring. Yes, now it grew clearer. Heavy footfalls on the stairs. They
were coming. Our neighbor, Rappaport, was a sick woman; she lay on
her table (there were no beds) and would not go anywhere; but not
everyone can be sick, we would have to go. Where were they taking
us, Ponar?* What should we take along? A slice of bread. And nothing
else? No clothing? . . .

One of them was an acquaintance—Wenig—a teacher in the Jewish
school, whose interesting talks on literature I used to attend with my
school chums or my father. He will surely recognize us and let us pass.
There are only two of us—my mother and I. The rest have gone ahead.

---

[56] Dina Abramovitz, "Yom Kippur, 1941–45: Memories of the Vilna Ghetto."
Jewish Frontier, January 1947, pp. 18, 19, 20.

* In English, Ponary—a mass execution site outside Vilna where about 70,000
Jews were murdered.

"Wenig, don't you recognize us? We cannot go, Mother is too weak."

"Yes, yes, but you cannot stay, you must go. Our heads will answer for it." . . . As we went forward the crowd grew thicker—a whole mass streaming through the narrow streets. Many were carrying bundles; a few, large packs. And here were uncle, aunt, and Georgie. Now we all walked together again with many of our friends, speaking in whispers. It was obvious we were being herded outside the ghetto. We were already near the gate on Rudnitzki Street. But it was nighttime and no one told the mass of men, women and children where we were going. It must be something horrible. Ponar, this thought flashed through all our minds. . . . A few suddenly vanished from the ranks. Where did they go to? . . . We went out, we were all standing pressed to the wall like shadows. And we saw the people push slowly through the gate, vanish forever.

People turned to look at us. Why are you standing there, we are all going. Lithuanian policemen noticed the stiff group, and one shoved mother so that she fell. We lifted her up. A young officer in a black uniform approached us. A German. He explained . . . that our refusal was senseless. The operation was being conducted under orders of the supreme German authority, which could not permit a Jewish ghetto to remain in the center of so large a town. . . .

Something happened elsewhere and his presence was demanded there. We stayed where we were. . . . We stood there for a while, unable to conceive at first that we were being let alone, and then began to work our way slowly back. We crawled into one gate, waited a while trembling, and then came into the street again. Files of people were still streaming toward the gate, but now there were more and more dark figures who emerged from secret holes and sprinted down the street in the opposite direction. Upon Disna Street we attached ourselves to such a group of "deserters from death" and together with them managed to get into a temporary "hide-out" (a hole somewhere covered over with a board) where we sat for about an hour listening to the sounds outside. . . . At length it was all quiet outside. We dared to creep out of the hole: the ghetto streets were empty, the first stage of the liquidation of the ghetto was completed. . . .

1942

YOM KIPPUR, 1942, came in late autumn, on a sunny day, but to the whistling of a keen, cold wind. We were freezing in our homes and in the shops where we worked. . . . I sat on a window-sill cramped between two long book-shelves, and tried to warm up a bit in a few stray rays of sun which found their way into the narrow shut-in streets of the ghetto. I can still see the view from that window: a dirty, crooked road like an alley in a small town. On the same street urchins; mothers straggling, tin can in hand, to the communal kitchen for a portion of thin soup for their children; and the most wretched of the wretched— the old, once someone's mothers and fathers, grandmothers and grandfathers, now illegal, scarcely tolerated burdens on the ghetto. . . .

1943

The nightmare of a liquidation period occurred. . . . Jews expelled from the Vilna ghetto were assembled by the Germans in the ravines of the mission monastery on Subac in order to be sorted. . . . In the damp ravines of the cloister, near the artificial fish pond which the monks had excavated, we sat a day and a night under a cold, penetrating autumn rain. The next day about noon we were ordered to rise and march out. We had to climb quickly, loaded with heavy packs, up a steep clayey hillside. There was shoving and haste to bring us the sooner to our end, but many remained behind, unable to climb up . . .

On Yom Kippur of 1943, the Vilna ghetto and the Vilna Jews no longer existed. There remained only a small group of Jews in the block of the furriers and in the HKP block (another German unit which still needed Jewish workers). The train depot of the city of Vilna bore the inscription *"Judenrein."*

I had had enough. I was ready to escape at any price, preferring death on the platform to reliving again the death-agonies of the ghetto in miniature. I jumped off the train in which we were to be brought to Riga while it was passing through the furriers' block. The train rolled by. I will always have a nightmare-sharp impression of that human ant heap, stirred up, confused, driven to madness by fear of death. . . .

READING NO. 44

THE DESTRUCTION OF THE RIGA GHETTO[57]

Riga, the capital of Latvia, one of the oldest and most distinguished Jewish centers in Eastern Europe, and where, ironically, most Jews spoke German and admired German culture, was invaded by the German army on July 1, 1941. Its Jewish population of 40,000 was quickly liquidated:

γ   γ   γ

. . . The Latvians made the Germans' job an easy one by committing unbelievable atrocities against the Jews. Many Latvians even joined the SS, so as to be part of the German machine. . . .

One week after having arrived in the city, *Einsatzgruppe A* organized a pogrom in Riga. Pictures were taken to show how the natives took self-cleaning actions. The Central Jail and the Riga Police Prefecture, presided over by Roberts Stiglics, became the site of brutal murders. The *Perkonkrusti*, a Latvian fascist organization, under the leadership of Victor Arajs, murdered at least two-thousand Jews during July alone, concentrating on the well-to-do, so as to confiscate their property. In the Great Synagogue of Riga, a gang led by that same Victor Arajs and Herbert Cukurs, burnt several hundred Jews alive. The press in Riga also did its best to encourage the populace in their hatred against Jews. Articles referred to Jews as ''destroyers of the nation'' and asked for their death.

By October 25, 1941, all Jews living in Riga were contained within the ghetto, located in the dilapidated Moscow suburb. 33,000 people lived in a space big enough for perhaps a third of that number and the fear of epidemics was therefore great. The able-bodied men and women went to work. They were badly needed by the enormous war machinery. . . .

While there were enough doctors, there was only very little in the way of medication, and there was much trepidation about the coming winter when diseases would be rampant. The Jews need not have worried: The ghetto lasted only thirty-seven days.

[57] Gertrude Schneider, ''The Jews of Riga,'' *Jewish Frontier*, March, 1975, pp. 17–19.

On November 27 they were notified that they would be resettled and they were told to assemble by November 29 for that purpose. Already the previous evening, their ghetto had been made smaller by herding them closer together. The Latvian SS, led by Herbert Cukurs, and the German SS, led by *Sturmbannfuehrer* Dr. Rudolf Lange, swarmed into the streets and terrorized the inmates. Children were thrown out of windows, women and older people were massacred, and over 15,000 were forced to walk toward the Rumbula forest. There, graves had been prepared by Soviet prisoners. The victims were told to disrobe and slowly, over a period of several days, they were exterminated. On their way to the forest, in spite of being closely guarded, one nameless victim managed to write a little note, later found and brought back into the ghetto. It said ''don't forget us—take vengeance'' and it was this note which prompted the Latvian Jew Max Kaufmann to write *''The Destruction of Latvian Jewry''* once the war was over.

In the ghetto, meanwhile, the remaining Jews had cleared the streets and apartments of corpses and had buried them in the old cemetery. The next day it was back to work as usual. The carnage was repeated in almost the same way on December 8; the victims were once more herded towards the forest, and while the Germans provided expert guidance, it was the Latvians who did the ''dirty'' work. At his trial after the war, *Obergruppenfuehrer Friedrich Jeckeln*, who was attached to all the *Einsatzgruppen* with his mobile killing units, credited the Latvians with ''strong nerves for executions of this sort.'' . . . Dr. Stahlecker, the head of *Einsatzgruppe A*, estimated that about 28,000 had been finished off; he includes a transport of one thousand Jews from Berlin, who left that city on November 27, and arrived just in time to share the fate of their Latvian brethren.

READING NO. 45

EVIDENCE OF THE BABI YAR MASSACRES[58]

One day in March 1942, Blobel and a Gestapo companion, Albert Hartel, were driving in the vicinity of Babi Yar. Hartel noticed an unusual shaking of the earth's surface and expressed astonishment. Blobel knew the cause and said with considerable pride, ''Here my Jews are buried.'' The movement had been set off by gases chemically released from the decaying corpses of the thousands who had been murdered. By the summer, Himmler was concerned about the problem of exposure of the massacres to the world. A special unit under Blobel was ordered to erase the traces of the Einsatzgruppen executions. He formed a special unit to dig up the bodies and burn them and at first used dynamite at Chelmo. But this method was not successful. He then tried constructing vast pyres of iron rails and wooden sleepers. At Babi Yar, in August 1943:

γ   γ   γ

The task force dug up the entire area, and selected commandos examined each corpse for rings, earrings and gold teeth—the potential evidence that was carefully removed.

Huge, wooden crematoria were built. The decaying bodies and skeletons were stacked alternately with logs and doused with gasoline in large pyres. Each took two nights and one day to burn. The bones that remained were crushed, mixed with earth and scattered over the area. The blazing fires lasted almost six weeks, the stench saturating and polluting the entire region.

But the evidence could not be suppressed. Disclosures of a hidden eyewitness, revelations of a survivor, captured Einsatzgruppen records first made public at the Nuremberg war-criminal trials of 1947–48, and the fourteen-month trial of ten Babi Yar killers in the Federal Republic of Germany, beginning in October 1967, all focused a glaring searchlight upon the extraordinary horror of this frenzied act of savagery . . .

The massive crime of Babi Yar was first brought to light in a Soviet Foreign Ministry memorandum dated January 6, 1942, and made available to Western allies, but information was extremely limited. A

[58] William Korey, ''Forty Years Ago at Babi Yar: Reliving the Crime,'' *Present Tense, Autumn 1981*, pp. 27–28, 30.

fuller account was prepared in the postwar period by a state Special Commission headed by Nikita Khrushchev. A fictional version of the Babi Yar episode, partly based on official information, appeared in Ilya Ehrenburg's *The Storm*, published in 1947, which won the Stalin Prize. A wealth of information about Babi Yar, drawn from Soviet sources appears in the documentary novel *Babi Yar*, written by Anatoly Kuznetsov and published in a three-part monthly serial form in the journal, *Yunost'*, beginning in August 1966.

The Nuremberg trials of 1947–1948 provided a more detailed account of the *Einsatzgruppen* operations in Kiev and elsewhere, when the court imposed the death sentence on Colonel Paul Blobel (executed in 1951) and other *Einsatzgruppen* leaders.

The most elaborate documentation of the Babi Yar massacre was presented in Courtroom 214 of the district court building in Darmstadt, the capital of the West German province of Hesse. Three judges sat here every Monday and Tuesday, beginning on October 2, 1967 and continuing for 14 months. Testimony was given by 175 witnesses concerning the crimes of eleven surviving apprehended members of Einsatzgruppe C, Sonderkommando 4A. One of the defendants died during the proceedings. The remaining ten were convicted and sentenced to long prison terms.

READING NO. 46

MASS KILLINGS IN THE BALTIC STATES AND WHITE RUSSIA[59]

"Indispensability" of skilled Jewish workers was not a valid enough reason to stop killing them:

γ γ γ

TOP SECRET
[Geheime Reichssache]
SPECIAL PURPOSE GROUP "A"
[Einsatzgruppe A]

* * * *

III
Jews

The systematic mopping up of the Eastern Territories embraced, in accordance with the basic orders, the complete removal if possible, of Jewry. This goal has been substantially attained—with the exception of White Russia—as a result of the execution up to the present time of 229,052 Jews (see Appendix). The remainder still left in the Baltic Provinces is urgently required as labour and housed in Ghettos . . .

Einsatzgruppe A did not take over this area [White Russia] until after the heavy frost had set in, which made mass executions much more difficult. A further difficulty is that the Jews live widely scattered over the whole country. In view of the enormous distances, the bad conditions of the roads, the shortage of vehicles and petrol and the small forces of Security Police and SD, it needs the utmost effort in order to be able to carry out shootings in the country. Nevertheless 41,000 Jews have been shot up to now. This number does not include those shot in operations by the former Einsatzkommandos. From estimated figures about 19,000 partisans and criminals, that is in the majority Jews, were shot by the Armed Forces [Wehrmacht] up to December 1941. At the moment approximately 128,000 Jews must still be reckoned with in the area of the Commissariat-General. In Minsk itself—exclusive of

[59] 2273-PS, *Nazi Conspiracy and Aggression*, vol. IV, 1946.

Reich Germans—there are about 1,800 Jews living, whose shooting must be postponed in consideration of their being used as labour.

The Commander in White Russia is instructed to liquidate the Jewish question as soon as possible, despite the difficult situation. However a period of about 2 months is still required—according to the weather.

The shutting up of all the remaining Jews in special Ghettos is also almost completed in the towns in White Russia too. They will be used for work to the fullest extent by the authorities of the Armed Forces, the Civil Administration and German Authorities.

The feeding of the Jews in the Ghettos causes considerable difficulty, especially in White Russia but also in Lithuania. Together with the general decrease in working capacity, there is increased susceptibility to all contagious diseases.

READING NO. 47

SOVIET SILENCE ABOUT NAZI ATROCITIES[60]

A German intelligence report of July 12, 1941, reveals a German officer's astonishment:

γ   γ   γ

The Jews are remarkably ill-informed about our attitude toward them. They do not know how Jews are treated in Germany, or for that matter, in Warsaw, which after all is not so far away . . . Even if they do not think that under German administration they will have equal right with the Russians, they believe, nevertheless, that we shall leave them in peace if they mind their business and work diligently.

---

[60] *Reichskommissar Ostland* to *General-kommissar* White Russia, August 4, 1941, enclosing report by Sonderführer Schröter, OCC E 3a-2, in R. Hilberg, *The Destruction of the European Jews.* Chicago, 1961, p. 207.

READING NO. 48

GÖRING'S ORDER TO HEYDRICH TO PLAN THE "FINAL SOLUTION"[60]

Having exhausted emigration and "evacuation" measures, and having set in motion the mobile killing units in the Soviet Union, Heydrich could now mobilize all forces necessary to completely eliminate Jews under German control:

γ   γ   γ

The Reich Marshal of the Greater German Reich
Commissioner for the Four Year Plan
Chairman of the Ministerial Council for National Defense
Berlin, 31 July 1941
To: The Chief of the Security Police and the Security Service; SS-Gruppenfuehrer Heydrich

Complementing the task that was assigned to you on 24 January 1939, which dealt with the carrying out of emigration and evacuation, a solution of the Jewish problem, as advantageous as possible, I hereby charge you with making all necessary preparations in regard to organizational and financial matters for bringing about a complete solution of the Jewish question in the German sphere of influence in Europe.

Wherever other governmental agencies are involved, these are to cooperate with you.

I charge you furthermore to send me, before long, an overall plan concerning the organizational, factual and material measures necessary for the accomplishment of the desired solution of the Jewish question.

signed: GOERING

---

[60] 710-PS, *Nazi Conspiracy and Aggression*, vol. III, 1946.

READING NO. 49

GAS VANS[61]

Killing by gas vans represented a "great ordeal" for the Einsatzgruppen, *according to Ohlendorf, because of the distorted faces and
excretions of the victims, who had to be buried. Furthermore, the gas
vans could kill only fifteen to twenty-five persons at one time, a rate
entirely inadequate for the scale Himmler had ordered. A description
of the operation of the gas vans was set forth in a captured Top Secret
document dated May 16, 1942, addressed to SS Obersturmbannführer
Rauff, 8 Prince Albrect-Straase, Berlin, from Dr. Becker, SS Unter-
sturmführer:*

γ   γ   γ

"The overhauling of vans by groups D and C is finished. While the
vans of the first series can also be put into action if the weather is not
too bad, the vans of the second series (*Saurer*) stop completely in rainy
weather. If it has rained for instance for only one half hour, the van cannot be used because it simply skids away. It can only be used in absolutely dry weather. It is only a question now whether the van can only
be used standing at the place of execution. First the van has to be
brought to that place, which is possible only in good weather. The
place of execution is usually 10 to 15 km away from the highways and
is difficult of access because of its location; in damp or wet weather it
is not accessible at all. If the persons to be executed are driven or led to
that place, then they realize immediately what is going on and get rest-
less, which is to be avoided as far as possible. There is only one way
left; to load them at the collecting point and to drive them to the spot.
I ordered the vans of group D to be camouflaged as house-trailers by
putting one set of window shutters on each side of the small van and
two on each side of the larger vans, such as one often sees on farm
houses in the country. The vans became so well-known, that not only
the authorities but also the civilian population called the van 'death
van', as soon as one of these vehicles appeared. It is my opinion the
van cannot be kept secret for any length of time, not even camouflaged."

[61] 501-PS *Nazi Conspiracy and Aggression,* vol. III, 1946.

* * * *

"Because of the rough terrain and the indescribable road and highway conditions the caulkings and rivets loosen in the course of time. I was asked if in such cases the vans should be brought to Berlin for repair. Transportation to Berlin would be much too expensive and would demand too much fuel. In order to save those expenses I ordered them to have smaller leaks soldered and if that should no longer be possible, to notify Berlin immediately by radio, that Pol.Nr. is out of order. Besides that I ordered that during application of gas all the men were to be kept as far away from the vans as possible, so they should not suffer damage to their health by the gas which eventually would escape. I should like to take this opportunity to bring the following to your attention: several commands have had the unloading after the application of gas done by their own men. I brought to the attention of the commanders of those S.K. concerned the immense psychological injuries and damages to their health which that work can have for those men, even if not immediately, at least later on. The men complained to me about headaches which appeared after each unloading. Nevertheless they don't want to change the orders, because they are afraid prisoners called for that work, could use an opportune moment to flee. To protect the men from those damages, I request orders be issued accordingly.

"The application of gas usually is not undertaken correctly. In order to come to an end as fast as possible, the driver presses the accelerator to the fullest extent. By doing that the persons to be executed suffer death from suffocation and not death by dozing off as was planned. My directions now have proved that by correct adjustment of the levers death comes faster and the prisoners fall asleep peacefully. Distorted faces and excretions, such as could be seen before, are no longer noticed.

"Today I shall continue my journey to group B, where I can be reached with further news.

"Signed: Dr. Becker, SS Untersturmfuehrer."

A letter signed by Hauptsturmfuehrer Truehe on the subject of S-vans, addressed to the Reich Security Main Office, Room 2-D-3-A, Berlin, and marked "Top Secret," establishes that the vans were used for the annihilation of the Jews. The message reads:

A transport of Jews, which has to be treated in a special way, arrives weekly at the office of the commandant of the Security Police and the Security Service of White Ruthenia. The three S-vans which are there are not sufficient for that purpose. I request assignment of another S-van (five tons). At the same time I request the shipment of twenty gas hoses for the three S-vans on hand (two Diamond, one Saurer), since the ones on hand are leaky already.

(signed) The Commandant of the Security Police and the Security Service, ''Ostland.'' (*501-PS*))

READING NO. 50

THE WANNSEE CONFERENCE, JANUARY 20, 1942[62]

On July 31, 1941, six weeks after the invasion of the Soviet Union and the first killing sweeps of the Einsatzgruppen, *Göring gave Heydrich absolute power to organize the "Final Solution" of the Jewish Question. Soon after Heydrich received this communication, Eichmann was summoned to Heydrich's office in Berlin and was told that "The Führer has ordered the physical extermination of the Jews." Eichmann was told to see Globocnik in Lublin, who was ordered to liquidate a quarter of a million Polish Jews. Meanwhile, Himmler told Rudolf Höss, commandant of Auschwitz, that his camp was to become an important death center. Heydrich now wanted to assure the cooperation of all government agencies and coordinate the necessary details. For this purpose the Wannsee Conference was called:*

γ   γ   γ

Secret Reich Business!
Protocol of Conference

I   The following took part in the conference on the final solution of the Jewish question held on January 20, 1942, in Berlin, Am Grossen Wannsee No. 56–58:

Gauleiter Dr. Meyer and Reich Office Director Dr. Leibbrandt	Reich Ministry for the Occupied Eastern Territories
Secretary of State Dr. Stuckart	Reich Ministry of the Interior
Secretary of State Neumann	Plenipotentiary for the Four Year Plan
Secretary of State Dr. Freisler	Reich Ministry of Justice
Secretary of State Dr. Bühler	Office of the Governor General
Undersecretary of State Luther	Foreign Office
SS Oberführer Klopfer	Party Chancellery

[62] Minutes of Wannsee Conference, January 20, 1942. NG-2586-G. *Trials of War Criminals Before the Nuremberg Military Tribunals,* XIII, Washington, D.C., 1952, pp. 210–11, 218–19.

Ministerial Director Kritzinger	Reich Chancellery
SS Gruppenführer Hofmann	Race and Settlement Main Office
SS Gruppenführer Müller	Reich Security Main Office
SS Obersturmbannführer Eichmann	
SS Oberführer Dr. Schöngrath, Commander of the Security Police and the SD in the Generalgouvernement	Security Police and SD
SS Sturmbannführer Dr. Lange, Commander of the Security Police and the SD in the General District of Latvia, as representative of the Commander of the Security Police and the SD for the Reich Commissariat for the Ostland	Security Police and SD

II   At the beginning of the meeting the Chief of the Security Police and the SD, SS Obergruppenführer *Heydrich,* announced his appointment by the Reich Marshal, as Plenipotentiary for the Preparation of the Final Solution of the European Jewish Question, and pointed out that this conference had been called to clear up fundamental questions. The Reich Marshal's request to have a draft sent to him on the organizational, substantive, and economic concerns on the final solution of the European Jewish question necessitates prior joint consideration by all central agencies directly concerned with these questions, with a view to keeping policy lines parallel.

Primary responsibility for the handling of the final solution of the Jewish question, the speaker stated, is to lie centrally, regardless of geographic boundaries, with the Reichsführer SS and the Chief of the German Police (Chief of the Security Police and the SD).

The Chief of the Security Police and the SD then gave a brief review of the struggle conducted up to now against this enemy. The most important aspects are:

a. Forcing the Jews out of the various areas of life of the German people;

b. Forcing the Jews out of the living space of the German people. . . .

Since then [October 31, 1941,] in view of the dangers of emigration during wartime and in view of the possibilities in the East, the Reichsführer SS and Chief of the German Police has forbidden the emigration of Jews.

III   Emigration has now been replaced by evacuation of the Jews to the East as a further possible solution, in accordance with previous authorization by the Führer.

However, these actions are to be regarded only as provisional options; even now practical experience is being gathered that is of major significance in view of the coming final solution of the Jewish question. . . .

In connection with this final solution of the European Jewish question, approximately 11 million Jews may be presumed to be affected.[5] They are distributed among the individual countries as follows:

Country	Number
A. Altreich	131,800
Ostmark	43,700
Eastern Territories	420,000
Generalgouvernement	2,284,000
Bialystok	400,000
Protectorate of Bohemia & Moravia	74,200
Estonia—free of Jews	
Latvia	3,500
Lithuania	34,000
Belgium	43,000
Denmark	5,600
France: Occupied territory	165,000
Unoccupied territory	700,000
Greece	69,600
The Netherlands	160,800
Norway	1,300
B. Bulgaria	48,000
England	330,000
Finland	2,300
Ireland	4,000
Italy, including Sardinia	58,000
Albania	200

Croatia		40,000
Portugal		3,000
Rumania, including Bessarabia		342,000
Sweden		8,000
Switzerland		18,000
Serbia		10,000
Slovakia		88,000
Spain		6,000
Turkey (European part)		55,500
Hungary		742,800
U.S.S.R.		5,000,000
Ukraine	2,994,684	
White Russia, excluding	446,484	
Bialystok		
TOTAL	over	11,000,000

. . . Under appropriate direction, in the course of the final solution, the Jews are now to be suitably assigned to labor in the East. In big labor gangs, with the sexes separated, Jews capable of work will be brought to these areas, employed in roadbuilding, in which task a large part will undoubtedly disappear through natural diminution.

The remnant that may eventually remain, being undoubtedly the part most capable of resistance, will have to be appropriately dealt with, since it represents a natural selection and in the event of release is to be regarded as the germ cell of a new Jewish renewal. (Witness the experience of history.)

In the course of the practical implementation of the final solution, Europe is to be combed through from west to east. The Reich area, including the Protectorate of Bohemia and Moravia, will have to be handled in advance, if only because of the housing problem and other socio-political necessities.

The evacuated Jews will first be brought, group by group, into so-called transit ghettos, to be transported from there farther to the East.

An important prerequisite for the implementation of the evacuation as a whole, SS Obergruppenführer *Heydrich* explained further, is the exact determination of the category of persons that may be affected.

The intent is not to evacuate Jews over 65 years of age, but to assign them to a ghetto for the aged. Theresienstadt is under consideration.

Along with these age groups (of the approximately 280,000 Jews who on October 31, 1941, were in the Altreich and the Ostmark, approximately 30 per cent are over 65 years old), Jews with serious wartime disabilities and Jews with war decorations (Iron Cross, First Class) will be taken into the Jewish old-age ghettos. With this efficient solution, the many interventions . . . will be eliminated at one stroke.

The beginning of each of the large evacuation actions will depend largely on military developments. With regard to the handling of the final solution in the European areas occupied by us and under our influence, it was proposed that the appropriate specialists in the Foreign Office confer with the competent official of the Security Police and the SD . . . [The specific situations in various countries of Europe are noted.]

IV   In the implementation of the final-solution program, the Nuremberg Laws are to form the basis, as it were; and in this context, a solution of the questions concerning mixed marriages and *Mischlinge* is a precondition for complete settlement of the problem. . . . [Treatment of *Mischlinge* and intermarried follows. Dr. Stuckart recommended compulsory sterilization.]

Secretary of State D. *Bühler* stated that the Generalgouvernement would welcome it if the final solution of this problem *were begun in the Generalgouvernement*. . . . He had only one request, he said: that the Jewish question in this territory be solved as quickly as possible . . . Dr. *Meyer* and Secretary of State Dr. *Bühler* took the position that certain preparatory tasks connected with the final solution should be performed right in the territories concerned, but that, in doing so, any alarm among the population must be avoided.

With a request by the Chief of the Security Police and the SD to the conference participants that they afford him appropriate support in carrying out the tasks connected with the solution, the conference was concluded.

READING NO. 51

RELIGIOUS RESISTANCE[63]

The Nazis aimed at erasing Judaism as well as Jews and, therefore, prohibited religious prayer and study as soon as local officials began to implement the policy of physical annihilation. Many Jews in camps and ghettos were killed after they were discovered at prayer. Others found momentary solace by transcending the brutality and degradation through spiritual uplift:

γ   γ   γ

"I remember," tells a witness, "how on Friday nights we would assemble in a barracks that was filled with 'beds' three tiers high. In the beds lay people with typhus and other diseases; all were hungry, suffering, and fearing for their lives daily. In conditions that defy all description, Goslar would sit on one of the upper bunks and speak to us about Sabbath rest, about the joy of Sabbath, about the holiness of Sabbath. True, we were far removed from any Sabbath rest; we were forced to toil on the Sabbath as any other day of the week. But we were listening to the words of Goslar who spoke to us with a face shining with the light from another world, his voice ringing with the trust of a steadfast faith, entirely transfigured by a great joy, we forgot our gruesome state and on the wings of his inspiring words we were transposed to the tables in our fathers' houses on the Sabbaths and Holy Days of times gone by . . . Goslar raised us from the depths of filth and defilement to the heights of faith, of joy, holiness and rest . . . Often we would burst out into the traditional Sabbath *Zemirot* (table songs). Though our voices were subdued because of the guards, yet we sang with trembling, and how happy we were!"

[63] Eliezer Berkovits, *With God in Hell.* New York, 1979, pp. 15–16.

READING NO. 52

CULTURAL LIFE IN THERESIENSTADT[64, 65]

A rich supply of talent was available in many ghettos, but artistic and musical activity was especially noteworthy in Theresienstadt among the children as well as adults. There were lectures, courses, debating and drama groups, wall newspapers, and musical programs. One instructor recalled:

γ   γ   γ

We took every opportunity to celebrate the Festivals. We wanted to give the children some way to cast a few rays of light on their drab life. Not only were the lessons given around the theme of the approaching Festival, but its special atmosphere was captured through decorating the house and the like. In addition to the celebrations held by each house alone, the children of these houses put on plays they had written for all the children in the Ghetto. They would be very excited about their performances and would carry out their rehearsals meticulously and with the utmost patience. We considered the presentation of plays on the stage of special importance because it gave the children a momentary escape from every day reality . . .

"While many of the Czech houses had Christmas trees at Christmas, we lit Hanukah candles in our houses. For eight days we carried out a programme full of joy and seriousness . . . The main attraction of the plays of our house was 'Mary Stuart' which was rehearsed over a long period and was a great success, even though it was presented by children who had never been to a theatre in their life. During the 'reception' for the artists after the play, the actors were given enough food to stay their hunger for the first time since they entered the Ghetto. . . .

* * * *

"By giving the children of the Ghetto an education," Mr. Schmiedt writes, "the inmates gave expression to the spiritual revolt against the

---

[64] Quoted in Shlomo Schmiedt, "Hechalutz in Theresienstadt: Its Influence and Educational Activities," *Yad Vashem Studies*, VII, 1968, p. 120.

[65] *Ibid.*, p. 119.

German oppressors who forbade all teaching activity. The teachers were required to adopt various stratagems in order to circumvent this prohibition. In some houses, history, geography and even mathematics were studied with the aid of playing cards made in the Ghetto. While lessons were in progress one child stood on guard outside the building, while another was posted outside the classroom door. Whenever anyone in uniform approached, the boy on guard informed the instructor immediately. As soon as the signal was given the children hid their execise books or the papers they had been using and the teacher "continued" reading them a story from a book ready at his side for the purpose.

READING NO. 53

DR. EZEKIEL ATLAS, DOCTOR-FIGHTER IN WHITE RUSSIA[66]

When the war broke out, Dr. Ezekiel Atlas fled with his parents and sister to Lvov, then Slonim, where he worked as a doctor. In the spring of 1942, Germans massacred Jews in the area and Atlas' parents and sister were killed. Atlas was spared because he was useful to the Germans as a doctor. In the village of Wielka-Wolia, in a dense forest, he also treated peasants and learned that some Soviet soldiers who had refused to surrender were still in hiding. Atlas contacted them and provided them with arms, secured from the peasants:

γ   γ   γ

When the war broke out, he fled with his parents and a younger sister to Lvov, then occupied by the Russians, and later to Slonim, where he worked as a doctor. He also worked in the hospital of the neighboring town of Kozlowszczyna. In the spring of 1942, the Germans massacred the Jews here and Atlas' parents and sister were killed. The Germans spared Atlas only because they needed doctors; he was immediately transferred to the village of Wielka-Wolia in an area of dense forests. Peasants from the entire district came to Atlas to be treated. From them, the young physician learned that some Russian soldiers who refused to surrender were still hiding in the forests. Atlas contacted them and provided them with arms, which he secured from the peasants, as well as medical care.

The soldiers asked Atlas to join them but he had resolved to go into the woods only if he could take Jews with him. On July 24, 1942, the ghetto of the little town of Dereczyn in the area was wiped out. About 300 men, women and children succeeded in escaping, some of them reaching Atlas in Wielka-Wolia. Atlas provided them with shelter and arms, and led them into the forest—a Jewish unit of 120 men. This detail became part of a mixed division later known as Brigade *Pobieda* (Victory). Atlas then prevailed on the Russian chief Boris Bullat to allow his group to spearhead an attack on the German garrison in Derec-

---

N. Levin, *The Holocaust: The Destruction of European Jewry, 1933–45*, New York, 1973, pp. 368, 369, 370.

zyn to avenge the liquidation of the ghetto. One night in August, the Jewish partisans marched on the town.

The attack lasted for several hours. Atlas' men took 44 Germans, mostly police, and executed them in the same square in front of the mill where the Germans had slaughtered the Jews in the ghetto three weeks before.

Besides appeasing the need for vengeance, this action helped to change the accepted image of the Jew as a coward or worthless fighter. After the Dereczyn attack, Atlas began turning over in his mind possibilities of sabotaging German communications and made his first attempt in the middle of August. He extracted the explosives from two large artillery shells and with several of his men walked to the railway station of Rozhanka and blew up a German train—the first such sabotage action in the area. Several days later, Atlas and four others bombed and destroyed a long bridge over the Niemen River—a bridge of strategic importance—and killed three German soldiers.

Atlas himself could be seen in a tattered army uniform, wearing oversized boots, armed with a submachine gun and pistol, with several hand grenades bulging from his pockets. Survivors have testified that he was enormously popular with his men and with the Dereczyn refugees whom he protected. . . .

His men became demolition experts. They rebuilt abandoned cannons, unearthed boxes of ammunition and repaired old German trucks. They roamed the countryside for arms not only for themselves but for Jews who had fled the massacre of Zetl and had found refuge in the forests of Lipczany. On September 28, they rushed a grounded German plane and destroyed it as well as the pilot. On October 5, combined partisan bands, including Atlas' unit, attacked the German garrison in Ruda-Yovarska. In this action 127 Germans and collaborators were killed, 20 were taken prisoner and 25 wagonloads of arms were captured.

READING NO. 54

THE BIELSKI FAMILY CAMP[67]

Tobias (Tuvia) Bielski was a Vilna Jew who had fought in the Polish army in 1927 and 1928. He and his brothers fled the city and ghetto of Novogrodek when the Germans began to murder Jews and organized a fighting unit in the White Russian forests:

γ   γ   γ

Tobias Bielski, a Vilna Jew who had served in the Polish Army in 1927 and 1928, fled to the home of his parents in a little village near Novogrodek. When German units swept in, the family moved to Novogrodek itself. The Germans came there, too, and surrounded the house where Bielski was living. At the last moment, he managed to escape in a cart driven by a peasant girl and hid in the forest. His two brothers joined him and they decided to try to buy arms. When the Jews of Novogrodek were pushed into a ghetto, the brothers made plans to move their parents into the forest with them, but in December 1941, before they could act, their parents were massacred, together with 5,000 other Jews. Still, they managed to round up fifteen Jews, friends and relatives from the neighboring villages. The Bielski group now numbered eighteen, including a nine-month-old infant and six men of fighting age. They had no arms as yet, but after much prodding coaxed a peasant into selling them six rifles. The day of the successful purchase, they shot a German guard and took his rifle and ammunition.[18] These were the very modest beginnings of the famous "Tobias Bielski Division" of Jewish forest fighters, a protected family camp and successful guerrilla unit. . . . Meanwhile, others began to stream in, women and children as well as men. The winter months passed in acquiring arms and training. No acts of any kind were undertaken until the spring of 1942. By the end of 1942, there were 500 fighting men in his unit and they came to be dreaded by the police in the area of Novogrodek, Lida and Zelwa. They destroyed telephone connections, dynamited railroads and laid ambushes.

Bielski's operations were encumbered by many old men, women

[67] N. Levin, *The Holocaust: The Destruction of European Jewry, 1933–45*, New York, 1973, pp. 372, 373, 374.

and children who sought his protection, but he flatly refused to forsake them. Food had to be bought, foraged or requisitioned. The "family partisan camp" was protected by armed sentries and a small militia, but the noncombatants had important functions themselves: they worked, cooked, built barracks and lived as a community in the woods. The skills and previous training of all "civilians" were put to use in the organization of a school for children and a modest infirmary. The camp also boasted its own bakery and soap factory. . . . Stories of Bielski's exploits soon spread and his name became respected and feared. His prestige mounted in the fall of 1942. At that time, the Germans had seized the local harvest and made preparations to thresh the wheat and send bread to the front. But Bielski's men planned to wreck the huge German granaries and burn the estates and *kolkhoz* farms that the Germans had taken over. The skies above the forest and fields blazed red. Russian planes returning from bombing enemy lines saw the burning fields and dropped their remaining bombs. Panic spread among the Germans who believed that Bielski's fighters must be coordinated with the Russian command. Rumors that he had a large army concealed in the forest filled the countryside, and a reward of 10,000 marks was put on his head. These Jewish partisans finally had become part of the war against Hitler and were avenging the hundreds of thousands who had no avengers.

In March 1943, Bielski's independent career ended. A Soviet detachment was sent by the High Command of the Red Army on a special mission to unite all partisans in a fighting force. Bielski met with one hundred other unit commanders in the Gluboki forest. The meetings lasted over a week. Bielski was asked to eliminate all noncombatants—he had acquired almost a thousand by now—but he refused. He did agree, however, to incorporate his unit into the Vladimir-Lenin Brigade and to operate under a unified command.

READING NO. 55

CHILDREN IN PARTISAN GROUPS—EXODUS FROM MINSK[68]

One famous Soviet unit commanded by Semion Goczenko included Jewish children who had grown up to be fighters and helped to establish the Zorin family camp in the forest. Boys and girls aged from 12 to 14 learned to use weapons and act as guides for the adults. One boy, Banko Hammer, went back to the Minsk ghetto ten times to bring out elderly Jews. These children came to the ghetto armed, their pistols always loaded, determined not to fall into the hands of the Germans alive. When Banko had gathered the people and supplies, he addressed them like a military commander:

γ   γ   γ

In two hours we will be leaving the ghetto. From that moment on, you are partisans. Until I deliver you into the hands of the partisan chief of staff you must obey my every command. The order of the journey is as follows: I go first and you follow behind me in a single file, according to the numbers I gave you. If we should run into a German patrol there is no way back because it would endanger the Jews in the ghetto. If the situation becomes critical, we resist. Those who receive grenades will throw them at the Germans, and those who have pistols will open fire on them . . . The Germans will not pursue us far because they are afraid of the night. Under no conditions must you abandon the knapsacks which you carry on your backs. Anyone who creates panic or refuses to obey my command will be shot without warning. I hope that all will go well and that in a few hours you will be free people without yellow badges.

[68] Yuri Suhl, *They Fought Back: The Story of the Jewish Resistance in Europe*. New York, 1975, pp. 243–244.

READING NO. 56

FRENCH JEWISH SCOUTS IN MILITARY RESISTANCE[69]

The German occupation confronted the Eclaireurs Israélites de France *(EIF) with urgent, new tasks and imbued the movement with a heightened Jewish national spirit. Children's homes created in 1939 as temporary shelters became centers for workshops in plumbing, carpentry, and electrical work. Agricultural training farms for youths who wanted to go to Palestine functioned until mid-summer 1942 when there were violent round-ups of Jews. By 1943, the EIF and other Jewish youth movements moved to armed resistance:*

γ   γ   γ

The Jewish youth organizations—the Zionist Youth Movement (M.J.S.), the Eclaireurs Israélites de France, the Jewish Fighters' Organization (O.J.C.)—all initially engaged in social assistance and welfare work. At first their main operations consisted of helping Jews to hide or ''submerge,'' and survive. After 1943, however, they moved towards armed, military resistance. . . .

While only 1 per cent of the population of France were Jews, their share in the French Resistance organizations was much higher—up to 20 or 25 per cent of the total forces. They were fighting under the French flag, but those who did battle in the ranks of the O.J.C.—the Organisation Juive de Combat, at first called Forces Armées Juives— or the Eclaireurs Israélites de France were at the same time also fighting under the Blue and White flag, the symbol of the Jewish homeland.

These organizations played a major role in making the Jewish youth of France aware of its origin and heritage. They were responsible for setting up the specifically Jewish Maquis, which in the course of the winter of 1943/44 sprang up in Toulouse, Lyons, St. Etienne, etc. Each of these Maquis had its own Jewish chaplain, and during the morning parade saluted both the French and the Jewish national flag before proceeding to the day's work: military training, Hebrew and

[69] Joseph Ariel, ''Jewish Self-Defence and Resistance in France During World War II,'' *Yad Vashem Studies,* VI, 1967, pp. 240, 241, 242–243.

general Jewish studies, courses in underground social welfare work, etc.

Dozens of members of the M.J.S., O.J.C. and E.I.F., under the command of staff headquarters at Toulouse, would every day set out for different parts of France to offer such assistance as could not be accomplished by mail: to carry arms, to place Jewish children in safe refuge in other parts of the country or across the border, and to smuggle them into Switzerland and from there to Palestine. With the aid of these youngsters a secret postal service was set up with Switzerland, with the help of the railway staff on the Lyons-Geneva line.

The Jewish military organizations established contact with the Forces Françaises de l'Intérieur (F.F.I.), the Local French Fighting Forces, who recognized the O.J.C. and E.I.F., supplied them with arms, and issued military instructions for their cooperation in the general actions in which all these young fighters took an active share.

In addition to their own independent Maquis the Jewish organizations set up their special Groupes Francs, urban commando troops, which were active in Paris, Lyons, Grenoble, Toulouse, Nice, Limoges and Chambon. . . .

The general objective of the O.J.C. was to prepare trained cadres which, after the landing of the Allies in occupied Europe, would be able to join the British Army and set up a Jewish Brigade, similar to the Palestinian Jewish Brigade. This plan was unfortunately foiled by a German secret agent, who presented himself to the O.J.C. as an agent of the British Intelligence and wormed himself into the confidence of staff headquarters. Several weeks before the liberation some twenty of the O.J.C.'s top commanders accordingly met at a certain place in Paris from which they were supposed to proceed to an underground airfield and to fly to London. Instead, however, their path led straight to one of the prisons of the Gestapo. A few days afterwards they were deported to an extermination camp. A few of them managed to jump the train and to return to Paris after many hazardous adventures.

Many of the members of the Jewish Fighters' Organization fell in action or were arrested and deported, and frequently savagely tortured by the Gestapo before they met their end.

In 1943 the Eclaireurs Israélites de France joined the Organisation Juive de Combat (O.J.C.), but this was not a complete merger, because in fact they continued their independent existence. They maintained their own military command and organizational structure and followed their own course of action, with separate Maquis posts. Their independent *Corps Francs*—called *Companie Marc Haguenau*—became famous through its successful attack on a German military train in Mazamet in the south-west of France, and its participation, under the command of Captain Robert Gamzon, in the attack against the German garrison of some 4,000 in the town of Castres, which it successfully liberated.

The Eclaireurs paid a high toll for their rescue and resistance operations. Their losses were considerable: 124 of their active Resistance members were killed—21 were shot by the Germans, 30 fell in battle and 73 met their death in the extermination camps. As against this heavy toll they managed to hide several thousands of Jewish men, women and children. They found them shelter and food, and sometimes even helped to teach and educate them. Many were smuggled over the border to safety in Switzerland and Spain . . .

Among the different movements of the Jewish underground, the Scout movement was the one which distinguished itself most by its scope, efficiency and fighting spirit.

READING NO. 57

JEWISH RESISTANCE IN GERMANY—
THE BAUM GROUP[70]

*After 1933, any active anti-Nazi resistance in Germany was prob-
lematical as well as perilous. The earliest persecutions fell upon left-
wing political parties, including Jews in the Socialist and Communist
parties, who were generally remote from organized Jewish life. Jewish underground activities after 1933 were often associated with Com-
munist-directed groups and included members of Zionist and non-
Zionist youth groups. Their chief aim was to sabotage the German war
effort. The best-known is the Baum Group of thirty-two original members, most of whom were from 11 to 14. Herbert Baum and his wife
Marianne were nineteen. They and their comrades recruited several
hundred members at the Siemens plant and became especially active
after the German invasion of the Soviet Union:*

γ   γ   γ

. . . they issued an appeal to Berlin housewives refuting Nazi propaganda, and an appeal to Berlin doctors whom they urged to see their
duty in the preservation rather than destruction of life. Furthermore
they sent letters to the front and distributed a six-page newspaper
which they produced themselves with the help of a duplicating machine in the cellar of Baum's home. The stencils were prepared by the
two non-Jewish members of the group, the German Irene Walter and
the Frenchwoman Suzanne Wesse, at their place of work. Jews were
not allowed to possess typewriters. . . .

The Zionists of the group evidently fitted themselves into the active
anti-fascist struggle of their Communist comrades, for they were confronted by the same alternative: either death at the hand of the Nazis or
overthrow of the regime. . . .

Among the most dangerous operations carried out by the group were
the nocturnal operations of bill-posting and painting of slogans on
walls and house façades. These activities required not only courage
and skill but also a dedicated readiness for sacrifice, since capture by

[70] Helmut Eschwege, "Resistance of German Jews against the Nazi Regime," *Leo
Baeck Yearbook,* XV, London, 1970, pp. 172, 173, 174, 175.

the Gestapo in such circumstances would for a Jew have meant certain death. Nevertheless, all the actions carried out between summer 1941 and May 1942 proceeded without loss. Frequently these operations were mounted jointly with the members of the friendly non-Jewish resistance group of the Kaiser Wilhelm Institute. This constituted a great gesture of solidarity with the Baum group which, in spite of everything, was feeling isolated and lonely.

It clearly emerges from the leaflets that the Baum group was at all times excellently informed about Germany's economic, political and military situation. The leaflets always made use of the latest reports from Moscow and London. As early as November 1941 they presented an accurate analysis of the situation and foresaw the final defeat of Nazi Germany. In their publications they consistently denounced the crimes committed against Soviet prisoners of war. . . .

The sympathy and support extended by the Berlin Jews to the Baum group raised the morale and consciousness of the group and saved them from a sense of loneliness. Berlin Jews placed their flats at the disposal of the group for their clandestine meetings. The woman in charge of the Jewish children's home not only allowed Kochmann and Jakob Berger, leading members of the group, to live on her premises but she actually made the gymnasium of the home available for meetings.

In March 1942 the Baum group was divided into three detachments in which strict discipline was observed. Members of different detachments avoided contacts with one another. Externally the group had close links (already referred to) with the resistance group at the Kaiser Wilhelm Institute under the leadership of the engineer Joachim Franke, with Werner Steinbrink acting as liaison man. Steinbrink and Herbert Baum together drafted an appeal intended to rouse the Berlin population from its passivity, to spur it on to an active struggle against the regime. The Franke group also provided generous help in financing the political work of the Baum group and enabled it to obtain "legal" identity documents. That was not so easy, as a false French or Belgian identity document cost 140 *Reichsmark* . . .

At the beginning of 1942 Goebbels organised at the Lustgarten in the centre of Berlin an anti-Soviet exhibition under the name "The Soviet Paradise". The exhibition was opened with a solemn ceremony. The German resistance groups believed that the main purpose of the exhibition was to deflect the attention of the German people from the German defeat outside Moscow and its consequences, such as the economic difficulties caused by the prolonged war. As usual, the anti-

Soviet campaign was accompanied by an equally virulent antisemitic campaign.

All the Berlin resistance groups considered the appropriate ways of reacting to the exhibition. The Schulze-Boysen-Harnack group distributed special leaflets exposing the true aims of the propaganda exhibition and pasted them up on the walls at night. The Baum group decided to distribute leaflets among the population at the very exhibition. When that proved impracticable, Baum proposed burning down the exhibition. After an exchange of opinions that plan was adopted by all groups . . .

Part of the exhibition was burnt out. . . .

Yet, though the operation of the Baum group was a success it met with no response among the population, as the press—presumably on higher orders—kept silent about the incident.

This fire-raising operation at the anti-Soviet exhibition marked the culminating point of the activities of the Baum group. It was to have been a clarion call summoning the German working class to resistance against the regime. The group wanted to place on record the active role of the Jewish anti-fascists, and that purpose they achieved. The arson at the exhibition was one of the most successful operations mounted by the resistance movement in Germany. It aroused admiration and enthusiasm in all anti-fascist circles. Yet it must not be concealed that some misgivings were expressed as to whether it had been right for a Jewish group to tackle a job of that kind, since the Gestapo would use the incident as a pretext to intensify its terror against all Jews.

Before long the Gestapo actually succeeded in arresting all those directly involved in the incident, and seized 500 other Jews. Goebbels personally took a hand in compiling the list of hostages.

All but two of the group were beheaded, executed, or perished at Auschwitz.

READING NO. 58

THE WARSAW GHETTO UPRISING—
FIRST ACTIONS[71]

There were many disappointments and betrayals in the search by the Jewish fighters for weapons, but the shock of the January action led the Germans to over-estimate the numbers and arms of the fighters. They also feared that the revolt would spread to the Polish quarter and to other ghettos. General Jurgen Stroop, who directed the action against the ghetto, described the first few days:

γ   γ   γ

I myself arrived in Warsaw on 17 April 1943 and took over the command of the action on 19 April 1943, 0800 hours, the action itself having started the same day at 0600 hours.

Before the large-scale action began, the limits of the former Ghetto had been blocked by an external barricade in order to prevent the Jews from breaking out. This barricade was maintained from the start to the end of the action and was especially reinforced at night.

When we invaded the Ghetto for the first time, the Jews and the Polish bandits succeeded in repelling the participating units, including tanks and armored cars, by a well-prepared concentration of fire. When I ordered a second attack, about 0800 hours, I distributed the units, separated from each other by indicated lines, and charged them with combing out the whole of the Ghetto, each unit for a certain part. Although firing commenced again, we now succeeded in combing out the blocks according to plan. The enemy was forced to retire from the roofs and elevated bases to the basements, dug-outs, and sewers. In order to prevent their escaping into the sewers, the sewerage system was dammed up below the Ghetto and filled with water, but the Jews frustrated this plan to a great extent by blowing up the turning off valves. Late the first day we encountered rather heavy resistance, but it was quickly broken by a special raiding party. In the course of further operations we succeeded in expelling the Jews from their prepared resistance bases, sniper holes, and the like, and in occupying during the

---

[71] 1060-PS "The Warsaw Ghetto Is No More", *Nazi Conspiracy and Aggression*, vol. III, 1946.

20 and 21 April the greater part of the so-called remainder of the Ghetto to such a degree that the resistance continued within these blocks could no longer be called considerable.

The main Jewish battle group, mixed with Polish bandits, had already retired during the first and second day to the so-called Muranowski Square. There, it was reinforced by a considerable number of Polish bandits. Its plan was to hold the Ghetto by every means in order to prevent us from invading it. The Jewish and Polish standards were hoisted at the top of a concrete building as a challenge to us. These two standards, however, were captured on the second day of the action by a special raiding party. SS Untersturmfuehrer Dehmke fell in this skirmish with the bandits; he was holding in his hand a hand-grenade which was hit by the enemy and exploded, injuring him fatally. After only a few days I realized that the original plan had no prospect of success, unless the armament factories and other enterprises of military importance distributed throughout the Ghetto were dissolved. It was therefore necessary to approach these firms and to give them appropriate time for being evacuated and immediately transferred. Thus one of these firms after the other was dealt with, and we very soon deprived the Jews and bandits of their chance to take refuge time and again in these enterprises, which were under the supervision of the Armed Forces. In order to decide how much time was necessary to evacuate these enterprises thorough inspections were necessary. The conditions discovered there are indescribable. I cannot imagine a greater chaos than in the Ghetto of Warsaw. The Jews had control of everything, from the chemical substances used in manufacturing explosives to clothing and equipment for the Armed Forces. The managers knew so little of their own shops that the Jews were in a position to produce inside these shops arms of every kind, especially hand grenades, Molotov cocktails, and the like. . . .

Moreover, the Jews had succeeded in fortifying some of these factories as centers of resistance. Such a center of resistance in an Army accommodation office had to be attacked as early as the second day of the action by an Engineer's Unit equipped with flame throwers and by artillery. The Jews were so firmly established in this shop that it proved to be impossible to induce them to leave it voluntarily; I therefore resolved to destroy this shop the next day by fire.

READING NO. 59

STROOP BURNS OUT
THE WARSAW GHETTO[72, 73]

*Unable to pull out Jews in hiding for deportation, Stroop had to re-
sort to fire. Marek Edelman, a Jewish unit leader, has described the
inferno:*

γ   γ   γ

Flames cling to our smouldering clothes. The pavement melts to a
sticky black tar beneath our feet. Broken glass cuts into our
shoes . . . One by one we stagger through the conflagration. From
house to house, courtyard to courtyard, half-choked, a hundred ham-
mers beating in our skulls, burning rafters falling over us, we finally
pass the area under fire . . . What the Germans could not do, the om-
nipotent flames now accomplished. Thousands perished; the stench of
burning bodies was everywhere. Charred corpses lay on balconies, in
window recesses, on unburned steps . . . Hundreds committed suicide by leaping from fourth and fifth-story windows.

* * * *

Stroop describes the burning ghetto and continuing resistance:

The resistance put up by the Jews and bandits could be broken only by
relentlessly using all our force and energy by day and night. *On 23
April 1943 the Reichs Fuehrer SS issued through the higher SS and Police Fuehrer East at Cracow his order to complete the combing out of
the Warsaw Ghetto with the greatest severity and relentless tenacity.*
I therefore decided to destroy the entire Jewish residential area by setting every block on fire, including the blocks of residential buildings
near the armament works. One concern after the other was systemati-

---

[72] Quoted in Leo W. Schwarz, ed., *The Root and the Bough.* New York, 1949, pp.
61–62.

[73] 1061-PS *Nazi Conspiracy. . .III, and Aggression,* vol. 1946.

cally evacuated and subsequently destroyed by fire. The Jews then emerged from their hiding places and dug-outs in almost every case. Not infrequently, the Jews stayed in the burning buildings until, because of the heat and the fear of being burned alive they preferred to jump down from the upper stories after having thrown mattresses and other upholstered articles into the street from the burning buildings. With their bones broken, they still tried to crawl across the street into blocks of buildings which had not yet been set on fire or were only partly in flames. Often Jews changed their hiding places during the night, by moving into the ruins of burnt-out buildings, taking refuge there until they were found by our patrols. Their stay in the sewers also ceased to be pleasant after the first week. Frequently from the street, we could hear loud voices coming through the sewer shafts. Then the men of the Waffen SS, the Police of the Wehrmacht Engineers courageously climbed down the shafts to bring out the Jews and not infrequently they then stumbled over Jews already dead, or were shot at. It was always necessary to use smoke candles to drive out the Jews. Thus one day we opened 183 sewer entrance holes and at a fixed time lowered smoke candles into them, with the result that the bandits fled from what they believed to be gas to the center of the former Ghetto, where they could then be pulled out of the sewer holes there. A great number of Jews, who could not be counted, were exterminated by blowing up sewers and dug-outs.

The longer the resistance lasted, the tougher the men of the Waffen SS, Police, and Wehrmacht became; they fulfilled their duty indefatigably in faithful comradeship and stood together as models and examples of soldiers. Their duty hours often lasted from early morning until late at night. At night, search patrols with rags wound round their feet remained at the heels of the Jews and gave them no respite. Not infrequently they caught and killed Jews who used the night hours for supplementing their stores from abandoned dug-outs and for contacting neighboring groups or exchanging news with them.

Considering that the greater part of the men of the Waffen-SS had only been trained for three to four weeks before being assigned to this action, high credit should be given for the pluck, courage, and devotion to duty which they showed. It must be stated that the Wehrmacht Engineers, too, executed the blowing up of dug-outs, sewers, and concrete buildings with indefatigability and great devotion to duty. Officers and men of the Police, a large part of whom had already been at the front, again excelled by their dashing spirit. . . .

Of the total of 56,065 Jews caught, about 7,000 were exterminated within the former Ghetto in the course of the large-scale action, and 6,929 by transporting them to T*.II, which means 14,000 Jews were exterminated altogether. Beyond the number of 56,065 Jews an estimated number of 5,000 to 6,000 were killed by explosions or in fires.

* Treblinka, a death camp.

READING NO. 60

THE DESCENT INTO THE SEWERS[74]

Blueprints of the Warsaw sewer system had been carried to the command bunker by a PPR (Polish Workers' Party) member, but they arrived a day too late. Exhausted, trembling, and smeared with mud, some survivors stumbled to 20 Francis Kanska Street to a bunker. Here two men from the "Aryan" side led them through the sewers. The sewers were twenty-eight inches high:

γ γ γ

With heavy hearts we descended into the sewer. The sewer was an abyss of darkness. . . . I was overcome by a dreadful nausea there in the cold, filthy water . . . Very few could come with us. The aged and the children would only die on such a trip. They did not even ask to go along. Sixty people crawled through the narrow sewer, bent almost in half . . . Each held a candle. We half-walked, half-crawled like this for twenty hours, one behind the other, without stopping. . . . Some were unable to walk and we dragged them through the water on their hands and knees. . . . there is always the agonizing thought: how shall we explain, when we meet our comrades again, why we did not remain, why we are alive at all? All of us were poisoned by the thought of those we had left behind, and this robbed us of all possible joy in our good fortune. . . .

[74] Zivia Lubetkin, "The Last Days of the Warsaw Ghetto." *Commentary*, May 1947, pp. 408–409.

READING NO. 61

YOUTHS FACE DEATH
IN THE BIALYSTOK GHETTO[75]

From Bialystok, we have the record of a meeting of the executive committee of the Bialystok Hechalutz (pioneering) movement on February 27, 1943. The chairman was Mordecai Tenenbaum, who had come from the Vilna Ghetto to organize resistance in Bialystok. He began by saying:

γ   γ   γ

This meeting is historic or tragic, as you prefer, but certainly sad. The few people sitting here are the last chalutzim in Poland. We are entirely surrounded by the dead. You know what has happened in Warsaw: no one is left. The same is true of Benzin and Czestochowa, and probably everywhere else. We are the last. It's not a particularly pleasant feeling to be the last; on the contrary it imposes a special responsibility on us. We have to decide what to do tomorrow . . . What shall we do?

We can do two things: decide that with the first Jew to be deported now from Bialystok, we start our counter-attack, that from tomorrow on nobody goes to the factories, that nobody is allowed to hide during the action. Everybody will be mobilized. We can see to it that not one German leaves the ghetto alive, that not one factory is left standing.

Or we could decide to escape to the woods. We must consider the possibilities realistically. Two of our comrades were sent today to make a place ready; in any event, as soon as this meeting is over, a military alert will be instituted. We must decide now, because our fathers can't do our worrying for us. This is an orphanage . . .

[75] "On the Agenda: Death: A Document of the Jewish Resistance," *Commentary*, August 1949, p. 105.

READING NO. 62

POCKETS OF JEWISH RESISTANCE
IN 1943 IN GALICIA[76]

*Massive deportations from Galicia in 1943 also involved desperate
acts of individual and group resistance:*

γ   γ   γ

To: The Superior SS and Police Leader East SS Obergruppenfuehrer
and General of Police Krueger or deputy
Cracow

Enclosed I am submitting the 1st copy of the Final Report on the Solution of the Jewish Question in the District of Galicia for your information.

[Signed] KATZMANN
SS Gruppenfuehrer and Lt. Gen. of Police

. . . In the meantime further evacuation [Aussiedelung] was executed with energy, so that with effect from 23 June 1943 all Jewish
Residence Districts could be dissolved. Therewith I report that the District of Galicia, with the exception of those Jews living in the camps
being under the control of the SS & Pol. Leaders, is

Free from Jews

Jews still caught in small numbers are given special treatment by the
competent detachments of Police and Gendarmerie.

Up to 27 June 1943 altogether 434.329 Jews have been evacuated
[ausgesiedelt] . . .

Owing to the great number of Jews and the vast area to be combed
out these actions were performed with the assistance of detachments
from the Security Police, the Order Police, the Gendarmerie, the Special Service, and the Ukrainian Police, all acting together in numerous
single sweeps . . .

On the occasion of these actions, many more difficulties occurred
owing to the fact that the Jews tried every means in order to dodge
evacuation [Aussiedelung]. Not only did they try to flee, but they concealed themselves in every imaginable corner, in pipes, chimneys,

---

[76] Katzmann to Krüger, June 30, 1943, L-18, NCA, VII, pp. 756, 763, 766, 767–
768.

even in sewers, etc. They built barricades in passages of catacombs, in cellars enlarged to dug-outs, in underground holes, in cunningly contrived hiding-places in attics and sheds, within furniture, etc.

The smaller the number of Jews remaining in the district, the harder their resistance. Arms of all kinds, among them those of Italian make, were used for defense. The Jews purchased these Italian arms from Italian soldiers stationed in the District for high sums in Zloty currency . . .

Underground bunkers were found with entrances concealed in a masterly manner opening some times into flats, some times into the open. In most cases the entrances had only so much width that just one person could crawl through it. The access was concealed in such a manner that it could not be found by persons not acquainted with the locality. Here nothing succeeded but the assistance of some Jews to whom anything whatever was promised in exchange . . .

READING NO. 63

GLOBOCNIK'S PRIMITIVE GASSINGS[77]

In Lublin, where he was SS Police chief, Odilio Globocnik converted a number of Lublin's labor camps into half-way houses to annihilation centers. By July 1940, there were more than 30 such camps, the largest of which was Belzec. Maidanek, a labor camp near Lublin, was set up at the end of 1940, the site of Globocnik's gassing experiments. In the late summer of 1941, Heydrich ordered Eichmann to see Globocnik, who had already been ordered by Himmler to convert Maidanek into a death center and carry out Hitler's order for the "Final Solution." Eichmann reported that he used the phrase "Final Solution" as a kind of password and Globocnik showed him around:

γ   γ   γ

A German police captain there showed me how they had managed to build airtight chambers disguised as ordinary Polish farmers' huts, seal them hermetically, then inject the exhaust gas from a Russian U-boat motor. I remember it all very exactly because I never thought that anything like that would be possible, technically speaking. Not long afterward Heydrich had me carry an order to Major General Odilo Globocnik, S.S. commander of the Lublin district. I cannot remember whether Heydrich gave me the actual message or whether I had to draw it up. It ordered Globocnik to start liquidating a quarter million Polish Jews. . . .

---

[78] Editors of *Life*, "Eichmann Tells His Own Damning Story," *Life*, November 28, 1960, p. 102.

READING NO. 64

AUSCHWITZ[79]

The most efficient of the killing sites was Auschwitz, a landscape so foreign to normative human experience and the modern Western consciousness up to the time of the Holocaust that the unprecedented experiences of Nazi victims have been described as belonging to a new realm—Planet Auschwitz. The commandant of the murder factory at Auschwitz was Rudolf Hoess, a member of the SS Guard Unit, the so-called Deathshead Formation (Totenkopf Verband) since 1934. He was appointed commandant of Auschwitz May 1, 1940, and in his affidavit at Nuremberg, matter-of-factly described the operations he directed and the "improvements" over the method in Treblinka:

γ　　　　　　γ　　　　　　γ

. . . I commanded Auschwitz until 1 December 1943, and estimate that at least 2,500,000 victims were executed and exterminated there by gassing and burning, and at least another half million succumbed to starvation and disease making a total dead of about 3,000,000. This figure represents about 70% or 80% of all persons sent to Auschwitz as prisoners, the remainder having been selected and used for slave labor in the concentration camp industries. Included among the executed and burnt were approximately 20,000 Russian prisoners of war (previously screened out of Prisoner of War cages by the Gestapo) who were delivered at Auschwitz in Wehrmacht transports operated by regular Wehrmacht officers and men. The remainder of the total number of victims included about 100,000 German Jews, and great numbers of citizens, mostly Jewish from Holland, France, Belgium, Poland, Hungary, Czechoslovakia, Greece, or other countries. We executed about 400,000 Hungarian Jews alone at Auschwitz in the summer of 1944 . . .

Mass executions by gassing commenced during the summer 1941 and continued until fall 1944. I personally supervised executions at Auschwitz until the first of December 1943 and know by reason of my continued duties in the Inspectorate of Concentration Camps WVHA

---

[79] 3868-PS, *Nazi Conspiracy and Aggression*, vol. VI, 1946.

that these mass executions continued as stated above. All mass executions by gassing took place under the direct orders, supervisions, and responsibility of RSHA. I received all orders for carrying out these mass executions directly from RSHA. . . .

The "final solution" of the Jewish question meant the complete extermination of all Jews in Europe. I was ordered to establish extermination facilities at Auschwitz in June 1941. At that time, there were already in the general government three other extermination camps; Belzek, Treblinka, and Wolzek. These camps were under the Einsatzkommando of the Security Police and SD. I visited Treblinka to find out how they carried out their extermination. The Camp Commandant at Treblinka told me that he had liquidated 80,000 in the course of one-half year. He was principally concerned with liquidating all the Jews from the Warsaw ghetto. He used monoxide gas and I did not think that his methods were very efficient. So when I set up the extermination building at Auschwitz, I used Cyclon B, which was a crystallized prussic acid which we dropped into the death chamber from a small opening. It took from 3 to 15 minutes to kill the people in the death chamber depending upon climatic conditions. We knew when the people were dead because their screaming stopped. We usually waited about one-half hour before we opened the doors and removed the bodies. After the bodies were removed our special commandos took off the rings and extracted the gold from the teeth of the corpses.

Another improvement we made over Treblinka was that we built our gas chambers to accommodate 2,000 people at one time, whereas at Treblinka their 10 gas chambers only accommodated 200 people each. The way we selected our victims was as follows: we had two SS doctors on duty at Auschwitz to examine the incoming transports of prisoners. The prisoners would be marched by one of the doctors who would make spot decisions as they walked by. Those who were fit for work were sent into the Camp. Others were sent immediately to the extermination plants. Children of tender years were invariably exterminated since by reason of their youth they were unable to work. Still another improvement we made over Treblinka was that at Treblinka the victims almost always knew that they were to be exterminated and at Auschwitz we endeavored to fool the victims into thinking that they were to go through a delousing process. Of course, frequently they realized our true intentions and we sometimes had riots and difficulties due to that fact. Very frequently women would hide their children under the clothes but of course when we found them we would send the

children in to be exterminated. We were required to carry out these exterminations in secrecy but of course the foul and nauseating stench
from the continuous burning of bodies permeated the entire area and
all of the people living in the surrounding communities knew that exterminations were going on at Auschwitz. . . .

[signed] Rudolf Hoess
RUDOLF FRANZ FERDINAND HOESS
Subscribed and sworn to before me this
5th day of April 1946, at Nurnberg, Germany.
[signed] Smith W. Brookhart Jr.
SMITH W. BROOKHART, JR.,
LT. COLONEL, IGD.

READING NO. 65

DEPORTATIONS FROM WARSAW, JULY 1942[80, 81]

On July 20, the head of the Jewish Council, Czerniakow, was ordered to prepare for the Aussiedlung *(resettlement) of ''non-productive'' elements, beginning July 22. Sixty Jews, including some council officials, were kept as hostages. Ukrainian and Lithuanian militia replaced German guards. Jews involved would report voluntarily to an evacuated hospital at the* Umschlagplatz, *the transfer station near the railway where freight cars would take them ''to the East.'' Hans Hoefle of ''Einsatz Reinhard'' said that resettlement would be limited to 60,000 non-productive workers, 6,000 per day and that the Council members would hang if they did not carry out the order. The first day's quota was filled, but on the 23rd, Czerniakow committed suicide, having failed to save orphans in institutions from the deportation. After July 29, few Jews reported voluntarily, so the Germans used a bread and marmalade ruse—3 kg. of bread and 5 kg. of marmalade. A young woman in the resistance observed:*

γ   γ   γ

They are loaded with sacks, baskets, suitcases, they drag with them the last remnants of their poor belongings, and they are all marching in the same direction—towards the Umschlagplatz. . . . Some of them are walking slowly, with drooping heads; others move nervously ahead, with unsteady, frightened eyes, seemingly in a hurry, as if they were afraid of being forced to go back. Nobody holds them back, nobody hinders them from moving forward. . . . Scarcely anyone in the ghetto is surprised at this quiet, resigned marching. From the hiding places and the shops people look at them with deep sorrow, sometimes mixed with a feeling of admiration. . . . ''They have found the strength to take a decision.'' . . . Crushed under the burden of ghetto life, shriveled or swollen from starvation, haunted by the constant fear

---

[80] Quoted in Philip Friedman, ed., *Martyrs and Fighters: The Epic of the Warsaw Ghetto.* New York, 1954, p. 155.

[81] Marek Edelman, *The Ghetto Fights.* New York, 1946, p. 21.

of being seized, these Jews could no longer go on with their fight. . . . How enticing were these three brown loaves!

* * * *

By the end of July, 59,000 Jews had been deported, but the raids on apartments did not stop. Hoefle had lied. Everyone was vulnerable. People either came out or were shot. A survivor has described a typical deportation order:

People run from all staircases. Nervously, on the run, they clothe themselves in whatever is handy. Some descend as they are, sometimes straight from bed, others are carrying everything they can possibly take along, knapsacks, packages, pots and pans. . . . Trembling, they form groups in front of the house. They are not allowed to talk but they still try to gain the policemen's pity. From nearby houses similar groups of trembling, completely desperate people arrive and form into one long column. . . . Two, three shots signify the death of those who did not heed the call and remained in their homes. The ''blockade'' is finished.

READING NO. 66

THE DEPORTATION OF JANUSZ KORCZAK AND HIS CHILDREN[82]

On August 12, 1942, the orphanage of Janusz Korczak was "evacu-ated." Dr. Korczak was a Polish-Jewish neurologist, but was better known in Poland as a writer and educator of advanced progressive ideas. He devoted his life after 1912 to directing the Jewish orphanage at 92 Krochmalna Street, with Stefania Wilczyńska as his chief assis-tant. Teachers and social workers from all over Poland came to ob-serve his unusual philosophy at work. After the German invasion of Poland, Korczak served in the Polish army, and after its defeat, he rushed back to care for the orphanage, determined to keep the children alive and well, and maintain an island of safe-keeping and warmth de-spite the savagery outside. The constant narrowing of the ghetto forced the orphanage to move several times and Korczak, to battle hunger and typhus engulfing the ghetto. On July 18, in the midst of preparations for the "journey", Tagore's highly symbolic play Dak Ghar *(The Post Office) was performed by and for the children and on August 12, they are ordered to leave the orphanage. They form a long line of small, emaciated children, some carrying shabby packages and schoolbooks, eyes turned toward Korczak at the head. An eye-witness at a first-aid station at the* Umschlagplatz *recalled:*

γ   γ   γ

It was an unbearably hot day. I put the children from the home at the far end of the square, near the wall. I thought that I might manage to save them that way at least until the afternoon, and possibly until the next day. I suggested to Korczak that he come with me to the ghetto officials and ask them to intervene. He refused, because he didn't want to leave the children for even a minute. They began loading the train. I stood by the column of ghetto police who were putting people in the boxcars and watched with my heart in my mouth in the hope that my stratagem would succeed. But they kept packing them in and there was still room left. Urged on by whips, more and more people were

[82] Joseph Arnon, "The Passion of Janusz Korczak," *Midstream,* May 1973, pp. 52–53.

jammed into the cars. Suddenly Schmerling—the sadistic ghetto police officer whom the Germans had put in charge of the *Umschlagplatz*—commanded that the children be brought to the cars. Korczak went at their head. I'll never forget the sight to the end of my life. It wasn't just entering a boxcar—it was a silent but organized protest against the murderers, a march like which no human eye had ever seen before. The children went four-by-four. Korczak went first with his head held high, leading a child with each hand. The second group was led by Stefa Wilczyńska. They went to their death with a look full of contempt for their assassins. When the ghetto policemen saw Korczak, they snapped to attention and saluted. "Who is that man?" asked the Germans. I couldn't control myself any longer, but I hid the flood of tears that ran down my cheeks with my hands. I sobbed and sobbed at our helplessness in the face of such murder.

READING NO. 67

HIMMLER'S "UNWRITTEN PAGE OF GLORY"—"THE EXTERMINATION OF THE JEWISH RACE"[83]

On October 4, 1943, Himmler exhorted SS major-generals to carry on their "hard task" of exploiting non-German peoples and eliminating Jews in a speech at Posen:

γ　　　　　γ　　　　　γ

. . . It is basically wrong for us to infuse all our inoffensive soul and spirit, our good-nature, and our idealism into foreign peoples. . . . This is true since the time of Herder who clearly wrote "Voices of the Nations" [Stimmen der Voelker], in a state of drunkenness, thereby bringing on us, who come after him, such immeasurable sorrow and misery. This is true for instance, of the Czechs and the Slovenes to whom we gave their consciousness of nationality. They were just not capable of it themselves; we had to discover it for them.

One basic principle must be the absolute rule for the *SS* man: we must be honest, decent, loyal, and comradely to members of our own blood and to nobody else. What happens to a Russian, to a Czech does not interest me in the slightest. What the nations can offer in the way of good blood of our type, we will take, if necessary by kidnapping their children and raising them here with us. Whether nations live in prosperity or starve to death [verrecken—to die—used of cattle] interests me only in so far as we need them as slaves for our Kultur; otherwise, it is of no interest to me. Whether 10,000 Russian females fall down from exhaustion while digging an anti-tank ditch interests me only in so far as the anti-tank ditch for Germany is finished. . . .

I also want to talk to you, quite frankly, on a very grave matter. Among ourselves it should be mentioned quite frankly, and yet we will never speak of it publicly. Just as we did not hesitate on June 30th, 1934, to do the duty we were bidden, and stand comrades who had lapsed, up against the wall and shoot them, so we have never spoken about it and will never. . . speak of it. It was that tact which is a matter

[83] 1919-PS, *Nazi Conspiracy and Aggression*, vol. IV, 1946.

of course and which I am glad to say, is inherent in us, that made us never discuss it among ourselves, never to speak of it. It appalled everyone, and yet everyone was certain that he would do it the next time if such orders are issued and if it is necessary.

I mean the clearing out of the Jews, the extermination of the Jewish race. It's one of those things it is easy to talk about—"The Jewish race is being exterminated", says one party member, "that's quite clear, it's in our program—elimination of the Jews, and we're doing it, exterminating them." And then they come, 80 million worthy Germans, and each one has his decent Jew. Of course the others are vermin, but this one is an A-1 Jew. Not one of all those who talk this way has witnessed it, not one of them has been through it. Most of *you* must know what it means when 100 corpses are lying side by side, or 500 or 1000. To have stuck it out and at the same time—apart from exceptions caused by human weakness—to have remained decent fellows, that is what has made us hard. This is a page of glory in our history which has never been written and is never to be written . . .

READING NO. 68

DANES IDENTIFY FATE OF JEWS WITH THEIR OWN[84]

The unique balance of forces which gave Denmark the status of a "model protectorate" came to an end in the summer of 1943. A dramatic change came about as a result of the increasing strength of the Danish underground:

γ   γ   γ

. . . With the outbreak of the crisis, the internal struggle among the different German factions competing for control of Denmark also intensified, and the plan for the deportation of the Jews became a tactic as well as a goal. The goal was to expel the Jews from Denmark in preparation for its inclusion in the "European Order." The tactic was to bring in German police forces to carry out the deportation, but even more important to strengthen the position of Plenipotentiary Werner Best in his struggle with the army.

The Danes indeed feared that the failure of the "policy of negotiation" was liable to bring about the persecution of the Jews, yet the *Aktion* of the night following *Rosh ha-Shanah* nevertheless came as a shock. The shock, however, did not paralyze the Danish public, but rather aroused the forces opposed to the Germans into action. For two or three weeks, the Danes, identifying the Jews' fate with their own, became totally involved in the rescue operations. They viewed the rescue of the Jews as a manifestation of their national revolt against the Germans, and thus the rare situation was created in which it was not the Jews who were asked or sought to prove their identification with the host country, but rather it was the Danes who proved by their response and actions how great the identification was between their national interests and the fate of the Jews. Their existence as an independent nation and the rescue of the Jews became a single goal. This fact explains both the spontaneity and the unanimity of the action. The underground

[84] Leni Yahil, "The Uniqueness of the Rescue of Danish Jewry," *Rescue Attempts During the Holocaust.* Proceedings . . . April 8–11, 1974. Yad Vashem, Jerusalem, 1977, pp. 620–621.

was able to channel this revolt into new organizational frameworks which continued to function later on as well.

The rescue operation was an important lever in the development of the resistance in Denmark. Among its members were Danish Jews who had been rescued and were living in Sweden, as well as Swedish Jews who provided financial assistance and organizational help. . . .

READING NO. 69

DANISH PARCEL PROJECT[85]

Efforts to dispatch parcels of food and clothing to ghettos and camps were numerous but generally fruitless, with the exception of the Danes who persisted in maintaining contact with Danish Jews in Theresienstadt:

γ　　　　　　γ　　　　　　γ

. . . A systematic operation was planned on the basis of a list of deportees, preliminary and incomplete though this was. Professor Ege and his helpers contacted the Ministry of Social Welfare or the social welfare services of the city of Copenhagen and with their assistance prepared parcels consisting of the deportees' own clothes. The dispatch of these parcels was organized through the offices of the Danish Red Cross and with the knowledge of the Germans, who gave their permission in November 1943, though they refused to allow the dispatch of food parcels. The sending of letters was also permitted. The organizers managed to add some medicine to these parcels. Moreover, Professor Ege was an expert in nutrition, and under his guidance several pharmaceutical firms produced large quantities of multivitamin pills. The total amount was sufficient for five hundred persons for a year. As stated, the Germans officially forbade the dispatch of food and medicine. The head of the Danish Red Cross, Helmer Rosting. . . . was a boyhood friend of Professor Ege, who succeeded in convincing him that vitamin pills were not forbidden by the German orders, since they were neither food nor drugs. Receipt of the parcels was acknowledged by special cards on which the deportees succeeded, by hints incomprehensible to the Germans, in emphasizing the need for food parcels. Regards were sent, for example, to a well-known grocer in Copenhagen or to a sausage factory. Repeated requests to the Gestapo in Copenhagen to allow food parcels were refused; nor was the approach of the Danish chargé d'affaires to the German Foreign Ministry any more successful.

Professor Ege and his friends, however, did not despair and sought

[85] Leni Yahil, *The Rescue of Danish Jewry: Test of a Democracy*. Philadelphia, 1969, pp. 292–293.

means of circumventing the German ban. The Fund of 1944 was set up with the support of several parties, in particular the clergy's underground movement. With the help of this fund the dispatch was begun of apparently private and unofficial food parcels. Since the number of the deportees' relatives remaining in Denmark was quite small, a group of people was organized to act as consignors for the parcels. Many of these "patrons" were priests. A large number of them were prepared to cover the cost of the parcels themselves and even requested to do so. In all instances, however, where expenses were not adequately covered, the director-general of the Ministry of Social Welfare and National Insurance, H. H. Koch, undertook to make up the difference from the Fund of 1944.

READING NO. 70

DUTCH WORKERS STRIKE, FEBRUARY 25, 1941[86]

Piet Nak and William Kraan, both sanitation workers in Amsterdam, were outraged by the brutal Nazi treatment of Jews as soon as the occupation started. They decided to call on fellow workers to strike in a gesture of protest:

γ   γ   γ

At 5:15 a.m. Monday, Feb. 24, 1941, in the emerging daylight, Piet Nak mounted an impromptu platform near the workers' assembly yards and speaking from his heart, called for a strike of all the sanitation and manual laborers of Amsterdam to protest the mistreatment of their fellow citizens of the Jewish faith . . . However, this call for action was not successful . . . That evening he again spoke . . . "I see a man not as Jewish or different in race or religion. Can we question difference when we see a man drowning? Do we not owe him what aid we can provide? We must strike to show our protest." . . . That evening appointed couriers sped all over Amsterdam declaring a strike, reprisals be damned!

* * * *

As Tuesday morning, Feb. 25, 1941 arrived, the sanitation and dock laborers went out on strike. By 8 a.m. this was apparent to all of Amsterdam, and word of mouth conveyed the reason for the strike.

By 9 a.m. the workers on the wharfs lay down their grapple hooks and the harbor and canals were still. No ships moved for the first time in Amsterdam's 666-year history. By 9:30 a.m. the last barge tied up.

Postal workers returned to their stations, mail undelivered. By 10 a.m. the trams and bus service stopped. The vehicles were returned to their depots. By 11 a.m. most shops and service businesses locked their doors, and commercially Amsterdam had ceased operating.

Upon learning of the strike and its reason when they left for lunch at noon, most factory workers returned to their homes as best they could

---

[86] Max Kaplan, "Chronicle of Courage," *Jewish Exponent,* April 2, 1976 (*Friday Forum* Supplement).

and not to their places of employment. Governmental offices did not entirely close, but operated with mostly pro-Nazi employees. By mid-afternoon it was apparent that for the first time a captive German city had shown open defiance by voluntarily stopping its operation.

By Wednesday, Feb. 26, 1941, the strike had spread to other parts of Holland, and the country approached total paralysis.

The strike showed a feeling of outrage at the barbarous conduct of the Nazis, and it showed that the Nazi beast could be defied. The pamphlets found their way to the Dutch underground and stiffened its resolve to harass the German war machine.

* * * *

The Germans at first tried to disguise the strike as one for higher wages, but the pamphlets and signs soon dispelled this myth.

When the higher pay myth faded away, the German occupational force was beside itself with anger. The Gestapo suspected the sanitation workers as being instigators of the strike, which of course was true, and arrested random groups for interrogation to ascertain the leadership cadre behind the strike.

Kraan and Nak were among those arrested. For three days the interrogations went on as even more strikers were brought in. Finally the arrestees were released; no information could be gotten. Nak's eyes lit up as he said proudly, ''So many were arrested and mistreated, yet no one gave any information.''

This was only the beginning for Kraan and Nak, who, with their wives, joined the Dutch underground forces to try and resist the Nazis in every possible way.

William Kraan was arrested and executed on Nov. 19, 1942, and yet, while being tortured and prepared for execution, he did not shed a tear as he had when he saw the helpless Jews being mistreated. Says Nak, ''Make no mistake, William Kraan was my best friend—the bravest man one could ever know.''

Nak was imprisoned four times for periods ranging from two to six months. Each time he was badly beaten to force a confession, which never came. The Gestapo had no proof and hoped the torture would break this slim, gentle-looking man. Often they offered him his freedom for the names of any underground members.

The last beating broke his already assaulted body, but not his spirit. He was forced to do pushups while being beaten about the head and body by wooden clubs. As his blood ran onto the floor, he was forced to lick it up as he had seen the Jews do on the streets of Amsterdam. The role of observer, then victim, had turned full cycle, yet he admitted nothing, betrayed no one.

By 1943 Nak was broken physically from the many beatings he had endured, and he could no longer perform on the job. This only acted to spur on his anti-German efforts. Four times he went into hiding to work on and distribute his pro-Jewish propaganda.

His closest brush with death was in November, 1943, while in hiding. Twenty-four suspected Dutch underground members were rounded up out of their quarters, and 18 were executed within 10 hours. Again no one betrayed anyone else.

In January, 1944, Nak was again arrested and spent six months in jail. During this time his wife Franceska was also imprisoned for two months on suspicion of hiding Jews from deportation.

Nak smiled as he recalled that, in the times he was not jailed, he resorted to being a street comic to earn money to feed his family. It was an excellent cover for his underground activities.

READING NO. 71

NAZIS CAMOUFLAGE THE TRUTH ABOUT BIRKENAU[87]

The Jewish Council in Amsterdam was reassured, for a time, about the nature of Birkenau when the first batch of letters came on August 13, 1942:

γ γ γ

. . . All of them appeared to have come from a place called Birkenau. It took the Council five days of searching the best available maps to discover that Birkenau lay in Upper Silesia. All of the 52 letters said more or less the same thing: the work was hard but tolerable, the food adequate, the sleeping accommodations were good, hygienic conditions were satisfactory and the general treatment correct. All this strengthened the Council's view, first gained from Schmidt's pronouncement, that the work-camps in Upper Silesia were nothing like the notorious Mauthausen extermination camp, which had been causing so much alarm ever since 1941. . . .

The 52 letters that had been sent to Amsterdam were dictated by the camp administration (they were identical in content) and gave an impression of camp life that made a complete mockery of the true situation. Words cannot describe what it meant to be an inmate, a *Haftling*, in Birkenau, during the summer of 1912, when this immense camp was being constructed. The food consisted of 2 pints of thin soup per day; there was no drinking water; roll-calls would often drag on deep into the night; people slept crowded together in stinking barracks crawling with lice; they worked all day at back-breaking tasks, under a blistering sun and at a killing tempo, and all that under the haughty supervision of the SS and under the direct control of vicious co-prisoners, most of whom had been professional criminals. "If a *Stubedienst* (barrack auxiliary) could buy vodka for ten rations of bread," wrote one of the few Dutch survivors, "he would think nothing of killing ten prisoners.

---

[87] Louis de Jong, "The Netherlands and Auschwitz: Why Were the Reports of Mass Killings So Widely Disbelieved?" *Imposed Jewish Governing Bodies Under Nazi Rule:* YIVO Colloquium, December 2–5, 1967. New York, 1972, pp. 13–14.

Every night, I could see some ten Hollanders lying dead in front of the *Block*. It was clear that all of us were gradually being weeded out. The boys kept drinking mud.'' And another: ''Eighty of us would leave for work, but only 55 would return. The rest had been clubbed down at work. One day we were stopped to be counted at the gate—there were 55 of us. Five too many, and so five were immediately battered to death.'' And a third: ''There were only 23 or 24 dirty old tins from which a thousand of us had to eat . . . When the commandos went out, we would hear that the guards would bring back seventy corpses tomorrow . . . Your life meant nothing in the camp. You were simply a number. You had nothing and you were nothing. All of us walked hand in hand with death.''

READING NO. 72

WOUNDED PRIDE OF FRENCH JEWS[88]

Like German Jews, French Jews were highly assimilated and ac-culturated. Their exclusion from accustomed social and economic relations was humiliating. Among the many letters of protest and distress is the following one from a Jewish scout leader Marc Haguenau:

γ   γ   γ

I submit this personal protest, along with that of so many of my Jewish and non-Jewish countrymen, to tell you of my sadness at the fact that an exceptional law should be passed for one category of Frenchmen. I count in my family too many generations of French Israelites who have lived under all regimes—monarchies, empires, republics—not to be capable of judging in a completely French spirit what a backward step this is for our country, as regards the respect for all spiritual values in which I was raised, and to which I remain attached.

I would have considered it contrary to my dignity not to make this brief and useless declaration.

---

[88] Quoted in Leon Paliakov, *Harvest of Hate*. Syracuse, New York, 1954, pp. 299–301.

READING NO. 73

FRENCH CLERGY PROTEST VICHY MEASURES[89]

French clergy were very active in protesting Vichy's anti-Jewish measures and in finding hiding places for Jewish children:

γ   γ   γ

. . . The Archbishop of Toulouse inveighed against the Nazi terror: ''Alas, it has been destined for us to witness the dreadful spectacle of children, women and old men being treated like vile beasts; of families being torn apart and deported to unknown destinations. . . . In our diocese frightful things take place. . . . The Jews are our brethren. They belong to mankind. No Christian dare forget that!''

The Primate of France and Archbishop of Lyon, Pierre Cardinal Gerlier, defied the authorities with his letter of sympathy to the Grand Rabbi of France, after a crude Nazi attempt to burn the synagogues of Paris in October 1941. Subsequently, in pastoral letters to the Catholics of France, Cardinal Gerlier called upon them to refuse to surrender the hidden children of deported Jews. It was Cardinal Gerlier who also sponsored *L'Amitié Chretienne* (*Christian Friendship*), an organization of Protestants and Catholics which placed Jewish children in Christian institutions, and promised not to attempt to convert them. Dozens of nuns, priests, and humble monks were arrested and even gave their lives in the efforts to rescue Jews, although Laval was determined not to have clerical interference ''in the internal affairs of the state of France.''

[89] Nora Levin, *The Holocaust: The Destruction of European Jewry, 1933–45*. New York, 1973 p. 435.

READING NO. 74

ITALIANS PROTECT JEWS
IN SOUTHERN FRANCE[90]

On March 20, 1943, Mussolini transferred jurisdiction over Jewish matters in the Italian zone in France from the Italian army to the Interior Ministry. This ministry established a Commissariat for Jewish Questions in Nice, headed by Guido Lospinoso. Lospinoso successfully evaded the Germans by sending lesser officials to confer with them, and they, in turn, pleaded insufficient authority. Lospinoso's chief aides were Father Marie-Benoit, a Capuchin monk, and Angelo Donati, a Jewish Italian banker. The Italian military were likewise interested in protecting Jews:

γ   γ   γ

24 May, 1943.

Confidential

To the Reich Security Head Office,
For the attention of S.S. Gruppenfuehrer Mueller,
Berlin.

Subject: The Jewish question in the French zone occupied by the Italians.

Reference: Conversation with S.S. Obersturmbannfuehrer Eichmann, on 28th. April 1943, and my telegram No. 26,162 of 4 May 1943.

In view of the fact that Inspector-General Lospinoso of the Italian police has still not come to see me, and that we know nothing of his possible presence in the Italian zone, I ordered enquiry to be made in the Italian Embassy in Paris about this visit. The Italian Embassy has informed us that Lospinoso did not arrive, and that it is not aware of such a projected journey.

These facts only confirm my suspicion that certain Italian services are not at all interested in the solution of the Jewish question in France,

[90] Leon Poliakov and Jacques Sabille, *Jews Under the Italian Occupation*. Paris, 1955, pp. 84–85, 86, 87, 88. ,

and that they are applying in this regard—as far as possible—a delaying tactic.

Because of the importance of applying the anti-Jewish measures in the Italian zone as quickly as possible, I refer to my previous reports and conversations, and request you to ask the Italian Government again whether we can still count on Lospinoso's visit, and if so, at what date we may expect it.

I enclose three copies in duplicate communicated by Bousquet, concerning the objections raised by the Italian military services against the anti-Jewish measures of the French Government.

The notes from the Italian authorities are significant and illuminating on the Italian attitude to the Jewish question.

I shall continue to keep you informed.

> (Signed): Dr. KNOCHEN.
> *S.S. Standartenfuehrer*
> *and Police Colonel.*

ANNEX 1.

1–47

GENERAL REPRESENTATIVE
SUPREME ITALIAN COMMAND
IN VICHY.

> *Vichy 2 March 1943.*

> To Admiral Platon,
> Secretary of State
> to the Head of Government.

Monsieur l'Admiral,

In the name of the Supreme Italian Command I have the honour to inform you of the following:

. . . the Supreme Italian Command cannot give its approval to the measures which were taken by the Prefects in regard to the arrests and the interning of Jews living in the Italian occupation zone in France, whether they are Jews of Italian, French or of foreign nationality.

These measures belong exclusively to the competence of the Italian military occupation authorities. For this reason the Italian Supreme Commander requires the French Government to annul all arrests and internments which have been ordered till now. An order should be issued to all Prefects of the territories controlled through the units of the

Italian Armies to stop these measures where they concern the internment of Italian, French or foreign Jews whose place of residence is in territory indicated.

(*Signed*): Carlo Avarna di GUALTIERI,
Brigadier-General.

ANNEX II

Vichy 29th. March 1943.
To Admiral Bourrague,
Director of the Armistice Services.

Admiral,

In the name of the Command of the Fourth Army I have the honour to inform you of the following:

. . . I emphasise that the Notes 679 and 857 of the 2nd and 17th inst. which I sent in the name of the Italian Supreme Command, and which require that every question concerning the policy in relation to the Jews in the French territory under Italian occupation lies exclusively within the competence of the Italian authorities and do not bear the character of a request or a proposal, but are a definite pronouncement to the French Government.

Please accept, Admiral, the expression of my highest regard.

(*Signed:*) Carlo Avarna di GUALTIERI.
Brigadier-General.

ANNEX III.

Vichy 27th. April 1943.
To Army Corps General Bridoux,
Secretary of State for Defence.

Excellency,

In reference to the Letter No. 1079 DN/SL of 27th. March 1943 and the Notes 670 and 857 dated respectively the 2nd. and 17th. March, in the name of the Supreme Italian Command, I have the honour to inform you of the following:

1. For reasons of military security the occupation authorities must reserve for themselves completely the measures relating to the Jews, without distinction of nationality.

2. When the French authorities proceed to arrest Jews, the Italian occupation authorities must be informed of the reasons which have

provoked the arrests, in order to determine whether the offence is subject to the civil penal code. If it falls—in conformity with the existing civil penal code—within the competence of a juridical authority active outside our occupation-zone, the accused can be transferred only after the Italian military authorities will have given the necessary permission in each separate case, and only to make possible the sentencing and the carrying out of the sentence in France itself.

3. The Supreme Italian Command insist that the French Government must annul the arrests and the internings of the Jews whose place of residence is in the zone occupied by us.

Accept, Excellency, the expressions of my high regard.

(*Signed:*) Carlo Avarna di GUALTIERI.

READING NO. 75

TRAUMAS OF CHILDREN IN THERESIENSTADT[91]

The shocks and deprivations in Theresienstadt were very severe for the many highly assimilated children, including those of mixed marriages:

γ γ γ

. . . I am here completely alone. Without Mommy and Dad and without my big brother whom I miss so much. I was fourteen years old not long ago and I had never been away from home before. . . . soon the war will be over and I'll go home. Every one said that I'm going for only a couple of months and perhaps I can hold out that long. My father is Jewish and my mommy is Aryan, so my brother and I are mixed and children of mixed marriages must, according to some German laws, go to Terezín. Why, I don't know, nor why it has to be us and not Dad, it's all a big mix-up. They say Mom saves Dad from being sent in a transport, but not us. It isn't clear to me, but nothing can be done about it, it's the stupid regulations. So I sit here in my bunk and write and am unhappy. . . .

. . . I still have no appetite. Most of the time I eat from my own supplies, but they are slowly disappearing. What will happen then? The food here stinks. I wonder that anyone can eat it. Gita says that in no time I'll be eating it, too. Perhaps I'll get a parcel soon. . . .

We manage to get only one kilogram of bread every three days. They bring it in old hearses pulled by people. Actually, that is the only transportation here. They also carry corpses in them. Sometimes we get mouldy bread and that's bad. We cut off the mouldy part and then we must slice the rest in very thin slices to make it stretch, and it doesn't matter at all that we have to eat dry bread. If only we get enough. Sometimes I'd cut off another slice, but I mustn't. Tonička is a good housewife. I'd just gobble it all down and then the third day I wouldn't have any. Now I've begun to think too much about food. I even eat the dis-

[91] "Excerpts from the Diary of Forteen-year Old Charlotte Veresova of Prague," *Terezin.* Prague, Council of Jewish Communities in the Czech Lands, 1965, pp. 109, 110, 111.

gusting soups sometimes, and only a little while ago I couldn't have imagined it.

. . . I've learned here to appreciate ordinary things that, if we had them when we were still free, we didn't notice at all. Like riding in a bus or a train, or walking freely along the road, to the water, say. Or to go buy ice cream. Such an ordinary thing and it is out of our reach.

. . . Transports are leaving for Poland. Three with 2,500 people in each. Eight girls are going from our room. It's sad. Children of mixed marriages are so far safe from transports; that means that it's probably worse in Poland than it is here. So many old people are going, and orphans must, too. We are arranging "Hilfsdienst," all of us, now. That means helping to pack wherever we are most needed. Mainly old people. The poor things, why don't they leave them in peace? After all, they are about to die and could just as well die here. Yesterday I helped a family with seven children and today one with three children whose mother has tuberculosis. This is supposed to be a model ghetto, so why do they send people away, especially old people, because it probably wouldn't look nice if some one saw them begging for that disgusting soup? The town is packed, and that also does not make a good impression, either.

The Germans are going to make a film here, so they are up to all sorts of monkeyshines. Sometimes we think it's a joke and it really is funny. To whom will they show us off? Are we something they can brag about? They should be ashamed but probably they don't know how to be. The sidewalks are being scrubbed and wherever there is even a tiny bit of earth they plant flowers. They carried earth to the main square and have made a park, but no one is allowed to go into it. They play music there at noon, too. It sounds nice, but it does not satisfy us and even with the music I am still very homesick. If not more so.

. . . It is rumoured that they are building gas chambers here. People whisper about it and they really are building something mysterious in the fortification catacombs with airtight doors. They say a duck farm. What for? Might it still be gas? I can't believe it. It is too terrible. Never before have I truly admitted the idea of death, and now gas all of a sudden . . .

But I won't give up. I am not a bug, even though I am just as helpless. If something starts, I'll run away. At least I'll try, after all, what could I lose? It would be better to be shot while trying to escape than to be smothered with gas. I'll take Tonička and we'll run away to Litoměřice together. Perhaps someone will take us in there. I know I'm not the only one, but still I'll not give up just like that, without resisting! No, I shan't give up, even if everyone else did, but not I! I want to live, I want to go back home, for after all I've done nothing to anyone, so why should I die? It's so unjust!

READING NO. 76

THERESIENSTADT: THE OLD[92]

Himmler's statistician, Dr. Richard Korherr, told him that the principal cause of the loss of 37,000 inmates in Theresienstadt during the first year was "the incidence of death." A judge who survived the ghetto-transit camp has described it:

γ   γ   γ

The new life was hardest on the old people. Many had been told in Germany that if they signed their property away, they would be sent to an old-age home. Instead they were brought here, to sleep on the floor, shorn of all their familiar possessions. Many of them had no close relatives left, and merely lived on, depressed and listless.

A dysentery epidemic broke out, and many of the older people were affected. The water came from wells, and few of the houses had modern hygienic plumbing. There were only two or three toilets for a hundred inmates, and people had to wait in line, writhing in pain and terribly ashamed if they could not wait long enough. Thousands were so weak that they could not get up, and literally died in their own excrement.

For many Theresienstadt was only a transit camp. The dreaded transports would eventually take them further east. "Transport" was a word of terror; it paralyzed all life and thinking. One heard the order, "Five thousand people to be processed!" Who would be called—your friend, your mother, your child, yourself?

[92] Heinrich Liebrecht, "Therefore Will I Deliver Him," In Eric H. Boehm, ed., *We Survived: The Stories of the Hidden and Hunted of Nazi Germany*. New Haven, 1949, p. 23.

READING NO. 77

THE "BEAUTIFICATION" CAMPAIGN IN THERESIENSTADT[93]

The Danish people doggedly worked at keeping in touch with their Jewish prisoners in Theresienstadt and tried to have them released as early as October 1943. Foreign Ministry officials and Ribbentrop himself were addressed. Five persons were released in January 1944. The Danes also succeeded in circumventing the ban on packages and pressed for permission to visit the camp, Finally, the date of the visit for the Danish Red Cross was set for June 23, 1944, and lasted eight hours. A 15-year old girl observed the preparations:

γ   γ   γ

The camp command issued new orders about the "beautifying campaign" that must be finished in two months.

It's ridiculous, but it seems that Terezín is to be changed into a sort of spa. I don't know why I was reminded of the fairy tale, "Table, set yourself!" But that is how everything seems to me. The orders are received in the evening, and in the morning everyone's eyes are staring with wonder, where did this or that thing come from? For three years it never occurred to anyone that streets might be named anything but Q and L. Where the Magdeburg barracks or the Jäger or any other barracks was, every little child knew. But all of a sudden the Germans had an idea and over night signs had to be put on every corner house with the name of the street, and at crossroads arrows pointed.: Zum Park, Zum Bad, etc. We don't say Magdeburg barracks any more, but BV; I don't live at L410, but Hauptstrasse 10. The school by the construction headquarters that had served as hospital up to today, was cleared out over night and the patients put elsewhere while the whole building was repainted, scrubbed up, school benches brought in, and in the morning a sign could be seen afar: "Knaben und Mädchenschule." It really looks fine, like a real school, only the pupils and teachers are missing. That shortcoming is adjusted by a small note on the door: "Holidays". On the square the newly sown grass is coming up, the

[93] "Excerpts from the Diary of Helga Weissova-Hoskova," *Terezin, op. cit.*, pp. 108–109.

centre is adorned by a big rose plot and the paths, covered with clean, yellow sand, are lined with two rows of newly painted benches. The boards we wondered about for so many days, trying to puzzle out what they were for, turned into a music pavilion. We even have a café with the fine sign "Kaffeehaus." And all the shops got new names of firms. The houses will also be painted, they have already started in Lange-strasse. The barracks behind "Magdeburg," where they had had pro-duction and processing of mica have become a "dining hall." The girls that are specially employed there to heat up the food must wear white caps and aprons. The physical culture hall was turned into a res-taurant with carved furniture, plush chairs in the foyer, and big vases with bouquets. On the second floor there is a library and reading room and little tables on the terrace with coloured sunflowers. They have al-ready got quite far in painting the houses. Some of the Danish inmates' rooms got equipment. In two of the barracks some bunks and shelves were painted yellow and they got blue curtains. In the park in front of the Infants' Home they put up a luxury pavilion with cribs and light blue, quilted covers. In one room there are toys, a carved rocking horse, and so on. Then there is a pool, a merry-go-round and see-saws. None of us can explain why they are doing all this. . . .

READING NO. 78

A RANSOM SCHEME FOR SLOVAKIAN JEWS[94, 95]

A proposal for rescuing the Jews of Slovakia was originally conceived by Rabbi Michael Dov Ber Weissmandel, a member of the Jewish Council "Working Group," who tried to save the rest of Slovakian Jewry after the June 1942 deportations. Gisi Fleischmann, a co-worker, carried on lengthy negotiations with Wisliceny over a ransom plan which Himmler promoted. Wisliceny told her:

γ   γ   γ

We have already done business, and I am now in a position to make more extensive proposals. If you can bring us two million dollars, we will stop the deportations throughout all Europe [except in Poland and Germany]. . . . The Jewish question in those lands must be settled once and for all. I cannot help you there. The result of my efforts in Berlin is a "Plan for Europe," which will apply to all the countries of Europe other than Germany and Poland. . . . If you bring us two million dollars, you may be certain that the Jews in Bulgaria, Rumania, France, Belgium, Holland, Greece and Scandinavia will survive this war.[94]

* * * *

From the negotiations conducted with Wisliceny, it appears that the SS-Chiefs would have agreed to put the plan into effect for two or three million dollars. There is reason to assume that the go-between, Wisliceny, was eager that the negotiations succeed. He himself was not an enthusiastic supporter of the "final solution", and may have believed that these successful negotiations would provide an alibi in the future. According to him, Eichmann opposed the "plan" from the beginning, but did not dare reject it outright; and so "against his wish" and out of certain considerations he forwarded the plan to Reichsführer Himmler. In November 1942, Himmler agreed to the transfer of 20,000 dollars, which Wisliceny had received from the Bratislava Group, as

---

[94] Quoted in Alexander Weissberg, *Desperate Mission: Joel Brand's Story*. New York, 1958, p. 56.

[95] Livia Rothkirchen, *The Destruction of Slovak Jewry: A Documentary History*. Jerusalem, 1961, pp. xxxiii, xxxiv, xxxv.

advance payment to the Chief Office for Economy and Administration of SS (SS–WVHA = Wirtschafts- u. Verwaltungshauptamt). Wisliceny was permitted to confer with Jewish representatives. . . . [He] as the emissary of RSHA together with Alois Brunner organized transports of Jews from Salonika and Macedonia to the death camps. Most likely the Nazis had rejected the plan from the very beginning, but kept negotiating for propaganda purposes. It is also possible that the SS-Chiefs wished to extort money from Jews and deceive them by illusory promises. After a few months' hesitation, Himmler annulled the ''Europa Plan'' in August 1943 . . . Wisliceny who kept making them believe that the Plan had good chances of success, insisted that it failed only because the leaders of Jewry abroad had not provided the money in time.[95]

READING NO. 79

MUSSOLINI'S OPPORTUNISTIC
ANTI-SEMITISM[96]

Italian anti-Jewish legislation shocked Italian Jews and caused them considerable suffering, but Mussolini's attitude toward Jews was far different from Hitler's, as was the great difference in their notions of race. This is indicated in the following reply to his sister, who criticized his racialist policy:

γ   γ   γ

In Italy, racialism and anti-Semitism were being made to appear as politically important as they are unimportant in their substance. The racial purity of this nation, over which have passed so many invasions and which has absorbed so many peoples from the four points of the compass and the Semitic peril in a nation like ours . . . are clearly absurd fables which should be left for certain fanatics to write [about].

But if circumstances had brought me to a Rome-Moscow Axis, I would perhaps have dressed up the Italian workers, who are so taken up with their jobs, just as promptly and with a detachment which the racialists might call Mediterranean, with the corresponding fable of Stakhanovite ethics and the happiness they bring. And in this case, too, it would have been a question of a showy but cheap token payment.

---

[96] Quoted in Meir Michaelis, "The Attitude of the Fascist Regime to the Jews in Italy," *Yad Vashem Studies*, IV, 1960, pp. 38–39.

READING NO. 80

GERMAN FEAR OF VATICAN STAND IN ROME[97]

Just before the deportation from Rome, Herbert Kappler, the SS Police Chief, demanded 50 kilograms of gold from Jews in Rome and threatened to take 300 hostages if the money was not raised. Not all of it could be collected, but Chief Rabbi Israel Zolli was able to arrange a loan from the Vatican. Pope Pius XII had also arranged to open convents and monasteries to fleeing Jews, but he did not take a public stand against the deportations. The rector of the German church in Rome, Bishop Ludwig Hudal, among others, feared that he might and sent a last-minute appeal to the German military commander to stop the seizures, which began October 15, 1943:

γ   γ   γ

I have just been informed by a high Vatican office in the immediate circle of the Holy Circle that the arrests of Jews of Italian nationality have begun this morning. In the interest of the good relations which have existed until now between the Vatican and the high German military command . . . I would be very grateful if you would give an order to stop these arrests in Rome and its vicinity right away. I fear that otherwise the Pope will have to make an open stand, which will serve the anti-German propaganda as a weapon against us.

[97] Gumpert to Foreign Office, enclosing message from Hudal, NG-5027.

READING NO. 81

GERMAN ARMY COMPLICITY IN SHOOTING JEWS AND SERBS[98]

Throughout the late summer and fall of 1941, Jews were crowded into camps near Belgrade and into the Belgrade ghetto. Eichmann proposed shooting them, and German troops were instructed to shoot with rifles, from a distance of eight to ten yards, aiming at the head or chest. Dr. Harald Turner, chief of the civil administration with a crucial role in handling Jewish matters, was proud of the "ruthless action" of the troops:

γ   γ   γ

Actually, it is false if one has to be accurate about it, that for murdered Germans—on whose account the ratio 1:100 should really be borne by Serbs—100 Jews are shot instead; but the Jews we already had in the camps—after all, they, too, are Serb nationals—and besides, they have to disappear. At any rate, I don't have to accuse myself that on my part there has been any lack of necessary ruthless action for the preservation of German prestige and the protection of members of the German Wehrmacht.

[98] Turner to Hildebrandt, October 17, 1941, NO-5810.

READING NO. 82

ITALIAN RESCUE EFFORTS IN CROATIA[99]

The Ustasi terror in Croatia aroused immediate and spontaneous rescue efforts on the part of the Italian army. Many of the actions were not recorded in documents, but there are numerous eye-witness accounts of help to Jews, and German anger at Italian "lack of cooperation" in German documents. In the summer of 1941, there was a secret discussion as to how to remove Jews hunted by the Ustasi. A young Italian lieutenant suggested that they be moved to safety in Italian tanks. The officers concerned were court-martialled but only sentenced to a few days' house arrest:

γ   γ   γ

There were countless instances like that. The Germans had no ground for mistaking the intentions of their Italian allies in this matter. General Vittorio Ambrosio had every right to say in his report to the General Staff on May 2nd. 1946:

"The Command of the Second Army, being fully informed of everything that was happening in the Second and Third Zone (of the Italian occupation area) not only acquiesced in all that its officers, N.C.O.'s and men were doing to save the lives of thousands of *Serb Orthodox Catholics* and Jews, but did nothing to hinder them using military transport for this purpose." . . .

The Jews, against whom the Croatian Government issued the special legislation of May 1941 (it was applied only in the German occupation zone) and who were subjected to terrible massacres during that summer by the Ustase, did all they could to escape over the demarcation line into the Italian zone.

Unfortunately only a few succeeded. But a year later, in the summer of 1942, the Jewish colony in the refuge zone counted about three thousand, concentrated mostly in Spalato, Zebenico and Cattaro. These Jews were enjoying complete liberty under the protection of the Italian flag. . . .

[99] Leon Poliakov and Jaques Sabille, *Jews Under the Italian Occupation.* Paris, 1955, pp. 133, 134, 135, 136, 142, 143, 145, 146, 148–149.

Luther says . . . that in Zagreb they were concerned about the attitude which the Italian Government would adopt with regard to the anti-Jewish measures now in preparation, especially the mass deportations. "So far as the Croatian side is concerned", Luther continues, "they are in principle in full agreement with the Jewish deportations; they consider of special importance the deportation of the four to five thousand Jews in the Second Zone, which is occupied by the Italians (including the important towns Dubrovnik and Mostar). They constitute—politically—a great hindrance, and their removal would ease matters generally."

This is the core of the problem. Luther says: "We have evidence of the effective resistance of the Italian authorities against the anti-Jewish measures of the Croatian Government.". . .

Luther concludes by informing the Minister that the German Ambassador in Zagreb, Kasche, is of the opinion that they should without further delay deport all Jews resident throughout Croatian territory, and that if these measures are taken they must be prepared for difficulties in the Italian occupation-zone.

[On October 3, 1942,] The Italians took the opportunity to suggest that Croatia "should propose to the Italian Government . . . that it should take over the Jews in the Second Zone."

Lorcovic [Croatian Foreign Minister] had told Kasche that "Croatia's agreement with Germany made it impossible for her to agree to the transfer of the Jews to Italy, without the consent of her German ally.". . .

Kasche added on his own account:

"I keep getting the impression that the Italian attitude is intended to drag the matter." He suggests that even Mussolini's reported approval of the German measures against the Jews is non-existent. "It is clear to me", he says, "that our Embassy was badly informed about the Duce's decision, or else the Italian officials disregard him."
. . . The Marquis d'Ajeta, the Italian representative in the negotiations . . . then announced the new decisions made by the Duce with a view to solving this problem:

"All Jews resident in the Italian zone in Croatia will be interned forthwith in the camps and will be subjected to a census. . . . "

As for the census, this was being carried on in the camps quietly and slowly. Of the 2,662 internees in the Italian occupation-zone only 863 were able to prove their claim to Italian nationality. Most of the others were Croatian. There were also Russians, Hungarians, Portuguese,

Poles, Czechoslovaks, Roumanians and Dutch. But there was never any question of handing anyone over to the Germans. . . .

The only result of the German pressure was the decision adopted by the Italian authorities in March 1943, in complete conflict with the Nazi demands, to concentrate all Jews in one camp, set up on the island of Arbe, in the Gulf of Carnaro, which was annexed by Italy, in order to protect the Jews from any danger that might follow on a change in the demarcation line between the two occupation zones.

This concentration of Jews on the island was started in May, and concluded in July, at the moment when the Fascist regime in Italy collapsed and Mussolini was arrested.

The regime which followed in Italy no longer felt it necessary to disguise its attitude of protecting Jews from the Germans. The new Secretary-General of the Foreign Ministry, Augusto Rosso, telegraphed on August 19th. 1943 to the Commander of the Second Army:

''We must avoid leaving behind the Croatian Jews or handing them over to the mercy of strangers, deprived of all protection, or exposed to the danger of repressions, except where they themselves express the wish to be given their freedom outside our occupation-zone.''

''The racial policy which was pursued by Italy'', he went on to say ''never prevented us from observing the principles of humanity, which constitute our inexhaustible spiritual legacy. Loyalty to these principles was never so urgent as now.''

READING NO. 83

JEWISH PARTISANS IN YUGOSLOVIA[100]

Early in 1943, the Italian command decided to send several thousand Jews in camps in their zone to the island of Rab (Arbe), in the Adriatic. There they were encamped near a camp of nationalistic Slovenes.

γ　　　　　　γ　　　　　　γ

The first inmates to be confined in the Jewish camp arrived at the end of May 1943, but already at the end of June the camp was full, housing 3,500 people with 500 children up to 15 years of age among them. From whichever angle one looks at the site, the buildings, the administration, it was for all practical purposes a concentration camp. . . . Among the inmates of the Rab camp there were also members of the Communist Party of Yugoslavia and of the Communist Youth Organization who formed their party organization headed by a committee. This committee found ways to be in touch with the committee in the Slovene camp and the two committees formed an Executive Committee for both camps which was responsible to make preparations for the liberation of the camps. The Jewish camp was represented in the Executive Committee by Viktor Hajon. Military units were formed and prepared for action on command. Within that framework a youth unit of 150 members was formed in the Jewish camp. This unit will be later the nucleus of the Jewish Rab Battalion. . . . On September 8, 1943, at a meeting of the inmates, a decision was taken to disarm the guard and to liberate the camp. After the meeting the inmates, although barehanded, disarmed the guard and came thereby in possession of their first firearms. During the next day military units were formed in both camps: four Slovene battalions and one Jewish battalion. . . . The Jewish battalion had 244 fighting men, including the medical unit of 40 members. Representatives of the two camps approached the Italian commanding officer on the island, colonel Cuiullio demanding from him to give order to the Italians to abandon the

[100] Jasa Romano, ''Jews in the Rab Camp and their Participation in the Liberation War,'' *Jewish Studies 2: Studies and Facts and Figures on the Participation of Jews in the People's Liberation War*. Belgrade, 1973, pp. 70–71.

military establishments and to hand over the arms and equipment. Cuiullio's objections notwithstanding the Italian units were disarmed, while he himself committed suicide in prison after his arrest. . . .

The four Slovene battalions were ordered to advance towards Slovenia while the Jewish brigade had to head for Otočac where the HQ has established itself. Thirtyfive Jewish nurses were sent with the Slovene battalion, while 18 medical doctors and 15 pharmacologists were attached to various other units. . . . The battalion was sent to the village of Lipa where the Staff Headquarters of the 7th Banija Division was housed. . . . Before the war ended 36 of these fighters died in combat. A number of former members of the Jewish battalion were given various political and military responsibilities in other units they joined. Nearly all the other inmates of the Rab camp, about 3000 of them, were brought to the liberated area of Lika, Kordun and Banija. . . . About 200 persons, mostly old and ill people, remained on the island of Rab. They were recaptured by the Germans and sent to death camp at Auschwitz. Out of those who were evacuated in good time 379 joined the Liberation Army. . . . Of these 86 died in the war (67 in combat, 19 as members of the supporting units) while 3 died due to illness. On the liberated area of Like, Kordun and Banija about 2400 Jewish emigrants found refuge. Out of these 648 joined the Liberation Movement and were given various noncombat duties. Before the war ended 33 of them died due to bombardments and capture, while 12 died due to illness.

READING NO. 84

MASS ANNIHILATION IN GREECE[101]

Eichmann's agent in Salonica, Wisliceny, has described the plan and execution of mass murder in Greece:

γ   γ   γ

16. In January 1943, I was ordered by Eichmann to go to Salonika and make arrangements with the military administration to find a final solution for the Jewish problem there. Shortly before my departure from Bratislava I was told to meet Hauptsturmfuehrer Brunner in Vienna. He showed me a "Marsch" order and told me that he had been given the assignment by Eichmann to arrange all technical matters and that I was to make contacts with the authorities and governmental agencies. We went to Salonika together on 2 February 1944, and conferred with the Chief of the Military Administration, War Administrative Counsellor Dr. Merten from the military command, Area Salonika-Aegeus. Also, the local branch office of the Secret Police and SD, the Criminal Commissioner Paschleben and Consul General Schoenberg. Dr. Merten was the decisive authority and said he wished the Jews in Salonika first be concentrated in certain areas of the city. This was done without difficulty during February-March 1943. At least 80 percent of the Greek Jews were workers, laborers, craftsmen or longshoremen, but a large proportion of them had tuberculosis and had also suffered of epidemics raging in their quarters. The Salonika Jews had lived in Greece since the 15th century when they had fled from the inquisition in Spain. On or about 10 March, Eichmann sent Brunner a message that the compulsory evacuation (Aussiedlung) of Jews was to start at once. Dr. Merten agreed to the action but requested 3,000 male Jewish workers for railroad construction work under the Organization Todt who were later returned in time for inclusion in the last transports. I talked to Eichmann by telephone in Berlin telling him that typhus raged among the Jews but he said his orders for immediate compulsory evacuation would stand. . . .

---

[101] Affidavit, C. Dieter Wisliceny, International Military Trubunal at Nuremberg, January 3, 1946. *Nazi Conspiracy and Aggression,* vol. VIII, 1946, pp. 611–612, 613.

18. Altogether, 60,000 Jews were collected from Greece and shipped to Auschwitz. I am sure that this figure is approximately correct. I know that twenty-four transports averaging approximately 2,300 human beings each were shipped from Salonika and surroundings between March and May 1943, under the supervision of Hauptsturmfuehrer Brunner and myself, while two transports of about 2,500 each were shipped from Athens in July 1944 under the supervision of Hauptsturmfuehrer Burger. The freight cars used in these transports were furnished by the Military Transport Command. The requests for these cars went from Hauptsturmfuehrer Novak in IV A 4 b to Department Counsellor Stange in the Ministry of Transport, Berlin and thence through; effecting the final solution of the Jewish problem commanded a sufficiently high priority to take precedence over other freight movements. All shipments were made on schedule, even in July 1944 when the Germans were evacuating Greece and rail transport needs were critical. Upon the departure of each transport a message was sent to Eichmann in Berlin stating the number of heads sent. I have seen copies of these cables in a folder kept by Brunner and upon completion of the movement of Jews from Northern Greece, Brunner made a summary report to Eichmann. I returned to Bratislava for several weeks and arrived again in Salonika at the end of May 1943 at which time Brunner was preparing the last shipment. The last transport left Salonika two days after my arrival and upon completion of the last shipment, Brunner was transferred to Paris for his new assignment.

19. During the period of collection into designated areas, the Jewish population was compelled to furnish their own subsistence. Upon arrival in the collecting camp, representatives of the Jewish community took over all cash and valuables from the inmates. Altogether, by August 1943, 280,000,000 drachmas had been deposited in the Greek National Bank for such purpose. This amount was appropriated by the German Military Administration. The property left behind, houses, businesses, apartments, movable belongings, etc., were administered by the Greek Governor General of Macedonia under the control of the Military administration.

20. In July 1944, Hoess, Commandant of Auschwitz, told Eichmann in my presence in Budapest that all of the Greek Jews had been exterminated because of their poor quality.

READING NO. 85

THE DOOMED MACEDONIAN TRANSPORTS[102]

On March 11, 1943, the Jewish quarter of Bitola in Macedonia, was divided into twenty-six sections and an army blockade was set up. Between five and six in the morning, Jews were told to be ready in an hour's time. At seven they left their homes under police escort and were taken to the railway station where all their valuables were seized. A witness has recalled:

γ   γ   γ

They loaded us into cattle wagons, fifty to sixty people in one wagon together with the luggage. There was not enough room and many had to stand. There was no water. The children kept on crying. . . . In one wagon a woman was in labor . . . and there was no doctor at hand. We reached Skoplje at midnight. . . . They opened the wagons and in the darkness pushed us into two big buildings. Our train had had the wagons carrying the Jews from Stip coupled to it. We kept stumbling over each other in the darkness, dragging along our luggage, the children, the aged and the sick. Squeezed in the mass and continuously beaten by the Bulgarian soldiers, we tried to get into the building. At dawn we learned that we were in Skoplje, in the Monopoly building, and that all the Jews of the whole of Macedonia had been rounded up that day.

In the Monopoly, 8,000 Macedonian Jews were confined to 30 rooms in four buildings. A doctor from Bitolj has described conditions there:

"In one room there were over 500 persons. . . . We and the Jews from Stip were kept locked in during the whole of the day because the plundering search of the Jews from Skoplje was still in progress. . . . When some of us tried to peep through the windows, a policeman fired in the air. . . .

On March 13, they opened the door for the first time and allowed us to go to the latrines. . . . They let out the 500 that were in our room and gave us half an hour, whereupon they locked us up again so that

---

[102] Declarations of Heskija Pijade, in Natan Grinberg, *Dokumenti*. Sophia, 1945, pp. 228–29, 230–231. Quoted in N. Levin, *The Holocaust*, pp. 556–557.

more than half the people never managed to relieve themselves or to get water. . . . The food was distributed once daily and it consisted of 250 grams of bread and usually a watery dish of beans or rice. . . . They gave us smoked meat from time to time, but it was so foul that we could not eat it in spite of our hunger. . . .

Under the pretext of searching us for hidden money, gold or foreign currency, they forced us sadistically to undress completely. . . . Sometimes they would even take away baby diapers.''. . .

READING NO. 86

THE MASSACRE AT JASSY[103]

On the eve of the war against the Soviet Union, the German High Command instructed Romania to remove all suspicious persons from the area of military operations to prevent sabotage and espionage. The Romanian Minister of Interior applied this order to Jews. There were extensive evacuations and arrests. Leaders in Jewish communities were held as hostages. A rumor circulated through Jassy, the capital of Moldavia and headquarters of the German military, that Soviet parachutes had landed near the city. A massacre followed involving German and Romanian soldiers and police. An Italian journalist, Curzio Malaparte, witnessed the scene:

γ   γ   γ

When I reached the top of the hill, I turned around. The town was ablaze. Thick clouds of smoke hung over the lower sections along the banks of the river. The houses and the trees close to the burning buildings stood out clearly and looked bigger than they were, like enlarged photographs. I could even discern the cracks in the walls, the branches and the leaves. There was something dead about the scene, and at the same time, something too precise, as in a photograph; I would have believed that I was facing a ghostly photographic backdrop, if it had not been for the confused din rising everywhere, the wailing hoot of sirens, the long whistling of steam engines and the rattling of machine-guns that imparted a vivid and immediate reality to that terrible sight. Up and down the narrow twisting streets leading towards the centre of town, I heard all about me desperate barking, banging of doors, shattering of glass and of china, smothered screams, imploring voices calling *mama! mama!*, horrible beseeching cries, . . . the sharp report of a shot, the whizzing of a bullet and the strident, frightful German voices. In Unirii Square a group of S.S. men kneeling by the Prince Gutsa Voda monument fired their tommy-guns towards the little square where the statue of Prince Ghiha in Moldavian costume stands with his great quilted coat and his brow covered by a tall fur cap. By the light of the fires a black, gesticulating throng, mostly women,

[103] Curzio Malaparte, *Kaputt*. New York, 1966, pp. 131–132, 134.

could be seen huddled at the foot of the monument. From time to time someone rose, darted this way or that across the square and fell under the bullets of the S.S. men. Hordes of Jews pursued by soldiers and maddened civilians armed with knives and crowbars fled along the streets; groups of policemen smashed in house doors with their rifle butts; windows opened suddenly and screaming dishevelled women in nightgowns appeared with their arms raised in the air; some threw themselves from windows and their faces hit the asphalt with a dull thud. Squads of soldiers hurled hand grenades through the little windows level with the street into the cellars where many people had vainly sought safety; some soldiers dropped to their knees to look at the results of the explosions within the cellars and turned laughing faces to their companions. Where the slaughter had been heaviest the feet slipped in blood; everywhere the hysterical and ferocious toll of the pogrom filled the houses and streets with shots, with weeping, with terrible screams and cruel laughter. . . .

I threw myself on to the bed and closed my eyes. I felt abased. All was over by now. The dead were dead. There was nothing more to do. *La dracu,* I thought. It was ghastly not to be able to do something. . . .

A couple of hours later I awoke. It was a brilliant morning; the air, cleansed and freshened by the storm of the previous night, glistened on everything like a transparent varnish. I went to the window and looked down Lapusneanu Street. Scattered about in the street were human forms lying in awkward positions. The gutters were strewn with dead bodies, heaped one upon another. Several hundred corpses were dumped in the centre of the churchyard. Packs of dogs wandered about sniffing the dead in the frightened, cowed way dogs have when they are seeking their masters; they seemed full of respect and pity; they moved about amid those poor dead bodies with delicacy, as if they feared to step on those bloody faces and those rigid hands. Squads of Jews, watched over by policemen and soldiers armed with tommy-guns, were at work moving the dead bodies to one side, clearing the middle of the road and piling the corpses up along the walls so they would not block traffic. German and Rumanian trucks loaded with corpses kept going by. A dead child was sitting up on the pavement near the *lustrageria* with his back against the wall and his head drooped on one shoulder. I drew back, closed the window and sat on the bed and began to dress very slowly. From time to time I had to lie flat on my back to fight down spasms of nausea. Suddenly, I thought I heard sounds of merry voices, of people laughing, calling and gaily answering each other. I forced myself to go back to the window. The road was crowded with people—squads of soldiers and policemen, groups of men and women, and bands of gypsies with their hair in long ringlets were gaily and noisily chattering with one another, as they despoiled the corpses, lifting them, rolling them over, turning them on their sides to draw off their coats, their trousers and their underclothes; feet were rammed against dead bellies to help pull off the shoes; people came running to share in the loot; others made off with arms piled high with clothing. It was a gay bustle, a merry occasion, a feast and a marketplace all in one. The dead twisted into cruel postures were left naked.

READING NO. 87

VATICAN HELP IN ROMANIA[104]

The papal nuncio in Romania, Andreia Cassulo, had tried a number of times to have the deportations stopped, especially of converts, but the Romanian government rejected any special concessions to the Church in this regard. The Chief Rabbi, Alexander Shafran, who had appealed to numerous political and religious officials for help, gave Cassulo a report and photographs of the terrible plight of orphans in Transnistria and urged him to visit the camp. Finally, in the spring of 1943, he was granted permission:

γ   γ   γ

. . . Cassulo later requested a meeting with Radu Leca, the commissioner of the Rumanian Government for Jewish affairs. From him he received a promise to grant ten requests. Six of them are mentioned by Martini: limitation of the deportations; the removal of the deportees from German-governed territory; the return of widows and people with special rights; different forms of relief work; the granting of more freedom to skilled workers in the ghettos to carry out their work; the dispatch to Palestine of a certain number of the orphans. . . . [but] the German authorities were totally opposed to any agreement of this nature and . . . tried especially to prevent the emigration of the young people. . . . The position of the Jews in Transnistria worsened sharply as the Rumanians prepared to withdraw from the area between the rivers Bug and Dniestr. On February 18, 1944, the Nuncio received a request from the Chief Rabbi of Palestine, Rabbi Herzog, which had reached him *via* the Papal Nuncio in Istanbul, Roncalli, the late Pope John XXIII. The Nuncio was asked to devote all his efforts to saving the remainder of the deportees in Transnistria whose position was threatened by the retreating German troops. This was an issue on which, together with Rabbi Shafran, Cassulo had already tried to intervene. Cassulo approached the Government on this matter already before the end of February, on his own initiative. He was at this stage

---

[104] Theodore Lavi, ''The Vatican's Endeavors on Behalf of Rumanian Jewry during the Second World War,'' *Yad Vashem Studies*, V, 1963, pp. 414, 415, 419–20.

seemingly working with the full knowledge of the Jewish leaders who were deeply concerned as to the fate of the deportees. . . .

[Shafran] describes the co-operation with the papal Nuncio in these words:

So our prime concern in those days was the vast problem of saving the remnants, the widows and orphans and the deportees of Transnistria. Nuncio Andreia Cassulo brought every problem we asked him about to the Government. I also asked him to arrange a visit to Transnistria and inspect for himself the conditions obtaining there, in that vale of tears. I also convinced him to request from the Vatican that they try to soften the heart of Mihai Antonescu when he visited Rome with Queen Elena. Cassulo also tried to soften the harsh approach of the German envoy to Bucharest, Manfred Killinger. This "righteous one of the nations of the world" neither rested nor kept silent until he had wrested from Antonescu's hand a promise of "return to the homeland." It sometimes happened that he appeared before them twice in one day on some burning issue. And it happened once, when he returned from an interview with Antonescu (I was waiting for him in his office) and showed me the "paper," a copy of some permit, tears flowed from his eyes, and he thanked me because I had given him the opportunity of doing a good deed.

READING NO. 88

HITLER LECTURES HORTHY ON HOW TO DEAL WITH HUNGARIAN JEWS[105]

Officials in Germany had anticipated early compliance with their demands, including the setting up of labor camps and ghettos. Kállay, however, stood firm. The Germans, meanwhile, insisted with Sztójay, the Hungarian minister in Berlin, that all Hungarian Jews be evacuated by the end of 1942. A high-level understanding was needed, and on April 17, 1943, the whole question of German demands was laid open by Hitler and von Ribbentrop in talks with Horthy in Klessheim Castle:

γ   γ   γ

PARTIAL TRANSLATION OF DOCUMENT D-736

Note Fueh. 25/43. Secret State Matter.

Notes   Secret Reich Matter.

. . . The Fuehrer then described to Horthy the German rationing measures which were carried out with perfect orderliness. There was no black market in Germany, and the peasants willingly delivered the quotas fixed for them. For produce which they placed at the Government's disposal over and above these quotas they were paid considerably higher prices by government offices in some cases even double the price, so that the peasants also had the possibility of getting hold of some money in this way. Horthy remarked to this that these problems were very difficult for Hungary. He had so far been unable to master the black market. The Fuehrer replied that it was the fault of the Jews who considered hoarding and profiteering as their main sphere of activity even during a world war, in exactly the same way as in England sentences for rationing offenses and the like now chiefly concerned Jews. To Horthy's counter-question as to what he should do with the Jews now that he had deprived them of almost all possibilities of livelihood, he could not kill them off—the Reich Foreign Minister declared that the Jews must either be exterminated or taken to concentration camps. There was no other possibility. To Horthy's re-

[105] D-736 *Nazi Conspiracy and Aggression*, vol. VII, 1946.

mark that it was easier for Germany in this respect, because she did not possess so many Jews, the Fuehrer quoted figures which showed the extraordinarily great predominance of Jews in certain professions. Horthy replied that he had not known this at all. In this connection the Fuehrer came to speak of the town of Nurnberg, which had not tolerated any Jews within its walls for 400 years, while Furth admitted Jews. The result was that Nurnberg flourished greatly and Furth degenerated completely. The Jews did not even possess organizational value. In spite of the fears which he (the Fuehrer) had heard repeatedly in Germany also every thing continued to go its normal way without the Jews too. Where the Jews were left to themselves, as for instance in Poland, the most terrible misery and decay prevailed. They are just pure parasites. In Poland this state of affairs had been fundamentally cleared up. If the Jews there did not want to work, they were shot. If they could not work, they had to succumb. They had to be treated like tuberculosis bacillae, with which a healthy body may become infected. This was not cruel, if one remembered that even innocent creatures of nature, such as hares and deer, have to be killed, so that no harm is caused by them. Why should the beasts who wanted to bring us Bolshevism be spared more? Nations which did not rid themselves of Jews, perished. One of the most famous examples of this was the downfall of a people who were once so proud—the Persians, who now lead a pitiful existence as Armenians. . . .

Salzburg, the 18th April 1943

(SCHMIDT)

READING NO. 89

EICHMANN'S KILLING UNIT IN HUNGARY, MARCH 1944[106]

On March 15, 1944, Horthy was again called to Klessheim Castle by Hitler and faced with an ultimatum of virtual arrest. Kallay would have to go and Hungary would have to choose between a German military occupation or a German-approved government. Horthy submitted to a German-approved government, but by the time he was allowed to return to Hungary on March 19, an army of German officials, including SS Police, were spread throughout the country and motorized army divisions were in full strength. Meanwhile, Eichmann had assembled a killing unit at Mauthausen:

γ   γ   γ

21. In connection with the movement of the German Army into Hungary in March 1944, it was agreed between Hitler and Horthy that the Army should not enter Budapest. No mention was made of the Security Police, however, and an Einsatz Group of about 800 members was secretly organized, under the leadership of Standartenfuehrer, later Oberfuehrer Dr. Geschke. The rank and file of the Einsatz Group consisted of members of the Security Police from all over Germany and occupied Europe, in addition about sixty men from the Waffen SS. Shortly after arrival in Budapest, a further battalion of Waffen SS was assigned to the Einsatz Group for guard purposes. Most of the experts on final solution of the Jewish question in IV A 4 b were organized under the designation "Special Action Commando Eichmann". This Special Commando was directly subordinated to the Chief of the Security Police and SK Kaltenbrunner. Both the Einsatz Group and the Special Commando were first activated about 10 March 1944. The personnel were assembled at Mauthausen in Linz, Austria, and moved later into Hungary 19 March 1944. Matters of personnel for the Special Action Commandos were handled by Geschke while all operations were directed by Eichmann personally. The Army had informed higher SS and Police Leader Winckelman as representative of Himm-

---

[106] Affidavit C. Wisliceny, Dieter, *Nazi Conspiracy and Aggression*, vol. VIII, 1946, pp. 613–614.

ler, and Oberfuehrer Piffrader and Dr. Geschke as representatives of RSHA, of the place and hour of the invasion of Hungary. I had advance knowledge of the action that was to be undertaken although it was kept secret from the rank and file of the group. I had seen Eichmann studying maps of Hungary in advance of the movement. We marched into Budapest on 19 March 1944 ahead of the Army and Eichmann arrived there on 21 March.

22. During the first days after arrival in Budapest, Eichmann, Hunsche and I conferred with Endre and von Baky who were Administrative State Secretary and Political State Secretary respectively of the Ministry of Interior for Hungary. Actions against Jews were discussed in the smallest detail. It was the purpose to start evacuation of Jews as soon as possible. In late March 1944, about 200 Jews prominent in the economical and cultural life of Hungary were taken as hostages on orders of Geschke. Thereafter in accordance with the agreement between Endre and Eichmann, Jews were concentrated in designated larger cities and towns in Karpato-Russia and Siebenbuergen (Transylvania), such actions being undertaken by the Hungarian Gendarmerie under Lt. Colonel Ferenzcy who had the same relative position for the Hungarian Ministry of Interior as I had for Special Action Commando Eichmann in the carrying out of these actions. Eichmann's delegates were sent to each of the larger collecting points.

READING NO. 90

ARROW CROSS ATROCITIES
IN BUDAPEST[107]

*Before their first exodus from Hungary, the Germans not only had
to eliminate Kallay and threaten Horthy, but exploit the Hungarian
fascists, the Arrow Cross, or Nyilas. Their murder of Jews began in
October 1944. A survivor recalls:*

γ   γ   γ

. . . The Arrow Cross took over. On the 16th of October the massacre
of Budapest Jews began. What happened—some of the Arrow Cross
and SS and SA came to the houses. We were still in the yellow star
houses and they took the people out and they killed the children—and
tortured [them]. Unbelievable torture was going on. . . .

The Russian army was approaching Budapest by November 6th, but
they were stopped . . . and that gave plenty of time to the Arrow Cross
to keep on massacring the Jews of Budapest. I am just picking up the
Jewish orphanage story. We had a Jewish orphanage with 200 orphans
and one Christmas night, it was a very bitter cold snowy night, and the
Arrow Cross people went into the orphanage to celebrate Christ's birth
and took each and every children and every teacher out of the orphanage. The children were in their nighties and barefooted. They marched
them through Budapest on that snowy night at midnight to the banks of
the Danube and they shot each and everyone of them, killing them into
the Danube, the frozen Danube. By that time the Danube was not the
blue or brown Danube, it was a red Danube because of the Jewish
blood. They said that we cannot send you to Auschwitz, we cannot
send you anywhere any more. . . . So we take care of you any way we
can.

---

[107] Testimony of Eva Bentley, March 8, 1985. Gratz College Holocaust Archives.

READING NO. 91

EVIDENCE OF MASS KILLINGS OF JEWS IN 1942 REPORTED IN THE WEST[108]

Many journalists, German soldiers, Vatican intelligence, the Polish underground, and neutral foreign ministry and consular officials, among others, had hard information about the annihilation of Jews in Europe, and much of it was reported or leaked to Western sources throughout 1942. But August 8, 1942 is generally considered to have been the date when knowledge of the Nazi official plan of mass destruction was made known to the West. This came about through a cable sent by Gerhardt Riegner, the representative of the World Jewish Congress in Geneva, through the American and British embassies in Switzerland to the WJC in London and New York. It was learned in 1983 that Reigner's source was a German industrialist, Edward Schulte. The cable was dismissed by the State Department and Whitehall as "unsubstantiated" and kept from the WJC leader in America, Rabbi Stephen S. Wise, until August 28.

γ   γ   γ

It presented the plan as an "alarming report" and added that "we transmit information with all necessary reservation as exactitude cannot be confirmed." It is not really surprising therefore that officials at the State Department should hesitate as to what to do about the report beyond asking for further verification . . .

However, there was still another report, at least as authoritative as the Riegner cable, which had reached the Western world some months previously, and which should have been far more effective in awakening both the Jewish and the non-Jewish worlds to what was going on in Poland . . .

It seems that the Polish Government in Exile in London took the report seriously. On June 2, 1942, the BBC broadcast the gist of the report to Europe, specifically mentioning the figure of 700,000, but not dwelling on the aspect of the report which indicates a concerted plan for physical extermination. . . . [See below, Report of Bund.]

---

[108] Yehuda Bauer, "When Did They Know?" *Midstream*, May 1942, pp. 51, 52, 53.

The Poles convinced the British Minister of Information, Mr. Brendan Bracken, to lend his hand, and on July 9 a press conference was held in which he participated, along with Stanislaw Mikolajczyk (Minister of Home Affairs in the Polish Government in Exile), Zygielbojm and Schwarzbart. At that conference the May report was fully utilized, along with other facts that had come to light in the meantime.

The problem remains as to what exactly was done with these reports, and whether they were utilized by Jewish or non-Jewish leaders to arouse public opinion or to map out a plan of action. The question as to the attitude of the press in this matter is therefore of vital importance. The only British daily that brought out some of the news concerning the May report was the conservative Daily Telegraph. In its issue of June 25, 1942, on page 5, it published the details of the report, including the report's conclusion that the Nazis intended to exterminate Polish Jewry, and gave details about the gassings at Chelmno. . . .

FOLDER NO. 15—POLISH UNDERGROUND STUDY— ITEM 26

REPORT OF THE BUND REGARDING THE PERSECUTION OF THE JEWS

From the day the Russo-German war broke out, the Germans embarked on the physical extermination of the Jewish population on Polish soil, using the Ukrainians and the Lithuanian fascists for this job. It began in Eastern Galicia, in the summer months of 1941. The following system was applied everywhere: men, fourteen to sixty years old, were driven to a single place—a square or a cemetery, where they were slaughtered or shot by machine guns or killed by hand grenades. They had to dig their own graves. Children in orphanages, inmates in old-age homes, the sick in hospitals were shot, women were killed in the streets. In many towns the Jews were carried off to "an unknown destination" and killed in adjacent woods. 30,000 Jews were killed in Lwów, 15,000 in Stanislawów, 5,000 in Tarnopol, 2,000 in Zloczów, 4,000 in Brzezany (there were 18,000 Jews in this town, only 1,700 are left). The same happened in Zborów, Kolomyja, Sambor, Stryj, Drohobycz, Zbaraż, Prezemyslany, Kuty, Sniatyn, Zaleszczyki, Brody, Przemyśl, Rawa Ruska and other places. . . .

In the months of October and November, the same began to happen in Wilno, in the Wilno area and in Lithuania. . . . The total number of the Jews murdered in a beastly fashion in the Wilno area and in Lithuania is 300,000, according to various estimates.

The killing of the Jews in the area of Slonim started in September. . . . In Rowne, the killing started during the first days of November. In three days over 15,000 people, men, women and children were killed. In Hancewicze (near Baranowicze) 6,000 Jews were shot. The action of killing Jews embraced all Polish territories beyond the San and the Bug. We have mentioned only some of the localities.

In November-December, the killing of Jews also began in the Polish territories incorporated into the Reich, the so-called Warthegau. The murder was accomplished by gassing in the hamlet of Chelmno, twelve kilometers from the town of Kolo (county of Kolo). A special automobile (a gas chamber) was used. Ninety persons were loaded each time. The victims were buried in special graves, in an opening in the Lubard Woods. . . . From November 1941 until March 1942, a total of 5,000 person were gassed at Chelmno, Jewish residents of Kolo, Dąbie, Bugaj, Izbica Kujawska, 35,000 Jews from the Lodz ghetto and a number of Gypsies.

The extermination of Jews in the territory of the so-called Government-General started in February 1942. . . . In March, the action of mass expulsion of the Jews out of Lublin started. Children and elderly people in the orphanages and old-age homes were murdered in a beastly fashion along with the patients in the hospital for general and epidemic diseases and numerous residents were killed in the streets and the homes. In all, there were over 2,000 victims. Some 25,000 Jews were carried off in ''an unknown direction'' out of Lublin, in sealed railway cars. They disappeared without a trace. Some 3,000 Jews were interned in barracks at Majdanek Tatarowy, a suburb of Lublin. No Jew has remained in Lublin. . . . It is estimated that the Germans have already killed 700,000 Polish Jews.

The above facts indicate without any doubt that the criminal German Government has begun to realize Hitler's prophecy that in the last five minutes of the war, whatever its outcome, he will kill all the Jews in Europe. . . . Millions of Polish citizens of Jewish extraction are in immediate mortal danger. . . .

We are, therefore, addressing ourselves to the Government of Poland. . . . immediately to take up the necessary steps to prevent the destruction of Polish Jewry. . . . The Governments of Poland and the

United Nations should let the German Government know of the application of the policy of retaliation. . . .

We are aware of the fact that we are requesting the Polish Government to apply unusual measures. This is the only possibility of saving millions of Jews from inevitable destruction.

READING NO. 92

U.S. GOVERNMENT ACQUIESCENCE IN THE MURDER OF JEWS[109]

On January 13, 1944, Morgenthau presented Roosevelt with an eighteen-page memorandum entitled ''Report to the Secretary on the Acquiescence of This Government in the Murder of Jews.'' It was a powerful document, written largely by Josiah Dubois, Jr., with the help of Randolph E. Paul and John W. Pehle, charging that State Department officials had utterly failed to prevent the mass annihilation of Jews. It began with a direct attack:

γ   γ   γ

One of the greatest crimes in history, the slaughter of the Jewish people in Europe, is continuing unabated.

This Government has for a long time maintained that its policy is to work out programs to save those Jews of Europe who could be saved.

I am convinced on the basis of the information which is available to me that certain officials in our State Department, which is charged with carrying out this policy, have been guilty not only of gross procrastination and wilful failure to act, but even of wilful attempts to prevent action from being taken to rescue Jews from Hitler.

I fully recognize the graveness of this statement and I make it only after having most carefully weighed the shocking facts which have come to my attention during the last several months.

Unless remedial steps of a drastic nature are taken, and taken immediately, I am certain that no effective action will be taken by this Government to prevent the complete extermination of the Jews in German controlled Europe, and that this Government will have to share for all time responsibility for this extermination.

The tragic history of this Government's handling of this matter reveals that certain State Department officials are guilty of the following:

(1) They have not only failed to use the *Governmental machinery*

---

[109] Transcript of pp. 212–213, *Diaries of Henry Morgenthau, Jr.* Franklin D. Roosevelt Library, Hyde Park, N.Y., 12538. Copy in Gratz College Holocaust Archives.

at their disposal to rescue Jews from Hitler, but have even gone so far as to use this Government machinery to prevent the rescue of these Jews.

(2) They have not only failed to cooperate with *private organizations* in the efforts of these organizations to work out individual programs of their own, but have taken steps designed to prevent these programs from being put into effect.

(3) They not only have failed to facilitate the obtaining of information concerning Hitler's plans to exterminate the Jews of Europe but in their official capacity have gone so far as to surreptitiously attempt to stop the obtaining of information concerning the murder of the Jewish population of Europe.

(4) They have tried to cover up their guilt by:

(a) concealment and misrepresentation;

(b) the giving of false and misleading explanations for their failures to act and their attempts to prevent action; and

(c) the issuance of false and misleading statements concerning the ''action'' which they have taken to date.

READING NO. 93

WAR REFUGEE BOARD REPORT ON GASSINGS IN AUSCHWITZ, APRIL 1942–APRIL 1944[110]

γ   γ   γ

Executive Office of the President
War Refuge Board
Washington, D.C.
Page 33.

German Extermination Camps—Auschwitz and Birkenau.

Careful estimate of the number of Jews gassed
In Birkenau between April, 1942 and April, 1944
(according to countries of origin).

Poland (transported by truck)	approximately	300,000
Poland (transported by train)	approximately	600,000
Holland	approximately	100,000
Greece	approximately	45,000
France	approximately	150,000
Belgium	approximately	50,000
Germany	approximately	60,000
Yugoslavia, Italy and Norway	approximately	50,000
Lithuania	approximately	50,000
Bohemia, Moravia and Austria	approximately	30,000
Slovakia	approximately	30,000
Various camps for foreign Jews in Poland	approximately	300,000
	approximately	1,765,000

[110] L-22, *Nazi Conspiracy and Aggression,* Vol. VII, 1946, p. 771.

READING NO. 94.

EICHMANN'S "BLOOD FOR GOODS" DEAL[111]

Eichmann's offer, directed by Himmler, was a continuation of the "Europa Plan," involving Wisliceny and Gisi Fleischmann in Slovakia. When the Jewish Council for Assistance and Rescue in Budapest learned that Wisliceny was in the same city, they felt encouraged for they knew about his involvement in the Europa Plan and had been urged by Rabbi Weissmandel of Slovakia to continue the contact. Joel Brand, a member of the Council, met with Wisliceny and started negotiations for the rescue of all Jews still alive. But the talks then continued with Eichmann. They met on April 25. Eichmann spoke in short, clipped sentences:

γ   γ   γ

I suppose you know who I am. I was in charge of the 'actions' in Germany, Poland, and Czechoslovakia. Now it is Hungary's turn. I have already investigated you and your people of the Joint and the *Sochnuth* [Jewish Agency], and I have verified your ability to make a deal. Now then, I am prepared to sell you one million Jews. Not the whole lot—you wouldn't be able to raise enough money for that. But you could manage a million. Goods for blood; blood for goods. You can take them from any country you like, wherever you can find them. From Hungary, Poland, the eastern provinces, from Terezin, from Auschwitz—wherever you want. Whom do you want to save? Men who can beget children? Women who can bear them? Old people? Children? Sit down and talk.

---

[111] Alexander Weissberg, *Desperate Mission: Joel Brand's Story*. New York, 1958, pp. 91–92.

READING NO. 95

ALLIED FAILURE TO BOMB AUSCHWITZ[112]

Aerial photos of Auschwitz taken from April 4, 1944, to January 14, 1945, clearly showed the camp's gas chambers and crematoria and prisoners at various stages of processing.

γ   γ   γ

The photographs, along with a scholarly treatise titled ''Holocaust Revisited,'' have just been turned over to the National Archives by the Central Intelligence Agency, which also passed the photographs on to the White House. It is understood that after seeing the photographs, President Carter sent them to Elie Wiesel, chairman of the Holocaust Commission and a survivor of Auschwitz.

Just why the CIA passed the pictures on to the archives is not clear. The authors of the CIA report accompanying the pictures said they were moved to research and write the report after seeing the television serial, ''The Holocaust.''

''My hope is that we stimulate the interest of historians in the use of photographs taken through aerial reconnaissance,'' Dino A. Brugioni, one of the authors of the CIA report, said yesterday. ''It is an untapped source of history.''

The immediate reaction to release and publication of the photographs may be primarily one of anger. Jewish scholars have long asked why the Allies did not bomb Auschwitz or the rail line leading to it, a question that is sure to be brought up again with the release of the pictures. . . .

Proponents of such an attack recognized that it would have killed many of the inmates, but the Germans were going to kill them anyway and destroying the camp might have saved other intended victims.

Destruction of the rail line would have hampered the transport of nearly 1 million Hungarian Jews, who were being moved to Auschwitz at the time.

In April 10, 1944, two Auschwitz escapees named Rudolf Vrba and Alfred Wetzler passed on detailed information to Jewish leaders in Switzerland that Auschwitz was a death camp for Jews. The Swiss Jews informed American diplomats in Berne that 12,000 Jews were

---

[112] '' '44 Photos Showed Auschwitz Camp,'' *Philadelphia Inquirer*, February 24, 1979.

being murdered every day at Auschwitz, information that reportedly reached Washington by June 1944.

A crucial question about the aerial reconnaissance pictures of Auschwitz is whether they were ever passed on to Washington by the U.S. Strategic Bombing Survey in Britain and Italy, where the planes were based that took the pictures.

The pictures of Auschwitz were almost an accidental byproduct of photographs taken of an I. G. Farben plant producing synthetic fuels less than five miles away. The plant was repeatedly bombed in the last year of the war by American and British planes.

There is little question that the Auschwitz photographs revealed the existence of a death camp. The question is whether the photo interpreters looking at the pictures recognized it as such and notified their superiors.

"Photo interpreters were unaware of Auschwitz at the time," Brugioni said. "They were looking for details of the Farben plant alongside Auschwitz, nothing else." . . . He said they were usually in a hurry to make judgments and often used shortcuts in making them. . . .

The pictures turned over to the archives by the CIA have lain in cans of aerial film stored at a Pentagon repository in Suitland, Md., for 30 years. The CIA acquired the film after "Holocaust" raised the Auschwitz issue last year.

The pictures illustrate what have been until now only "eyewitness accounts of the death process at Birkenau," which was the murder section of the Auschwitz camp, according to the CIA report. The pictures of the four gas chambers and crematoria at the camp "appear to be historically unique," the CIA report said.

"As far as we have been able to determine," the report's authors write, "no other photography of these facilities exists. The Birkenau gas chambers were special access facilities, even for most Nazis, and all photography was forbidden. The extermination facilities at the camp were destroyed by the Nazis prior to the camp's being liberated by the Red Army in January 1945."

Situated in a remote area south of Warsaw in Poland, the Auschwitz death camp was first opened in June 1940 to receive Soviet prisoners of war. It later became the main death camp for European Jews. By one count, 2.5 million Jews were killed at Auschwitz.

READING NO. 96

INTERNATIONAL RED CROSS ADMITS FAILURE TO SAVE MORE JEWS[113]

During World War II, the International Red Cross was confronted with unprecedented responsibilities in its efforts to alleviate the suffering of millions of people in Nazi-controlled Europe. German authorities opposed all relief and rescue programs designed to help local populations, especially if they were meant for Jews. At the same time, Germany needed Red Cross protection of German prisoners of war and interned German civilians. At times, this bargaining power could be used, but seldom was to help Jews. Nor did Jews obtain the status of "civilian internees" until October 2, 1944. The institution has often been criticized for not publicizing the atrocities in the camps, which it was aware of, and for its failure to inspect them. These failures have recently been acknowledged.

γ   γ   γ

TEL AVIV *(JTA)*—The International Committee of the Red Cross has admitted, in a special communication to the *Jerusalem Post,* that it could have saved more Jews from the Nazis.

The statement, published in last Wednesday's edition of the *Post,* was issued Tuesday in Geneva and signed by its director general, Jacques Moreillon.

It was released especially for publication in the Post in response to a report by the Israeli daily's London correspondent, David Horowitz, published last Sunday under the headline "Red Cross knew in '42 of massacre of Jews, but kept silent."

The ICRC admits for the first time that it could probably have saved more Jewish lives than it did, particularly in countries where the Nazis did not maintain total control, such as Hungary and Romania.

The *Post* reported that the ICRC itself hired Swiss Professor Jean-Claude Favez to investigate the matter. Following a six-year study of 350,000 Red Cross documents, Favez wrote, "The ICRC knew what was happening—that is quite clear. (But) it did not dare confront the Germans."

[113] Hugh Orgel, "Red Cross Admits Failing to Save Jews During the War," *The Forward* (New York), September 9, 1988, p. 24.

The ICRC's failure to inspect Nazi concentration camps has been reported before, including one inspection for which the Nazis propped up a false front at Theresienstadt, in Czechoslovakia.

The camp was presented as having healthful conditions, and the Red Cross fulfilled the Nazi illusion by only visiting the camp's orchestra and carefully prepared children's facilities.

Moreover, vans used by the Nazis for the mobile extermination of Jews were painted with a red cross on the side, thereby leading people to believe that the vans were actually Red Cross vehicles.

Favez has written a book on the subject of the ICRC's failure, titled "Silent Witness," and has appeared in a BBC documentary on the subject seen in England.

However, Favez' conclusion was challenged by Moreillon, who hired him, prior to the publication in the *Post* of the first article. At the time, Moreillon had said he did not believe an appeal would have helped Jews.

The Simon Wiesenthal Center in Los Angeles criticized Moreillon for defending the Red Cross in the BBC documentary.

But Tuesday's ICRC statement, titled "First Lessons Drawn by the ICRC," admits for the first time that it could probably have saved more Jews.

"In those countries, the ICRC today feels that it did not seek out, at that time, all the possible ways and means of protecting more of the victims," Moreillon wrote.

However, Moreillon refrained from unconditional apology by saying that in October 1942, the Red Cross had "mostly indirect and incomplete information regarding the fate of the Jews in Europe and was not conscious of Hitler's systematic plan to kill all the Jews."

But the ICRC also takes blame for not having asserted itself more in its contacts with the Allied and neutral powers, singling out the United States and Britain.

"The ICRC could no doubt have shown more imagination and greater firmness is order to persuade the Allies—especially the U.S. and Great Britain—and the neutral countries, to combat the policy of genocide and—particularly with regard to Switzerland—to relax their policies towards refugees, the Jews in particular, for whom admittance by neutral countries and by the Allies represented the only chance of survival," the statement says.

Moreillon told Swiss radio that the ICRC "did not do enough to save the Romanian and Hungarian Jews during World War II, but could not do more in favor of the Polish and Russian Jews under Nazi occupation.''

Moreillon also said that ''restricted documents'' concerning activities of the organization during World War II will be made available in the future to non-Swiss researchers.

''We made an exception and gave access to the documents to Arieh Ben-Tov, a Tel Aviv researcher,'' Moreillon said.

READING NO. 97

HELP TO JEWS FROM "ŻEGOTA" IN POLAND[114]

*Despite widespread anti-Semitism in Poland, various segments of the Polish population wanted to help save Jews from the deportations. The initiative came from Catholic circles and from a democratic group in the Polish underground. In August 1942, at the height of the massive deportations from Warsaw, the Catholic organization F.O.P. (*Front Odrodzenia Polski—*"Front for a Reborn Poland"*) published a protest condemning:*

γ   γ   γ

"the murder of millions of defenseless human beings which was being conducted amidst hostile general silence. The hangmen are silent, they do not exult in their deeds; England and America do not raise their voices—even the highly influential international Jewry, which was always so sensitive to every evil act directed against it, keeps silent; and the Poles are also silent . . . "

Under these circumstances, the proclamation continued, Polish Catholics must raise their voice in protest, although their feelings toward the Jews have not changed nor have they ceased to regard the latter as the political, economic, and ideological enemies of Poland. On the other hand, they have also noticed that the Jews hate them more than they do the Germans. Nevertheless they asserted that:

"this sensitive consciousness does not exempt us from denouncing the crime. We do not wish to be Pilates . . . we are unable to do anything against the murderous German action, we are unable to take action to save one person, but we protest from the depths of our hearts, full of compassion, anger and dread. This protest is demanded of us by the Almighty God who forbade killing. It is demanded by Christian conscience."

---

[114] Joseph Kermish, "The Activities of the Council for Aid to Jews ("Zegota") in Occupied Poland." *Rescue Attempts during the Holocaust*. Proceedings . . . April, 1977, pp. 369–370, 371, 374, 375, 378.

One of the principal initiators of the activities to help the Jews was the well-known Catholic writer Zofia Kossak-Szczucka, authoress of historic novels, who was active in the Polish underground and was later interned in Auschwitz (1913–1944). Although she was known for her right-wing, conservative, and religious views, the bitter fate suffered by the Jews made such an impression on her that she deemed it her Christian duty to help them. She set to work with great fervor and to a large extent was responsible for the formation, on September 27, 1942, of the "Konrad Żegota Committee," a code name for the Provisional Committee for Aid to Jews . . .

The Provisional Committee conducted its operations on a very limited scale, as it lacked broad public support. It received a very small subsidy—practically a token sum—of 50,000 zlotys per month from the Delegate of the Government-in-Exile. The Committee assumed responsibility for 180 Jews in hiding (mostly children), 90 of whom were in Warsaw. Aid was extended to a dozen people in Cracow, and three children were brought from there to Warsaw. . . . [This committee dissolved, but] a plan was drawn up for the creation of a Council which would have the broadest possible public support.

On December 4, 1942, a clandestine Council for Aid to Jews—the "Żegota" Council—was established by representatives of the Polish parties operating in the underground—socialist, peasants, democrats, and Catholics, as well as delegates of the Jewish Coordinating Committee. . . . Żegota produced thousands of birth certificates, baptismal documents, marriage certificates, pre-war identity cards . . . residence permits, a variety of work permits, etc . . . The Council was particularly concerned about the plight of Jewish children . . . The function of "Żegota's" special department for children . . . was first of all to care for orphaned and abandoned children and place them in institutions or with families . . . The Council also did a great deal to distribute underground publications on Jewish subjects—for propaganda purposes and to help Jewish relief operations. . . .

READING NO. 98

RAOUL WALLENBERG IN HUNGARY[115]

Wallenberg, a Young Swedish owner of an import-export firm, had visited Budapest a few times and had made friends as well as business contacts there. In response to requests by Jewish organizations, he consented to stay in Budapest in a quasi-official capacity to help Hungarian Jews. The Swedish Minister made him envoy extraordinary with the rank of Secretary of the Swedish Legation in Budapest.

γ   γ   γ

In 1944, Wallenberg became the counterforce to Eichmann in Budapest. The neutral embassies were the Budapest Jews' only lifeline. Switzerland, Spain, Portugal and the Vatican had assisted Jews, but on a far more limited scale than Wallenberg's operation. . . .

In all, the neutral embassies saved about 20,000 Jews.

Wallenberg had pulled together a staff of some 400, nearly all Jews, to give out passports, gather information, distribute supplies and protect the 32 safe houses he had set up on the Pest side of the Danube, where most of the city's Jews lived—plus special shelters housing 8,000 children. What is more, Wallenberg issued passports wholesale. Theoretically, these papers indicated that the holders were about to be admitted to the issuing countries; passport holders were deemed to be under the protection of the issuing countries and therefore exempt from deportation. It didn't always work. . . .

It was Wallenberg's shrewdness, courage and dedication that allowed him to succeed as much as he did. His role was twofold. He had to give terrified Jews the feeling that they could save themselves; and he had to deal with the Nazis, at times winning secret friends among them, and at other times confronting them with threats as to what would happen to them after the war. He could when necessary confront Nazis head on with a blaze of moral authority. For example, he confronted Arrow Cross thugs with their rifles poised and shouted, "Cowards! Slobs! What criminal arrogance! How dare you enter a Swedish-protected house! Nothing takes place here without my permission!" He dressed "Aryan-looking" Jewish young men in S.S. uniforms and

[115] Eleanor Lester, "The Lost Hero of the Holocaust," *The New York Times Magazine*, March 30, 1980.

set them to guarding safe houses. They hustled off groups of Jews headed for deportation and led them to safety, telling guards they had "higher orders from headquarters."

Wallenberg turned up along the route of death marches with his large car and his driver. The impact of his presence was described recently by Susan Tabor, a librarian at the Hebrew Union College.

"He gave us the sense that we were still human beings," she said. "My mother and I were among thousands taken one night to stay at a brick factory outside Budapest. There was no food, no water, no sanitation facilities, no light. Then Wallenberg appeared and said he would try to return with passports, or 'safety passes,' as we called them, and would also try to get medical attention and sanitation facilities. Soon afterward, some doctors and nurses came from the Jewish Hospital. . . . Wallenberg's presence on the scene was also a reminder to the Nazis that their depravity was being observed and recorded. He verbally reminded them that the United States had announced that it would treat those committing outrages against civilians as war criminals, not as soldiers. At one point, as the Russians were beginning to penetrate into Pest, the Germans and the Arrow Cross men plotted a last-minute extermination of the ghetto. However, one of Wallenberg's contacts, a member of the Budapest police department and a leader of the Arrow Cross, objected. He warned the German commander that if the action was carried out, Wallenberg would see to it that they would all be judged as murderers. The action was called off. Because of this episode, Wallenberg is also credited with indirectly saving an additional 70,000 Jews living in the central ghetto in Pest.

Russian units entered Budapest on Christmas Eve of 1944, taking the city house by house, the fighting raging on until February 14. Wallenberg was living on the Pest side of the Danube, near the two Jewish ghettos. On Jan. 10, his colleague at the legation, Per Anger, urged him to move with the Embassy to the safer Buda side, where the neutral embassies were located and where there was less chance of meeting up with the roving Arrow Cross gangs. Wallenberg refused. . . . On January 17, 1945, three and a half weeks after the Russians entered Budapest on Christmas Eve, Wallenberg and his driver, Vilmos Langfelder, and two Russian officers set out for Debrecen, some 120 miles east of Budapest. Wallenberg wanted to get the Russians' help in dealing with the Arrow Cross gangs. Neither he nor his driver ever returned. . . .

READING NO. 99

SMALL-SCALE RESCUE EFFORTS IN 1945[116]

The internal Nazi conflict over deals to save the remnant of Jews raged until the very end of the Third Reich. In the affidavit of Walter Schellenberg, a high-ranking Nazi intelligence officer, his negotiations with a Swiss official are aborted:

γ　　　　　γ　　　　　γ

19. Late in October 1944, Mr. Musy, former President of Switzerland, and his son visited Himmler at my instigation. In Musy's first discussion with Himmler, they went into the Jewish problem and he proposed to Himmler that all Jews still interned in concentration camps in Germany be discharged. It was suggested that Germany should receive in return for release of Jews a certain number of tractors, trucks and foreign currency. Himmler was undecisive during the negotiations and did not have the courage to make a basic decision. The decisions resulted in no binding agreement since Mr. Musy needed to clarify the issued with Jewish organizations. I was requested by Himmler to continue my contact with Mr. Musy and to aid with State Police officials in obtaining the release of individual Jews and Frenchmen whose release was authorized by Himmler.

20. I approached Mueller, Chief of Amt IV, and requested permission to take up individual cases personally. Mueller refused, saying that I was not a member of the Secret State Police and would therefore not be permitted to look into its internal activities. He directed me to State Police officials and I was permitted to get in touch with internees and bring about improvement in their living conditions. These included: Alien Thorel, Brothers Rottenberg, Family Donnebaum, Family Rosenberg, Dr. Stiassny and Helene Stein.

21. A second discussion between Musy and Himmler took place on 12 January 1945 at my instigation and thereafter a trainload of approximately 1200 Jews was to leave for Switzerland every 14 days. Himmler expected to bring about a change in the world propaganda against Germany. He also hoped to have certain sums of money made available to be used later. I was successful in convincing Himmler that this money should be turned over to the International Red Cross.

---

[116] *Nazi Conspiracy and Aggression,* vol. VIII, 1946. Affidavit D, pp. 627–629.

22. The first trainload of Jewish immigrants was delivered early in February. Thereafter Musy submitted a press story of 8 February from the New York Times and also submitted proof that he deposited 5,000,000 Swiss francs placed in trust later in February. Thereafter Kaltenbrunner, at the direction of Hitler, prevented further transports of Jews into Switzerland. Hitler threatened the death penalty for anyone attempting to further assist such transfers and ordered that not another Jew nor any American or British PW's should pass the border with the aid of any German.

23. Mr. Musy again visited Berlin and expressed great anger and bitter disappointment over the stopping of transfers. Musy and I suggested to Himmler that requests be made to the Western Powers for a 4 day armistice to permit sending all Jews and foreign internees through the front lines in an orderly manner. On my own responsibility I informed SS Obergruppenfuehrer Berger, Chief of War Prisoners, of the plan. He delayed sending many of Hitler's orders and thereby saved the lives of thousands of people who would otherwise have been evacuated from POW camps or executed where evacuation was impossible. Himmler favored the plan of an armistice but did not have the courage to suggest it to Hitler. I discussed it with Kaltenbrunner who replied to me on 3 April 1945: ''Have you too joined the idiots?''

24. Mr. Musy, Jr., returned to Germany to pick up a number of Jews from Buchenwald under authority granted by Himmler. He received unfavorable treatment from the camp commandant and returned to Berlin on 10 April, expressing horror at what he had observed in the evacuation of the camp. I looked into the matter and found that Himmler had been discredited with Hitler by Kaltenbrunner and that all camps were ordered to be evacuated. I reproached Himmler by telephone and found him embarrassed by the fact that a number of orders had bypassed him and that his course of action was blocked by contrary orders from Kaltenbrunner. Immediate energetic action by Himmler counteracted Kaltenbrunner's orders and saved many lives.

25. During March 1945, Dr. Burkhardt, President of the International Red Cross, with whom I had a contact through Swiss friends, indicated he wished to talk to Himmler about evacuation of various nationals held in Germany. I relayed this information to Himmler who talked with Hitler and was prohibited from having such a meeting. I then suggested that Himmler send Kaltenbrunner or myself. Kaltenbrunner was selected and he ordered me to draft a letter to Dr. Burkhardt. . . . Dr. Burkhardt wrote a long letter with concrete proposals

covering the categories and priorities for the exchange of internees from all Nations. Kaltenbrunner's comment on these letters was that it was a clever legal document and contained detailed proposals which he could not fulfill. . . . Kaltenbrunner kept me out of further participation in order to evade my insistent demands that Dr. Burkhardt be answered. I then discussed the matter with Himmler who also failed to take action. I sent one report to my friends in Switzerland and was thereafter unable to maintain communication and the proposed attempt to bring about a humanitarian evacuation was thus circumvented.

The above statements were made by me voluntarily and without coercion. They are true and correct to the best of my knowledge and belief.

[In handwriting of Schellenberg] ''I understand written English''

[signed] WALTER SCHELLENBERG

Walter Schellenberg

Subscribed and sworn to before me, this 23rd day of January 1946.

READING NO. 100

DEATH MARCH FROM HUNGARY TO GERMANY[117]

Eichmann returned to Budapest on October 17, 1944, and resumed his plan to deport Budapest Jews. He also negotiated with Hungarian officials to march 50,000 on foot, allegedly to work in Germany where there was a desperate labor shortage. They were to be marched to the Austrian border, 120 miles away. Men and women between 16 and 60 were seized from apartments marked with Jewish stars and on November 10, the seven-day trek began. Columns of men and women trudged through snow, sleet, and rain, without food toward Austria. Those who fell from exhaustion were shot or died from exposure. At Nuremberg, SS Lieutenant General Max Jüttner, whom Himmler had sent to watch the march, described what he saw:

γ   γ   γ

"Two-thirds of the way to Budapest we saw columns of Jewish women up to sixty years old, escorted by Honved guards. There were many stragglers lying in the road in the intervals between the columns. . . . I was told that the responsible man was Eichmann. I was aware that I might incur disagreeable consequences in sending for him, but he was not in Budapest, so I saw a captain whose name I do not recall and told him his business. He said he was not under my orders and I threatened to inform Himmler in order that this wrong which cried to heaven should be put right. Three days later I sent Himmler a strong report—apparently without result."

Jüttner also approached Otto Winkelmann, the Higher S.S. and Police Leader in Hungary, but Winkelmann said that he was helpless. Eichmann had jurisdiction over the deportations and was not under his command. Jüttner also complained to Eichmann's office and was told not to intervene, that Eichmann took orders from the RSHA exclusively.

Still uncurbed, Eichmann fumed against Jüttner, who, he said, "was not in any position to judge whether people who had been seven or eight days on the road would be treated as fit for work or otherwise."

[117] N. Levin, *The Holocaust: The Destruction of European Jewry, 1933–1945*, pp. 656, 657.

341

He had received only half of the 70,000 workers promised him by Szalasy. As for Wisliceny, who had returned some sick Jews to Budapest, Eichmann said he would bring him before a court-martial. . . .

Accompanying Jüttner en route from Vienna to Budapest, S.S. Lieutenant Colonel Rudolf Höss, the commandant of Auschwitz—no stranger to mass death—was also shocked by the brutality of the march and complained to Becher. Höss had come straight from Himmler's headquarters, where a new policy had been laid down as a result of Becher's meeting with Roswell McClelland, an American negotiator who had replaced Saly Mayer. Eichmann ignored all protests.

Some deportees were driven into the Danube. A Red Cross report describes a midwinter scene:

"In Gönyii, we saw that a part of the deportees were driven on board the ships anchored in the Danube over night. Many—in their great distress—committed suicide. In the still of the night one scream was followed by the other; the doomed people were jumping into the Danube which was covered with drifting ice. . . . With our own eyes we saw the gendarmes driving the Jews, who arrived in pitch darkness, over the narrow gangplank covered with ice, so that scores of them slipped into the icy river."

READING NO. 101

ESTIMATES OF JEWISH DEAD IN NAZI-OCCUPIED EUROPE[118]

γ   γ   γ

1. Anglo-American Committee of Inquiry Regarding the Problems of European Jewry and Palestine, April 1946.

Germany (1938 frontiers)	195,000
Austria	53,000
Czechoslovakia (1938)	255,000
Denmark	1,500*
France	140,000
Belgium	57,000
Luxembourg	3,000
Norway	1,000
Holland	120,000
Italy	20,000
Yugoslavia	64,000
Greece	64,000
Bulgaria (pre-1941 frontier)	5,000
Romania (pre-1940 frontier)	530,000
Hungary (1938 frontiers)	200,000
Poland (1939 frontiers)	3,271,000
U.S.S.R. (pre-1939 frontiers plus Baltic States)	1,050,000
	6,029,500
Less dispersed refugees	308,000
Total	5,721,500

* Chiefly refugees in Sweden.

2a. Losses Estimated by Raul Hilberg, *The Destruction of the European Jews*, 1961.†

	1939	*1945*
Austria	60,000	7,000
Belgium	90,000	40,000

[118] N. Levin, *The Holocaust, op. cit.*, pp. 715, 716—718.

Bulgaria	50,000	47,000
Czechoslovakia	315,000	44,000
Denmark	6,500	5,500
France	270,000	200,000
Germany	240,000	80,000
Greece	74,000	12,000
Hungary	400,000	200,000
Italy	50,000	33,000
Luxembourg	3,000	1,000
Netherlands	140,000	20,000
Norway	2,000	1,000
Poland	3,350,000	50,000
Romania	800,000	430,000
U.S.S.R.	3,020,000	2,600,000
Estonia	4,500	
Latvia	95,000	
Lithuania	145,000	
Yugoslavia	75,000	12,000
	9,180,000	3,782,500

† Statistics for 1939 refer to prewar borders. Postwar frontiers have been used for 1945. The figure of 80,000 for Germany includes 60,000 displaced persons. The estimate for the U.S.S.R. comprises about 300,000 refugees, deportees and survivors from newly acquired territories (Hilberg, p. 670).

2b. Statistical Recapitulation of Jewish Dead by Territory (Borders as of August 1939).

Reich-Protektorat Area	250,000
U.S.S.R.	700,000
Baltic States	200,000
Poland	3,000,000
Low Countries	130,000
France and Italy	70,000
Yugoslavia	60,000
Greece and Rhodes	60,000
Slovakia	60,000
Romania	270,000
Hungary and Carpatho-Ukraine	300,000
Total	5,100,000

(Hilberg, p. 767).

3. Estimates of Jewish Losses by Jacob Lestchinsky,
Balance Sheet of Extermination, American Jewish Congress, 1946.*

Country (Prewar borders)	Jewish Population September 1939	Number of Jews Lost
Poland	3,250,000	2,850,000
U.S.S.R. (Occupied Area)	2,100,000	1,500,000
Romania	850,000	425,000
Hungary	400,000	200,000
Czechoslovakia	315,000	240,000
France†	300,000	90,000
Germany	193,000	110,000‡
Austria	90,000	45,000
Lithuania	150,000	130,000
Holland	150,000	105,000
Latvia	95,000	80,000
Belgium†	90,000	40,000
Yugoslavia	75,000	55,000
Greece	75,000	60,000
Italy†	57,000	15,000
Bulgaria	50,000	7,000
Denmark, Estonia, Norway, Luxembourg, Danzig	15,000	5,000
Totals	8,255,000	5,957,000

* Revised in 1955, *Yad Vashem Bulletin*, No. 10, April 1961.

† Figures include refugees.

‡ Does not include Jewish victims killed between 1933 and 1939, estimated at between 30,000 and 40,000 by Lestchinsky.

SUGGESTED READINGS

Ainsztein, Reuben. *Jewish Resistance in Nazi-Occupied Europe*. New York, Barnes and Noble, 1975.

Allen, William Sheridan. *The Nazi Seizure of Power: The Experience of a Single German Town*, 1930–1935, Chicago, 1965.

Arnon, Joseph. "The Passion of James Korozak," *Midstream*, May 1973, pp. 52–53.

Auschwitz: Beginning of a New Era? Reflections on the Holocaust. Edited by Eva Fleischner. New York: KTAV, Cathedral Church of St. John the Divine and Anti-Defamation League of B'nai B'rith, 1977.

Baker, Leonard. *Days of Sorrow and Pain: Leo Baeck and the Berlin Jews*. New York: Macmillan Co., 1978.

Bartoszewski, Wladyslaw. *The Samaritans: Heroes of the Holocaust*. New York: Twain, 1970.

Bauer, Yehuda. *A History of the Holocaust*. New York: Franklin Watts, 1982.

Berkovits, Eliezer. *Faith After the Holocaust*. New York: KTAV, 1973.

Bierman, John. *Righteous Gentile: The Story of Raoul Wallenberg, Missing Hero of the Holocaust*. New York: Viking Press, 1981.

The Black Book: The Nazi Crime Against the Jewish People. New York: Duell, Sloan and Pearce, 1946.

Black Book of Localities Whose Jewish Population Was Exterminated by the Nazis. Jerusalem: Yad Vashem, 1965.

Bracher, Karl D. *The German Dictatorship: The Origins, Structure, and Effects of National Socialism*. New York: Praeger, 1971.

Braham, Randolph L. *The Destruction of Hungarian Jewry: A Documentary Account*. 2 vols. New York: Pro Arte for the World Federation of Hungarian Jews, 1963.

Broszat, Martin. *The Hitler State: The Foundation and Development of the Internal Structure of the Third Reich*. Translated by John W. Hiden. London: Longman, 1981.

Bullock, Alan. *Hitler: A Study in Tyranny*. Rev. ed. New York: Harper and Row, 1964.

Carstein, F. L. *Fascist Movements in Austria: From Schönerer to Hitler*. London: Sage, 1977.

Chary, Frederick B. *The Bulgarian Jews and the Final Solution, 1940–1944*. Pittsburgh: University of Pittsburgh Press, 1972.

Cohen, Ellie A. *Human Behavior in the Concentration Camps*. New York: Universal Library, 1953.

Cohn, Norman. *Warrant for Genocide: The Myth of the Jewish World Conspiracy and the Protocols of the Elders of Zion*. New York: Harper and Row, 1966.

Costanza, Mary S. *The Living Witness: Art in the Concentration Camps and Ghettos*. New York: Free Press, 1982.

Dawidowicz, Lucy S. *A Holocaust Reader*. New York: Behrman House, 1976.

———, *The War Against the Jews, 1933–1945*. New York: Behrman House, 1976.

Donat, Alexander. *The Holocaust Kingdom*. New York: Holt, Rinehart and Winston, 1965.

Des Pres, Terrence. *The Survivor: An Anatomy of Life in the Death Camps*. Oxford: Oxford University Press, 1976.

Dicks, Henry V. *Licensed Mass Murder: A Socio-psychological Study of Some SS Killers*. New York: Basic Books, 1972.

Dobroszycki, Lucian. *The Chronicle of the Lodz Ghetto*. New Haven, Conn., Yale University, 1984.

Dorian, Emil. *The Quality of Witness: A Romanian Diary 1937–1944*. Translated by Mara S. Vamos. Philadelphia: Jewish Publication Society of America, 1983.

Ehrenburg, Ilya, ed. *The Black Book: The Ruthless Murder of Jews by German-Fascist Invaders Throughout the Temporarily-Occupied Regions of the Soviet Union During the War of 1941–1945*. Translated by John Glad and James S. Levine. New York: Holocaust Publications, 1981.

Epstein, Helen. *Children of the Holocaust: Conversations with Sons and Daughters of the Survivors*. New York: G. P. Putnam Sons, 1979.

Ferencz, Benjamin B. *Less Than Slaves*. Cambridge, Mass.: Harvard University Press, 1979.

Feingold, Henry. *The Politics of Rescue: The Roosevelt Administration and the Holocaust, 1938–45*. New Brunswick, N.J.: Rutgers University Press, 1970.

Fisher, Julius S. *Transnistria: The Forgotten Cemetery*. New York: A. S. Barnes, 1969.

Frank, Anne. *Diary of a Young Girl*. New York: Pocket Books, 1953.

Friedlander, Saul. *Pius XII and the Third Reich*. New York: Alfred A. Knopf, 1966.

Friedman, Philip. *Their Brothers' Keepers: The Christian Heroes and Heroines Who Helped the Oppressed Escape the Nazi Terror*. New York: Holocaust Library, 1978.

Friedman, Saul S. *No Haven for the Oppressed*. Detroit: Wayne State University Press, 1973.

Gilbert, Martin. *Final Journey: The Fate of the Jews in Nazi Europe*. London: George Allen and Unwin Ltd., 1979.

Glatstein, Jacob, ed. *Anthology of Holocaust Literature*. Philadelphia: Jewish Publication Society of America, 1973.

Goebbels, Paul J. *The Goebbels Diaries*. Edited and translated by Louis Lochner. Westport, Conn.: Greenwood Press, reprint of 1948 ed.

Gutman, Yisrael. *Rescue Attempts During the Holocaust: Proceedings of the Second Yad Vashem International Historical Conference, April, 1974*. Jerusalem: Yad Vashem, 1977.

Hallie, Phillip. *Lest Innocent Blood Be Shed: The Story of the Village of Le Chambon and How Goodness Happened There*. New York: Harper and Row, 1979.

Harris, Whitney R. *Tyranny on Trial: The Evidence at Nuremberg*. Dallas, Tex.: Southern Methodist University Press, 1954.

Heiden, Konrad. *Der Fuehrer: Hitler's Rise to Power*. Boston: Beacon, 1969.

Hilberg, Raul. *The Destruction of the European Jews*. Chicago: Quadrangle, 1961. Rev. and enl. ed. published by Holmes and Meier in 3 vols., 1985.

Hirschmann, Ira. *Lifeline to a Promised Land*. New York: Vanguard Press, 1946.

Hitler, Adolf. *Hitler's Secret Conversations, 1941–44*. New York: New American Library, 1961.

———. *Mein Kampf*. Translated by Ralph Manheim. Boston: Houghton Mifflin, 1953.

International Military Tribunal. *Trial of the Major War Criminals Before the International Military Tribunal: Official Text*. 42 vols. Nuremberg: 1947–1949. Blue Series.

Jäckel, Eberhard. *Hitler's Weltanschauung: A Blueprint for Power*. Middletown, Conn.: Wesleyan University Press, 1972.

Kaplan, Chaim. *Scroll of Agony: The Warsaw Diary of Chaim Kaplan*. Edited and translated by Abraham Katsh. Rev. ed. New York: Macmillan Co., 1981.

Karski, Jan. *The Story of a Secret State*. Cambridge, Mass.: Riverside Press, 1944.

Klarsfeld, Serge. *Memorial to the Jews Deported from France 1942–1944*. New York: Beate Klarsfeld Foundation, 1983.

Kluger, Ruth. *The Last Escape*. Garden City, N.Y.: Doubleday, 1973.

Koehl, Robert L. *RKFDV: German Resettlement and Population Policy, 1939–1945*. Cambridge, Mass.: Harvard University Press, 1957.

Kogon, Eugen. *The Theory and Practice of Hell: The German Concentration Camps and the System Behind Them*. Translated by Heinz Norden. New York: Farrar, Straus and Cudahy, 1950.

Korczak, Janusz. *Ghetto Diary*. New York: Holocaust Library, 1978.

Kranzler, David. *Japanese, Nazies and Jews: The Jewish Refugee Community of Shanghai, 1938–1945*. New York: Yeshiva University Press, 1976.

Krakowski, Shmuel. *The War of the Doomed: Jewish Armed Resistance in Poland, 1942–1944*. New York: Holmes and Meier, 1985.

Laqueur, Walter. *The Terrible Secret: Suppression of the Truth about Hitler's 'Final Solution.'* Boston, Little, Brown and Co., 1980.

Latour, Anny. *The Jewish Resistance in France (1940–1944)*. Translated by Irene R. Ilton. New York: Holocaust Library, 1981.

Leboucher, Fernande. *The Incredible Mission of Father Benoit*. Translated by J. F. Bernard. New York: Doubleday, 1969.

Lederer, Zdenek. *Ghetto Theresienstadt*. New York: Fertig, 1983.

Lemkin, Raphael. *Axis Rule in Occupied Europe*. Washington, D.C.: Carnegie Endowment for International Peace, 1944.

Leo Baeck Institute. *Yearbook,* Vol. 1 -date. London: Martin Secker and Warburg, 1956–

Levi, Primo. *Survival in Auschwitz: The Nazi Assault on Humanity*. New York: Collier Books, 1961.

Levin, Nora. *The Holocaust: The Destruction of European Jewry, 1933–1945*. New York: Schocken Books, 1973.

Marrus, Michael R., and Robert O. Paxton. *Vichy France and the Jews*. New York: Basic Books, 1981.

Maser, Werner. *Hitler: Legend, Myth and Reality*. New York: Harper and Row, 1973.

Massing, Paul. *Rehearsal for Destruction: A Study of Political Anti-Semitism in Imperial Germany*. New York: Harper and Row, 1946.

Michaelis, Meir. *Mussolini and the Jews: German-Italian Relations and the Jewish Question in Italy*. Oxford: Clarendon Press, 1978.

Mitscherlich, Alexander. *Doctors of Infamy: The Story of the Nazi Medical Crimes*. New York: Henry Schuman, 1949.

Morley, John Francis. *Vatican Diplomacy and the Jews During the Holocaust 1939–1943*. New York: KTAV, 1980.

Morse, Arthur D. *While Six Million Died: A Chronicle of American Apathy*. New York: Random House, 1968.

Mosse, George L. *The Crisis of German Ideology: Intellectual Origins of the Third Reich*. New York: Grosset and Dunlap, 1964.

———. *Toward the Final Solution: A History of European Racism*. New York: Harper and Row, 1978.

Müller, Filip. *Auschwitz Inferno: The Testimony of a Sonderkommando*. Edited and translated by Susanne Flatauer. London: Routledge and Kegan Paul, 1979.

Nuernberg Military Tribunals. *Trials of War Criminals Before the Nuernberg Military Tribunals Under Control Council Law No. 10*. 15 vols. Washington, D.C.: 1949–1953. Green Series.

Patterns of Jewish Leadership in Nazi Europe, 1933–1945. Proceedings of the Third Yad Vashem International Historical Conference, April 1977. Jerusalem: Yad Vashem, 1979.

Pearlman, Moshe. *The Capture and Trial of Adolf Eichmann*. New York: Simon and Schuster, 1963.

Poliakov, Leon. *Harvest of Hate: The Nazi Program for the Destruction of the Jews of Europe*. New York: Holocaust Library, 1979.

Poliakov, Leon, and J. Sabille. *Jews Under the Italian Occupation*. New York: Fertig, 1983.

Presser, Jacob. *The Destruction of the Dutch Jews*. New York: E. P. Dutton, 1969.

Pulzer, Peter G. J. *The Rise of Political Anti-Semitism in Germany and Austria*. New York: John Wiley, 1964.

Ringelblum, Emanuel. *Notes from the Warsaw Ghetto: The Journal of Emmanuel Ringelblum*. Edited and translated by Jacob Sloan. New York: Schocken Books, 1974.

———. *Polish-Jewish Relations During the Second World War*. New York: Fertig, 1976.

Rousset, David. *The Other Kingdom*. New York: Reynal and Hitchcock, 1947.

Ryan, Allan A., Jr. *Quiet Neighbors: The True Story of Nazi War Criminals in America*. New York: Harcourt Brace Jovanovich, 1984.

Schoenberner, Gerhard. *The Yellow Star: The Persecution of the Jews in Europe 1933–1945*. Translated by Susan Sweet. New York: Bantam Books, 1979.

Schneider, Gertrude. *Journey into Terror: Story of the Riga Ghetto*. New York: Irvington Pub., 1981.

Seidel, Rachelle G. *The Outraged Conscience: Seekers of Justice for Nazi War Criminals in America*. Albany: State University Press of New York, 1984.

Senesh, Hannah. *Hannah Senesh: Her Life and Diary*. New York, Schocken Books, 1973.

Snell, John L., *The Nazi Revolution: Germany's Guilt or Germany's Fate?* Lexington, Heath and Co., Mass., 1959.

Snyder, Louis L. *Hitler's Third Reich*. Chicago, 1982.

Stern, Fritz. *The Politics of Cultural Despair: A Study of the Rise of the Germanic Ideology*. Berkeley: University of California Press, 1961.

Suhl, Yuri. *They Fought Back: The Story of Jewish Resistance in Nazi Europe*. New York: Schocken Books, 1974.

Syrkin, Marie. *Blessed Is the Match: The Story of Jewish Resistance*. Philadelphia: Jewish Publication Society of America, 1947.

Tec, Nechama. *When Light Pierced the Darkness: Christian Rescue of Jews in Nazi-Occupied Poland*. New York, Oxford University Press, 1986.

Trunk, Isaiah. *Judenrat: The Jewish Councils in Eastern Europe Under Nazi Occupation*. New York: Macmillan Co., 1972.

U.S. Chief of Counsel for Prosecution of Axis Criminality. *Nazi Conspiracy and Aggression*. 8 vols. Washington, D.C.: 1946–1948. Red Series.

The Warsaw Diary of Adam Czerniakow: Prelude to Doom. Translated by Stanislaw Staron, edited by Raul Hilberg. New York: Stein and Day, 1979.

Wasserstein, Bernard. *Britain and the Jews of Europe, 1939–1945*. Oxford: Oxford University Press, 1979.

Weissberg, Alexander. *Desperate Mission: Joel Brand's Story*. New York: Criterion, 1958.

Wiesel, Elie. *Night*. Translated by Stella Rodway. New York: Avon Books, 1969.

Wyman, David. *Abandonment of the Jews*. New York: Pantheon, 1984.

———. *Paper Walls: America and the Refugee Crisis, 1938–41*. Amherst: University of Massachusetts Press, 1968.

Yad Vashem Studies on the European Jewish Catastrophe and Resistance,
Vol. 1 -date. Jerusalem: Yad Vashem Martyrs' and Heroes' Remembrance
Authority, 1957–.

Yahil, Leni. *The Rescue of Danish Jewry.* Philadelphia: Jewish Publication
Society of America, 1969.

INDEX